Mobile Learning

MW00814461

Dear Saad,

    Thanks so much for the pointers you gave me & the connections you helped me make while I was researching this book — much appreciated!

        Mark

        Dec. 2014

New Language Learning and Teaching Environments

Series edited by **Hayo Reinders**

Titles include:

Hayo Reinders (*editor*)
DIGITAL GAMES IN LANGUAGE LEARNING AND TEACHING

Fred Dervin, Marie-Noëlle Lamy and Katerina Zourou (*editors*)
SOCIAL NETWORKING FOR LANGUAGE EDUCATION

Mark Pegrum
MOBILE LEARNING
Languages, Literacies and Cultures

New Language Learning and Teaching Environments
Series Standing Order ISBN 978–0230–28249–0 hardback
978–0230–8250–6 paperback
(*outside North America only*)

You can receive future titles in this series as they are published by placing a standing order. Please contact your bookseller or, in case of difficulty, write to us at the address below with your name and address, the title of the series and the ISBN quoted above.

Customer Services Department, Macmillan Distribution Ltd, Houndmills, Basingstoke, Hampshire RG21 6XS, England

---

Mobile Learning

Languages, Literacies and Cultures

Mark Pegrum

Graduate School of Education, The University of Western Australia

First published 2014 by
PALGRAVE MACMILLAN

Palgrave Macmillan in the UK is an imprint of Macmillan Publishers Limited, registered in England, company number 785998, of Houndmills, Basingstoke, Hampshire RG21 6XS.

Palgrave Macmillan in the US is a division of St Martin's Press LLC, 175 Fifth Avenue, New York, NY 10010.

Palgrave Macmillan is the global academic imprint of the above companies and has companies and representatives throughout the world.

Palgrave® and Macmillan® are registered trademarks in the United States, the United Kingdom, Europe and other countries.

ISBN 978–1–137–30979–2 hardback
ISBN 978–1–137–30980–8 paperback

This book is printed on paper suitable for recycling and made from fully managed and sustained forest sources. Logging, pulping and manufacturing processes are expected to conform to the environmental regulations of the country of origin.

A catalogue record for this book is available from the British Library.

Library of Congress Cataloging-in-Publication Data
Pegrum, Mark, 1969–
    Mobile learning : languages, literacies and cultures / Mark Pegrum.
       pages cm — (New Language Learning and Teaching Environments)
    Summary: "This book is a wide-ranging exploration of the use of mobile devices for teaching and learning language and literacies. It investigates the particular qualities of mobile devices which open up new educational possibilities, and examines the agendas behind the use of these tools in the developed and developing world alike. A history of the development of the hardware and software leads into a detailed study of how mobile devices can be used to teach language, which language areas and skills are already being taught around the world, and how the teaching of literacy, including digital literacies, can be supported. Eighteen case studies from across the globe are complemented by 13 vignettes by experienced mobile educators, thus building up a rich picture of contemporary mobile learning as well as sketching an outline of likely future developments"—Provided by publisher.
    ISBN 978–1–137–30979–2 (hardback)
    1. Language and languages—Study and teaching—Computer network resources.   2. Language and languages—Study and teaching—Computer-assisted instruction.   3. Language and languages—Study and teaching—Technological innovations.   4. Mobile communication systems in education.   5. Distance education.   6. Internet literacy.   7. Computer literacy.   8. Internet in education.   I. Title.
    P53.285.P44 2014
    418.0078′5–dc23   2014018509

For Second
谢谢您默默的支持。

Contents

Figures

Acknowledgements

People who work in mobile learning and related fields are often extraordinarily busy, dividing their time between teaching courses and seminars, giving conference papers and presentations, writing articles and books, researching new initiatives, and supporting policy development. On top of that, many of them run m-learning projects, ranging from exploratory initiatives whose participants number in their dozens to well-established programmes whose participants number in their millions. Their willingness to share their expertise has been invaluable in shaping the global overview of m-learning sketched out in this book, especially given the relative lack of published information about many current projects. It's been very encouraging to receive so much enthusiastic co-operation. If my experience while researching this book is any indication, then m-learning and MALL have a very promising (and very networked) future.

I'd like to thank the numerous people with whom I've conversed by phone, Skype and email, through Facebook, LinkedIn and Twitter – and occasionally in person! – and who have so generously given their time and support, shared their research and contacts, commented on early drafts of case studies and chapters, and helped me to chase up facts or tidy up translations: Carla Arena, Stephen Atherton, Shaheen Attiq-ur-Rahman, Samyuktha Balakrishnan, Neil Ballantyne, Stephen Bax, Ben Beaton, Adam Black, Diane Boulay, Işıl Boy, Fraser Cargill, Sangay Choden, Dorothy Chun, Daniel Churchill, Anna Comas-Quinn, Marisa Constantinides, Kate Donahue, Gavin Dudeney, Isabelle Duston, Yomna ElMeshad, Gai Fan, Eitan Geft, David Glance, Ben Gray, Mark Gregory, Laura Hakimi, Trude Heift, Nicky Hockly, Scott Isbrandt, Matthew Kam, Agnes Kukulska-Hulme, Richard Lace, Marie-Noëlle Lamy, Diana Laurillard, Mike Levy, Si Hui Lim, Raquel Mardomingo, Richard Mayer, Winda Wastu Melati, Lisa Merschel, Ichiro Miyazawa, Gary Motteram, Jayanti Nathan, Gilbert Ng, Grace Oakley, Lucas Paletta, Salomi Papadima-Sophocleous, Nik Peachey, Lyn Pemberton, Sobah Abbas Petersen, Png Bee Hin, Bhanu Potta, Lee Rainie, Hayo Reinders, Marie-Eve Ritz, Saad Rizvi, Tom Salmon, Paul Scott, Rose Senior, Prithvi Shrestha, James Simpson, Rangan Srikhanta, Corrie Staats, Graham Stanley, Glenn Stockwell, Julian Stodd, Tommy Sweeney, Julie Sykes,

Sharon Tham, Michael Thomas, Alexandra Tyers, Fakhar Uddin, Merel van der Woude, Willem van de Waal, Ozan Varlı, Jennifer Verschoor, Steve Vosloo, Simon Wardman, Danny Whitehead, Marcus Winter, Beyza Yılmaz and Ronda Zelezny-Green.

I'd also like to thank my series editor, Hayo Reinders, and my editor at Palgrave Macmillan, Olivia Middleton, for their advice and assistance from the conception of this project right through to the placement of the final full stop.

Of course, it's not possible to undertake a project like this without a lot of personal support. I want to thank my parents, Margaret and Brian Pegrum, and my friends for having the patience to continually ask how it was progressing – and to listen to the answers! The journey, at last, is complete... for now at least.

Permissions

Every effort has been made to trace the copyright holders of the material reproduced in this text. We would like to thank the following for permission to reproduce copyright material:

Business Insider Intelligence for permission to reproduce Figures 1.1, 1.3, 1.4, 3.1, 3.3, 3.5, 3.7, 4.3 and 4.5; Cisco for permission to reproduce Figure 1.2; Ruben Puentedura for permission to reproduce Figure 2.1; SIMOLA for permission to reproduce Figure 2.2; Carla Arena/Casa Thomas Jefferson, Brasília, for permission to reproduce Figure 2.3; Ichiro Miyazawa/UNESCO for permission to reproduce Figure 2.4; The British Council, Tripoli, for permission to reproduce Figure 3.4; Rockbench Publishing for permission to reproduce Figure 3.6; et4d for permission to reproduce Figure 3.8; Pearson for permission to reproduce Figure 4.1; Taylor & Francis for permission to reproduce Figures 4.2 and 6.1; Matthew Kam and the MILLEE team for permission to reproduce Figure 4.4; Chris Holden and Julie Sykes for permission to reproduce Figure 4.6; Nokia for permission to reproduce Figure 5.1; The British Council, Chennai, for permission to reproduce Figure 5.2; Nulu Languages for permission to reproduce Figure 5.3; Rangan Srikhanta/OLPC Australia for permission to reproduce Figure 6.2; Peter Ramspacher/ Joanneum Research, Graz, for permission to reproduce Figure 6.3; LDR Pte Ltd for permission to reproduce Figure 6.4; Surendra Gohil/Mobigam for permission to reproduce Figure 6.5; Prithvi Shrestha, The Open University, for permission to reproduce Figure 7.2; Merel van der Woude/Butterfly Works for permission to reproduce Figure 7.3; The British Council, Jakarta, for permission to reproduce Figure 7.4.

Abbreviations

1:1	one-to-one (one computing device per student)
1G	first generation (analogue wireless telecommunications standard)
2G	second generation (digital wireless telecommunications standard)
3G	third generation (digital wireless telecommunications standard)
4G	fourth generation (digital wireless telecommunications standard)
app	application (software)
AR	augmented reality
ARIS	Augmented Reality for Interactive Storytelling (software; see Case Study 8)
AusAID	Australian Agency for International Development
BCI	brain-computer interface
BMI	brain-machine interface
BYOD	Bring Your Own Device
BYOT	Bring Your Own Technology
CALL	Computer-Assisted Language Learning
CEFR	Common European Framework of Reference (for Languages)
CK	content knowledge (see: TPACK)
CMC	computer-mediated communication
DFID	Department for International Development (UK)
EFA	Education for All (UNESCO goals)
EGRA	Early Grade Reading Assessment
EIA	English in Action (see: Case Study 16)
e-learning	electronic learning
e-portfolio	electronic portfolio
ESL	English as a Second Language
ETSI	European Telecommunications Standards Institute
Gbps	gigabit(s) per second (data transmission speed)
GPS	Global Positioning System (satellite-based navigation system)
GSM	Global System for Mobile (Communications) (2G telecommunications standard)

GSMA	GSM Association
HTML5	HyperText Markup Language 5 (current web standard)
IADIS	International Association for Development of the Information Society
IAmLearn	International Association for Mobile Learning
ICALL	Intelligent CALL
ICT(s)	information and communication(s) technology/ies
ICT4D	ICT(s) for Development
IEEE	Institute of Electrical and Electronics Engineers
IGO	intergovernmental organisation
IM	instant message/ing
IMALL	Intelligent MALL
IMT-2000	International Mobile Telecommunications-2000 (3G telecommunications specifications)
IMT-Advanced	International Mobile Telecommunications-Advanced (4G telecommunications specifications)
iOS	i-operating system (Apple's mobile operating system)
ITU	International Telecommunication Union
iTunes	(Apple's digital content store and distribution platform)
iTunes U	(Apple's educational content distribution platform)
L2	second language
LOTM	Learning-On-The-Move (software; see Case Study 14)
LTE	Long Term Evolution (4G telecommunications standard)
M4D	Mobile(s) for Development
MALL	Mobile-Assisted Language Learning
MASELTOV	(partial acronym for) Mobile Assistance for Social Inclusion and Empowerment of Immigrants with Persuasive Learning Technologies and Social Network Services (see: Case Study 13)
Mbps	megabit(s) per second (data transmission speed)
MDGs	Millennium Development Goals (UN goals)
MILLEE	Mobile and Immersive Learning for Literacy in Emerging Economies (see: Case Study 7)
m-learning	mobile learning

MMOG	massively multiplayer online game
mMOOC	mobile MOOC
MMS	Multimedia Messaging Service
Mobigam	'Mobi' (mobile) + 'gam' (Gujarati for 'a rural setting') (see: Case Study 15)
MOBIlearn	Mobile Learning (project)
Mobiledu	Mobile Education (see: Case Study 6)
MOE	Ministry Of Education (including in Afghanistan, Bangladesh & Singapore)
MoEYS	Ministry of Education, Youth & Sport (in Cambodia)
MoLeNET	Mobile Learning Network (project)
MOOC	Massive Open Online Course
MP3	(digital audio format developed by the Motion Picture Experts Group [MPEG])
NED	Nokia Education Delivery (platform)
NFC	near field communication (wireless communications technology)
NGO	non-governmental organisation
NLP	Natural Language Processing
Nulu	New ('Nu') language for you ('u') (see: Case Study 11)
OCR	optical character recognition
OER	Open Educational Resources
OLPC	One Laptop Per Child (see: Case Study 12)
OS	operating system
P21	Partnership for 21st Century Skills
PC	personal computer
PD	professional development
PDA	personal digital assistant
PK	pedagogical knowledge (see: TPACK)
PLE	personal learning environment
p-learning	pervasive learning
PLN	personal learning network
QR	quick response (code)
SAMR	Substitution – Augmentation – Modification – Redefinition (teaching framework)
sat nav	satellite navigation
SD card	Secure Digital (memory) card
SIM card	Subscriber Identity Module card (mobile phone memory chip)

SIMOLA	Situated Mobile Language Learning (see: Case Study 1)
SLA	second language acquisition
SMS	Short Message Service (text message/ing)
TALULAR	Teaching And Learning Using Locally Available Resources (see: Case Study 18)
TCK	technological content knowledge (see: TPACK)
TED	Technology, Entertainment, Design (talks platform)
TK	technological knowledge (see: TPACK)
TPACK	Technological Pedagogical And Content Knowledge (teacher training framework)
TPK	technological pedagogical knowledge (see: TPACK)
TRAC	Total Reading Approach for Children (see: Case Study 5)
UKaid	(aid provided by DFID)
u-learning	ubiquitous learning
UN	United Nations
UNESCO	United Nations Educational, Scientific & Cultural Organization
USAID	United States Agency for International Development
VLE	virtual learning environment
VoIP	Voice over Internet Protocol (for internet telephony)
WAP	Wireless Application Protocol (for internet access on 2.5G networks)
WHO	World Health Organization
wifi	(wireless local area network technology)
WiMAX	Worldwide Interoperability for Microwave Access (4G telecommunications standard)
WSIS	World Summit on the Information Society (UN summit)
XO	(OLPC laptop or tablet device)

1
The Mobile Landscape

The years 2002 and 2013 stand out in the history of international telecommunications. In 2002, the number of mobile telephone subscriptions surpassed the number of fixed lines globally; and in 2013, the number of internet-enabled mobile devices is set to surpass the number of desktop and laptop computers (*The Economist,* 2012; Meeker, 2012). Welcome to the mobile age.

As of early 2013, mobile phone penetration was estimated at 96% globally and 128% in developed countries (ITU, 2013), reflecting individuals' ownership of more than one phone. There are already over a billion smartphone subscriptions and the penetration of tablets is growing rapidly, with media players and other handheld devices widely, if not evenly, distributed. There is also a strong trend towards ownership of multiple mobile device types, with 25% of mobile users expected to own a second device by 2016 (Cisco, 2012). This brings added mobility and flexibility, as users move seamlessly between fixed and mobile screens.

In the developing world, where mobile penetration is estimated to have already reached 89% (ITU, 2013), the proliferation of mobile devices may permit a leapfrogging of the desktop and laptop stages typical of developed countries. This doesn't mean that 89% of the population has phones, since the figures refer to subscriptions, not people, but it's true that large numbers of people are prepared to outlay a significant proportion of their income – estimated at 4–8% of average monthly income in India and Sri Lanka, for example (Deriquito & Domingo, 2012) – to own mobile phones. Access rates in developing countries are further bolstered by the common practice of sharing phones between family members and friends (GSMA, 2010a). Many of these devices, which often represent users' first gateway to the digital world, are basic or feature phones which operate on older second generation (2G) networks. Yet trends are shifting: in February 2013, China surpassed the USA with the largest number of active smartphones and tablets in the world, but in terms of growth it was placed only sixth, following Colombia, Vietnam, Turkey, the Ukraine and Egypt (Farago, 2013).

Globally, mobile traffic reached 15% of all internet traffic by the end of 2012 (see Figure 1.1) and is on track to surpass 25% in 2013/2014 (Cocotas, 2013; Meeker & Wu, 2013), accompanied by a corresponding decline in desktop and laptop traffic. This phenomenon isn't restricted to the developed world. Indeed, in 2012, mobile traffic in India, soon to be the world's second largest internet market, exceeded fixed internet traffic (Meeker, 2012). Worldwide, large increases in mobile traffic are predicted through to 2017 and beyond, with the Asia–Pacific region coming to dominate in the near future (see Figure 1.2).

It's not just our devices which are mobile; more and more, so are we. We can socialise, learn and work across multiple real-world settings. After centuries of growing immobilisation of the populace, which gradually became tethered to homes, schools and workplaces, we're seeing the rise of what *The Economist* calls 'the new nomadism' (Woodill, 2011: Kindle location 127). Thanks to mobile devices and their constant

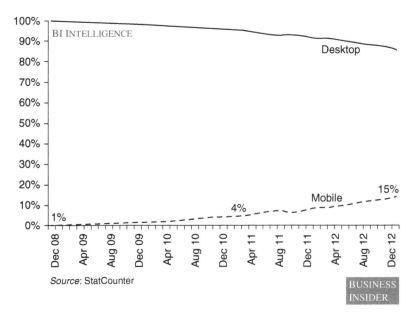

Figure 1.1 Global desktop vs mobile traffic 2008–2012. © Business Insider Intelligence, https://intelligence.businessinsider.com, reproduced by permission.

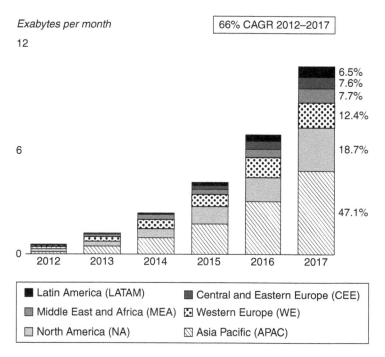

Figure 1.2 Global mobile data traffic by region 2012–2017 (forecast). © Cisco VNI Global Mobile Data Forecast 2012–2017, reproduced by permission.

connectivity we can access information and resources, connect to and communicate with others, and create and share media almost anywhere. While devices and connections in the developed world far surpass those in the developing world in both quantity and quality, more and more of the world is coming online (see Figure 1.3), and more and more of the newest users are accessing the internet predominantly or solely through mobile devices.

In the desktop era, the internet seemed like a separate place partitioned off from everyday life by monitor screens. Mobile devices, especially our multiplying smart devices, integrate the virtual and the real as we carry the net with us, entertaining and informing ourselves and sharing our thoughts and experiences while we navigate through our daily lives. Mobile devices also represent a return to embodiment, augmenting our brains and our senses as we interact with the world around us. For now, we keep them close to our bodies, waiting for the day when they'll migrate into our clothing and, eventually, under

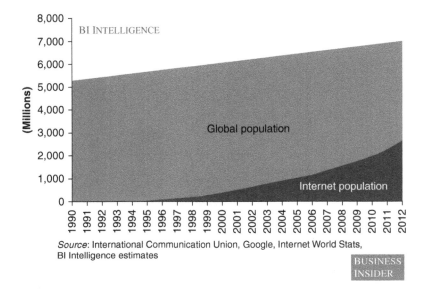

Figure 1.3 Global internet population 1990–2012. © Business Insider Intelligence, https://intelligence.businessinsider.com, reproduced by permission.

our skin. No longer will we enter cyberspace; cyberspace will enter us. With developed countries setting the pace, but developing countries acting as catalysts for innovations appropriate to their own contexts, we're in for some dramatic changes to our sense of space and time, our understanding of ourselves and others, and our ways of learning.

From e-learning to m-learning

The field of *e-learning* (electronic learning) is well-established. There's a whole area of scholarship built around the educational use of digital technologies like desktop and laptop computers, the web, and especially web 2.0. *M-learning* (mobile learning) shares enough common ground with e-learning that it features regularly in major e-learning conferences, journals and books. Yet we've also seen the emergence of dedicated conferences like mLearn (since 2002), International Association for Development of the Information Society (IADIS) Mobile Learning (since 2005) and MobiLearn Asia (since 2012); a professional organisation, the International Association for Mobile Learning (IAmLearn) (since 2007); journals like the *International Journal of Mobile Learning and Organisation* (since 2007) and the *International Journal of Mobile and Blended Learning* (since 2009); and growing numbers of book-length treatments.

Of course, the very form of the term 'm-learning' can't help but suggest parallels with 'e-learning' at the same time as it suggests there may be specific differences. Other recently popular terms like 'u-learning' (ubiquitous learning) and even 'p-learning' (pervasive learning) hint at the same kind of blend of commonalities and differences.

Similarly, the field of *Computer-Assisted Language Learning (CALL)* is a well-established subfield of e-learning, with its oddly old-fashioned moniker having seen off all challengers to gain global acceptance. In recent years, mainstream CALL conferences, journals and books have increasingly included mobile technologies in their purview, suggesting that in the language teaching community there's a general perception of continuity between the use of fixed and mobile tools. But perhaps the sense of continuity is most neatly captured in the term *Mobile-Assisted Language Learning (MALL)*. In the wake of George Chinnery's well-known 2006 article 'Going to the MALL', which brought the acronym to the attention of many teachers, it has continued to gain traction, surfacing at conferences, in journals and in books. As with 'm-learning', the form of the term 'MALL' suggests there may be both commonalities and differences with 'CALL'.

We've already noted that there are key differences between fixed technologies, which tend to be separate from daily life, and mobile technologies, which tend to be part of it. To decide how large the differences are, and how significant they are for education, we need to take a closer look at mobile devices. But this is a somewhat contested category. As a rule of thumb for differentiating what is mobile (which is included) from what is portable (which is not), we might use Puentedura's (2012) distinction that portable devices are normally used at Point A, closed down, and opened up again at Point B, while mobile devices may be used at Point A, Point B and everywhere in between, without stopping. While leaving a fuller discussion until Chapter 3, it's worth noting that laptops, with the exception of smaller devices like XOs, are not normally included. A representative list might include mobile phones, whether feature phones or smartphones, along with tablets, digital media players, e-readers and handheld gaming consoles.

A key theme of the recent m-learning literature has been that mobility does not refer only, or even primarily, to *devices*, but to *learners* (Pachler et al., 2010; Woodill, 2011) and even to *learning* itself (Traxler, 2007). Some suggest that it may also apply to the wider *society* and *era* in which the learning is taking place (Sharples et al., 2010; Traxler, 2007). Yet it's not easy to tease apart the mobility of the devices, the learners, the learning, the society and the era. Moreover, any definition of m-learning which doesn't view the devices as central risks straying into nebulous claims that all learning has always been mobile. While it's true that in some senses toys or books are mobile learning tools, such discussions go well beyond the scope of this book. Therefore, while bearing in mind that device mobility is not the be-all and end-all of mobile learning, taking a look at the affordances of the devices themselves is a logical way to begin unpacking the interlocking elements of mobility which underpin m-learning.

From affordability to affordances

In the discourses around digital technologies, we hear a great deal about the affordances of mobile devices, in terms of their social and educational impact and even, beyond this, their economic and political impact. But we must remember that *affordability* precedes *affordances*.

In the developed world, it's the affordability of mobile devices that has encouraged their spread throughout the population. This is why we're now in a position to discuss the social and educational affordances of smart devices, with their third generation (3G) or fourth generation (4G) connectivity and their smorgasbord of apps. On the other hand, it's easy to forget that lack of affordability remains an issue, leading to a patchy uptake of the iPods, iPhones and iPads that we hear so much about – along with other similar devices – and introducing equity challenges in Bring Your Own Device (BYOD) models.

But it's in the developing world that affordability matters most. As hardware prices continue to fall, a ' "mobile first" development trajectory' is becoming evident (World Bank, 2012, p.3). Africa has the world's highest growth rate in mobile phones (Isaacs, 2012a), which are described by the International Telecommunication Union (ITU) as the 'mass ICT technology of choice for Africa' (cited in ibid., p.12). In Latin America, meanwhile, there were an estimated 17 computers per 100 people in 2011, but there was already almost one mobile phone per person (Lugo & Schurmann, 2012). The limited affordability of desktop and laptop computers, along with the limited affordability and coverage of fixed telecommunications infrastructure, means that mobile devices are often the best, or only, option for internet access in the developing world (Deloitte/GSMA, 2012). This is borne out by statistics: although mobile devices accounted for 15% of global net traffic by the end of 2012 (see Figure 1.1), some 58% of web traffic was already mobile-based in Nigeria and Zimbabwe in that year (Deloitte/GSMA, 2012).

But affordability is relative. While an average European spends a little over 1% of their monthly income on mobile communication, an average

African spends 17% (STT & Grosskurth, cited in Vosloo, 2012). What's more, the average African gets a lot less for their money. The low-end phones typical of the developing world, with their limited functionality and connectivity, offer far fewer of the affordances we hear about in the developed world. By the end of 2011, 90% of the world's population was covered by 2G networks, but only 45% by 3G networks (ITU, 2012). In 2012, nearly 90% of mobile subscriptions in Africa were still restricted to older 2G or 2.5G networks (Gallen, 2012). We need to remember these limitations in projects that seek to broaden access to educational opportunities. Although it makes sense to plan with an eye to future mobile expansion in developing regions, our planning must remain grounded in the – long – present.

Of course, even when their *affordability* reaches a level that allows them to become widespread, new technologies don't lead to social changes by themselves (the technological determinism fallacy); nor can we say that social changes alone have led to the rise of new technologies (the social determinism fallacy). Rather, society and technology influence each other, a view often called a *social shaping* perspective (Baym, 2010; Selwyn, 2013; Williams & Edge, 1996). The social context promotes certain lines of technological development and certain uses of technologies; the technological context amplifies some social practices and constrains or undermines others. The obvious uses of new technologies, seen within a larger social framework, are what we might term their *affordances* – put simply, the purposes to which they seem most easily to lend themselves.

It's possible to identify certain affordances of mobile technologies which are bound up in the social and educational changes we see happening around us. Leaving aside for the moment the question of affordability, to which we'll return later, it's time to take a look at these affordances.

Where the local meets the global

In discussions of digital technologies, we often hear about an increased emphasis on the *global* but, especially since the advent of mobile phones, we've also heard about the increased salience of the *local*. While these points might at first seem contradictory, they're tightly intertwined with each other and with the ongoing transformation of our sense of space and place. Interestingly, the term 'm-learning' is sometimes seen as placing emphasis on mobility, seamlessness and the 'global', while the term 'u-learning', with which it's occasionally interchanged, may be seen as placing emphasis on contextualisation and embeddedness (Leone & Leo, 2011; Milrad et al., 2013) and thus the 'local'. But ultimately these are two sides of the same coin.

We've become used to accessing digital materials, digital communications and digital networks from whatever real-world locations we find ourselves in. As the developed world in particular shifts increasingly towards a digitally mediated *network society* structure (Castells, 2010) – predicated on mobile *networked individualism* (Rainie & Wellman, 2012) – our online and offline lives overlap more and more. Our mobile devices contribute considerably to the fact that we find ourselves living simultaneously in a local *space of places* and a global *space of flows* (Castells, 2010; Castells et al., 2007). In other words, we live in local real-world contexts and at the same time in online networks, which provide a permanent, pervasive, global context for our thoughts and actions. As Manuel Castells (2008) writes of our era of mobile communication: 'We never quit the networks, and the networks never quit us; this is the real coming of age of the network society' (p.448).

Some m-learning focuses on global materials, communications and networks, and ignores the local context. As a result, the physical setting may be irrelevant to the substance of the learning (if not to its organisational, psychological or affective aspects). Connectivity permitting and distractions notwithstanding, it's possible to learn anywhere: in a school, a café, a park or a train. This kind of *seamless learning* (Chan et al., 2006; Looi et al., 2010) across different physical spaces is a more flexible version of e-learning, untethered from desktop computers. Some educational institutions are already exploiting this flexibility by reconfiguring the traditional 'built pedagogy' (Monahan, 2002) of classrooms, making them into adaptable spaces which teachers or students can reshape to suit newer pedagogies and interactions mediated by mobile devices.

But m-learning may equally entail a heightened focus on context. In the past, a contextual focus was present in limited ways in excursions and field trips. Now, education can emerge much more fully from the classroom as we begin 'to utilise our everyday life-worlds as learning spaces', as Pachler et al. (2010, p.6) put it. They go on: 'the world has become the curriculum populated by mobile device users in a constant state of expectancy and contingency' (p.25). As we become more mobile and travel more, opportunities arise for learning, including language learning, across contexts. But contexts aren't just simple shells made up of the locations or times in which events occur. They're dynamic configurations of *where*, *when* and *who*, combined with numerous other elements such as *what* (activity) and *why* (purpose), and they even incorporate the technologies we use (Dourish, 2004; Luckin, 2010; Sharples et al., 2010). Context-aware users, especially those with mobile context-sensitive devices, can engage in *contextual(ised) learning* (JISC, n.d.; Petersen et al., 2009) or *situated learning* (Comas-Quinn et al., 2009; Traxler, 2007) or indeed *embodied learning* (Driver, 2012; Klopfer, 2008). More precisely, we might say that contextualised learning, situated learning or embodied learning can occur when people produce their own *user-generated contexts* (Cook, 2010) or *learner-generated contexts* (ibid.; Luckin, 2010) on the fly by intentionally turning their real-world contexts into *learning contexts* via their actions (Wong, 2013). This is a process greatly aided by mobile devices which can highlight, capture and share the interconnected elements of a context that are most relevant to a given learning experience. Outside of formal classrooms, learning contexts don't exist a priori; they're created in the moment of learning.

Such context-aware approaches represent an extension of *seamless learning* – one that suits the originally intended meaning of the term and, even more, its evolving usage (Milrad et al., 2013; Wong, 2013) – by fostering increased engagement with the local without forsaking the benefits of global connections. In short, these approaches enable locally embedded but globally informed (and globally communicated) learning, centred very much on the experience of each individual learner. This can dramatically increase the effectiveness of situated language learning and literacy practice, for example, especially when enhanced by the augmented reality (AR) technologies that are now becoming commonplace. And, as individuals move across communities, there's potential for local cultural encounters, which are often surprising and sometimes unsettling – but also informative, if simultaneously viewed from a global intercultural perspective.

When context-aware m-learning and MALL make the most of the affordances of mobile technologies for combining the local and the global, and for learning *in* the real world rather than just learning *about* it, they begin to diverge from e-learning and CALL. However, by its nature, the learning enabled by mobile devices is often informal and contingent, and so needs careful structuring and guidance if it is to feed into formal learning and assessment systems. This may be achievable with the help of recently popular platforms like *personal learning networks (PLNs)* and *personal learning environments (PLEs)*, which might be viewed as stable *user-generated online contexts*, interlinked with other learners' self-generated contexts and designed to endure over time (see Chapter 4). Here, students can review and reconceptualise learning in interaction with teachers and peers. But as yet, formal and informal learning are not well aligned, and we need to explore further ways of building bridges between them.

Where the episodic meets the extended

The received wisdom in discussions of new technologies is that all things mobile should be small in size, succinct in style, and short in duration. By implication, mobile learning should be *episodic*, that is, delivered in brief episodes. But education as we know it, even when designed specifically for mobile devices, relies explicitly or implicitly on *extended* learning over time. As with the global and the local, however, the episodic and the extended are very much interwoven in our digital mobile era.

In tandem with a new sense of space and place, a new sense of time is emerging, again especially in developed countries. In a world of *timeless time* (Castells, 2010; Castells et al., 2007), new technologies, and notably our mobile devices, allow us to uncouple time both from the biological clock and from the traditional sequencing of events. Our lives are characterised by multitasking activities and conversations undertaken quasi-simultaneously, as work and leisure blur into each other. Just as fluid space allows conversations to flow unhindered across geographical settings, fluid time allows them to flow across temporal settings. Conversations are no longer restricted to isolated, if typically extended, blocks of time. Rather, our mobile devices permit 'a constant flickering of conversation' (Sheller cited in Traxler, 2010, p.6) in the background of our lives, with brief episodes strung into extended chains of meaning stretching across places and times.

E-learning with fixed devices involves an older style of interaction. As John Traxler (2010) points out, such interaction typically 'takes place in a bubble, and in dedicated times and places where the user has his or her back to the rest of the world for a substantial and probably pre-meditated episode' (p.5). Consequently, as he goes on to say, 'desktop technologies operate in their own little world while mobile technologies operate in *the* world' (ibid.; italics in original). Naturally, mobile devices can be used in fixed places and at fixed times, as well as over extended periods, but this simply replicates e-learning on smaller screens. It's only when we shift away from fixed places and times that we begin to fully exploit the affordances of mobile devices. It's about using them on the move. And that means they need to slot into the in-between spaces and times in our lives, the places where we wait, the moments we kill, but which the right tools let us turn into learning contexts.

It's not surprising that 'small', 'succinct' and 'short' are commonly used adjectives, along with their more cosmopolitan cousins: m-learning is frequently described as *bite-sized* (Klopfer, 2011; Traxler, 2007), *granular* (Quinn, 2012; Woodill, 2011) and *chunked* or *in chunks* (Quinn, 2012; Stodd, 2012; Traxler, 2010; Woodill, 2011). Mobile devices, says Klopfer (2011), 'aren't only for long focused sessions, but can also be used for bite-sized interactions taking place for mere seconds in the context of some other related (or unrelated) activity'. If the interaction occurs during an unrelated activity, it's likely that we're once again talking about displaced e-learning, such as using an app to revise vocabulary during a bus journey home, where a mobile device may add flexibility (since the learning can occur anywhere and anytime) and efficiency (in the case of spaced revision of learning). But it's when the interaction occurs during a related activity that m-learning comes into its own, that is, when the context is drawn into the learning experience or, more exactly, when the learner establishes their own user-generated context that incorporates elements of their real-world context. If tied to particular places at particular times, the learning that arises is almost inevitably episodic. It could occur in *push mode*, with context-sensitive devices delivering relevant prompts and support to students so they don't pass up learning opportunities. It could occur in *pull mode*, with students seeking support for desired learning experiences from online resources or networks of contacts. It could also take the form of students creating and annotating multimodal records of (potential) learning experiences, and disseminating and discussing them through digital networks, either at the moment they occur or at a later time when there is more leisure for reflection.

But it's not only about episodes, because episodes add up over time. As with conversation, mobile devices allow a constant flickering of learning to go on in the background – and sometimes, episodically, in the foreground – of our lives. With structuring and guidance, these episodes can be linked into a coherent whole and, depending on the situation, unified within a more formal educational structure like a PLN or PLE. In this way formal learning can be enriched by drawing on informal, spontaneous, real-world learning grounded in the experience of each learner. And going beyond the bounds of formal education, mobile devices can support lifelong learning which, even if episodic, is effectively unbounded. Of course, as learning becomes integrated not only with the *where* but the *when* of life, m-learning and MALL diverge further from e-learning and CALL.

Where the personal meets the social

In the discourses around digital technologies, we also hear regularly that mobile is *social* and, simultaneously, that it's *personal*. Once again, though apparently at opposite ends of the spectrum, these turn out to be closely interrelated.

'Mobile is the needle; social is the thread', states Kathryn Zickuhr (2012). Mobile devices have helped drive the growth of social media and social networking over recent years (Udell, 2012). The numbers speak for themselves: mobile social media consumption is outstripping personal computer (PC) social media consumption (see Figure 1.4). Mobile is, notably, an ever larger driver of Facebook use (Ballvé, 2013), while there is some evidence emerging that Facebook is in turn a driver of mobile use (Pimmer et al., 2012). Indeed, CEO Mark Zuckerberg claims that Facebook has now become a mobile company (Facebook, 2013). As the world's largest social networking site, Facebook is both a mirror of and a catalyst for wider changes in our network society: changes which bring benefits (such as the value we draw from our ever present global connections) as well as concerns (like the erosion of traditional distinctions between the private and the public). But if mobile has ushered in a more social era, it's also ushered in a more personal era where, within certain limits, our decisions about who to socialise with are much more open. Networked individuals, certainly in the developed world,

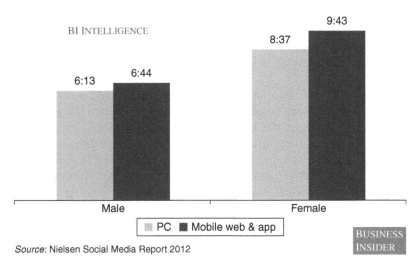

Figure 1.4 US social media consumption on PCs vs mobile devices, 2012 (hours and mins per month). © Business Insider Intelligence, https://intelligence.businessinsider.com, reproduced by permission.

can increasingly join and identify with diverse networks of their choice, rather than being assigned community membership and identity on the basis of history or geography (Pegrum, 2010).

In some ways, education can be much more personal in our era, too. M-learning is often seen as promoting *personalisation* (Berge, 2011; Squire, 2009), *individualisation* (Cook, 2010; Melhuish & Falloon, 2010) and *customisation* (Quinn, 2012). Increased engagement is a widely noted effect of one-to-one (1:1) learning with individual devices, especially if users own and can personalise their devices and determine how they're used (Burden et al., 2012; Pachler, 2009). Customisation of learning may involve *automated adaptation*, with voice recognition software adapting to a user's accent, Intelligent CALL (ICALL) software adjusting difficulty levels to a learner's developing skills, or AR software pushing information to a user based on their learning history and context. Customisation of learning may also involve *user tailoring*. Learners can select their own hardware, rather than being restricted to one-size-fits-all technology. They can select their own software and make choices within it to cater to personal preferences or needs, including special needs or disabilities. They can select their own resources from app stores or the wider internet, without waiting for information to be distributed to them. They can capture, create and curate their own *user-generated content* (or *learner-generated content*). And they can select real-world places and times in which to put all of the above into action, setting up their own user-generated contexts which include the learners themselves, their chosen tools, and their individual goals, and are therefore highly personal. After all, as noted earlier, learning contexts are not just about *where* and *when*, but about *what* and *why*, and indeed *who*.

In brief, m-learning empowers individuals as agents and (co-)designers of their own learning. Of course, it's important not to confuse consumerist choices among colours and covers (typical of current mobile hardware) or superficial selections among preset options and templates (typical of current mobile software) with deeper levels of personalisation. While colour choices may increase a sense of ownership, and menu choices may increase the relevance of learning, what matters most is that learners can make real decisions about their goals, approaches and materials, and generate their own learning contexts and content. This carries the potential to enhance their sense of agency, control and ownership, while simultaneously requiring them to take on more responsibility for their own learning.

Nevertheless, m-learning doesn't only involve personalisation. Having observed the confluence of the mobile and the social in our era, we shouldn't be surprised to hear it said that by its very nature, m-learning is social (Stodd, 2012; Udell, 2012). Mobile devices, above all the mobile phones that are coming to dominate our thinking about m-learning, are fundamentally social communication tools. When we introduce them into learning, we also introduce a sense of informal connectedness, via voice calls, Short Message Service (SMS) texts, instant messaging (IM), and social networking platforms. Learners have become used to carrying mobile social networks with them wherever they go, drawing on them whenever they need support, and sharing through them whatever they experience. But m-learning isn't just about learning in online social networks, it's about learning in everyday social realities – and it's about learning at the crossover point between the two. While formal learning (often including e-learning) has to build connections with the real world, informal learning (often including m-learning) already takes place in the real world, albeit a real world overlaid with digital networks. Many m-learning initiatives involve students using contextualised digital data to support engagement with real-world settings and the people who inhabit them. Other initiatives involve students recording real-world learning experiences and sharing them digitally through social media platforms. And if teachers, peers and wider audiences then go on to offer differentiated feedback on this individual learning, they help close the loop between the social and the personal.

The meeting of the personal and the social is perhaps most clearly seen in the current educational trend towards building PLNs and PLEs. These personalised but networked learning platforms are based on the idea of individuals learning at the centre of, and supported by, their own social networks. PLEs have come into their own in the mobile era (Johnson et al., 2012) as handheld devices have opened up anywhere, anytime access, and multiplied learning input and output options. In fact, mobile devices have been called *learning hubs* (Wong et al., 2010), and we might see them as omnipresent gateways to PLNs and PLEs, allowing students to fuse local and global learning, episodic and extended learning, and personal and social learning, as they build narratives of their learning journeys which are highly individual but shared with, responded to, influenced by and ultimately embedded in their social and educational networks.

M-learning, suggests Agnes Kukulska-Hulme (2013a), is a '[p]aradoxical new learning' which is 'individual yet social'. It fits perfectly with a society of networked individuals. Obviously, e-learning on desktop or laptop computers, especially when it has a web 2.0 orientation, can also be personal (involving, for example, building PLEs and receiving differentiated feedback) and social (involving collaboration and co-construction of understanding in social networks). However, the trend towards the integration of the personal and the social is not just *mobilised* but also *intensified* by mobile devices. M-learning can be more personal: the hardware and software are typically more customised by, and to, the individual user, who can exploit their devices to generate learning contexts and content in a range of real-world settings. M-learning can also be more social: the hardware and software have social origins, are often already embedded in users' regular social interactions, and make it easy to support and share learning through mobile social networks. With the right connectivity, no mobile learner ever has to learn alone. Their digital networks are ubiquitous and, with AR software, will soon be right in front of their eyes wherever they go. Here again, m-learning and MALL pull further away from e-learning and CALL.

A fuzzy concept of mobile learning

It's become clear that m-learning differs from e-learning, and MALL from CALL, because of the affordances of the devices involved. We've seen that the apparently contradictory attributes of mobile devices often turn out to be complementary, and that they can work together in such a way as to give m-learning considerable reach and power. As we now come back to the question of exactly what constitutes m-learning and MALL, and how they're shaped by the interplay of their affordability and their affordances, it's time to start elaborating our theoretical answers with references to real-world practice drawn both from the case studies reported in this book and the wider literature.

In an early definition in 2000, Clark Quinn described m-learning as: 'elearning independent of location in time or space'. By the time of the EU MOBIlearn project (2002–2005), the concept had been unshackled from e-learning and broadened to cover: '[a]ny sort of learning that happens when the learner is not at a fixed, predetermined location, or learning that happens when the learner takes advantage of the learning opportunities offered by mobile technologies' (O'Malley et al., 2005). In the later UK MoLeNET project (2007–2010), m-learning was equally broadly defined as: '[t]he exploitation of ubiquitous handheld technologies, together with wireless and mobile phone networks, to facilitate, support, enhance and extend the reach of teaching and learning' (*MoLeNET*, 2010). In a widely cited definition from the year MoLeNET began, interaction and context were foregrounded in a description of m-learning as: 'the processes of coming to know through conversations across multiple contexts among people and personal interactive technologies' (Sharples et al., 2007, p.225). In short, it's very difficult to capture m-learning, with its evolving technologies, emerging uses and varying cultural settings, in a way that is both succinct and comprehensive. Indeed, suggests John Traxler (2007), m-learning 'is inherently a "noisy" phenomenon where context is everything'.

It may be best, then, to view mobile learning less as a category than a *fuzzy concept* which allows for different degrees of mobility of the devices, the learners and the learning. The greater the overall degree of mobility, the more conspicuous the example of m-learning. By extension, MALL is also a fuzzy concept, referring to language learning scenarios in which varying degrees of mobility pertain to the devices, the learners and the learning experience itself.

When the devices are mobile

In some scenarios, although the *devices* are mobile in principle, the learners typically move little if at all during the learning experience, which takes place in one or two fixed and largely unchanging locations. Thus, the principle of mobility applies to the devices but not to the learners or the learning experience:

☑ devices   ☒ learners   ☒ learning experience

For example, mobile devices are an affordable way to set up *connected classrooms* where students can access the internet, download apps, create content, and communicate with each other and the world; sets of devices may be moved between classes and classrooms as desired, as can be seen in the Casa Thomas Jefferson iPads for Access project in Brazil (see Case Study 2). Or, in increasingly popular *flipped classroom* models, where more pedagogically traditional content transmission or behaviourist activities are completed outside class to free up in-class time for active learning (Johnson et al., 2012; UNESCO, 2013c), students may be expected to use their mobile devices not only in the classroom but at home as well. Mobile devices can also *become the classroom* in various kinds of distance learning, where they serve as an affordable supplement to, or substitute for, desktop and laptop devices. We see this in the arrival of mobile options for accessing global Massive Open Online Courses (MOOCs), sometimes referred to as mobile MOOCs (mMOOCs) (de Waard, 2013). We see it, too, in local services for potential students who don't have easy access either to PCs or to teachers, but who do have phones, which can be turned into classrooms in certain places and times. That might mean Pakistani girls in rural homes, as in UNESCO'S Post-literacy project (see Case Study 3); or it might mean upper-caste Indian boys who are supervising lower-caste boys working in the fields, or lower-caste Indian girls who are grazing goats, as in the MILLEE project (see Case Study 7).

In the above cases, the mobility of the devices may be little exploited. To return to Puentedura's (2012) definition, the devices are treated as portable rather than mobile. Actually, m-learning at this level might be seen as a kind of portable e-learning. In a connected classroom, students may remain at their desks in one fixed location, although the devices are rotated between classes from time to time. In a flipped classroom model, students may use their devices across two fixed locations, namely the classroom and home, but not while actually moving. In distance learning, too, students often use their devices in just one or two fixed locations where they can focus without distractions, whether that's in an air-conditioned office or under a tree in a field. In all of these settings, the mobility/portability of the devices is crucial since they must be transported between locations, but the students are not mobile while learning, and the learning experience itself is unaffected. Yet in many of these cases, the learners can choose to more fully exploit the mobility of their devices when they feel ready (or when they're encouraged to do so by teachers). At this point they themselves become mobile, taking m-learning to the next level.

When the learners are mobile

In some scenarios, the *learners* are mobile, even if the learning experience itself isn't affected by changing locations. Here, the principle of mobility applies to the devices and the learners, but not to the learning experience:

☑ devices   ☑ learners   ☒ learning experience

A certain amount of movement can be explicitly introduced into connected classrooms with pair work or group work activities centred on collaborative, creative software and apps. Moreover, collective learning often emerges spontaneously, with students migrating around the room with their devices, forming groups around users who have discovered something new, sharing insights, and offering each other peer support. Similar phenomena have been observed in the Brazilian iPads project mentioned above (see Case Study 2) and iPad classrooms from Scotland to Australia (Burden et al., 2012; Oakley et al., 2012), as well as in XO laptop classrooms from Australia to Uruguay (see Case Study 12; Hourcade et al., 2009).

Naturally, mobile devices can also be used on the move outside the classroom. There are regular patches of downtime in everyday settings, whether you're going for a walk, waiting for a bus, commuting on the underground, or taking time out in a café – or some similar combination or sequence of activities. Given the distractions of real-world contexts, says Julian Stodd (2012), 'the environment conspires against complexity, at least for learning' (Kindle location 927). That's why content consumed in everyday settings, and especially on the move, should ideally be granular, notwithstanding the risk of fragmented understanding. Both push and pull vocabulary services – with content automatically delivered at regular intervals in the first case, and requested manually by learners in the second – work on this principle of granularity, as seen in the British Council's Learn English SMS services in Sudan and Libya, and the British Council/Nokia Life Learn English project in China (see Case Studies 4 & 9). Similarly, Nulu Languages' chunked Spanish and English news stories in the Americas (see Case Study 11) make it easy for mobile users to process them on the go.

The above cases are examples of *independent learning*, which is self-determined and, in pull services, self-paced. But it's possible to take independent learning a step further and free it completely from the oversight of teachers or the strictures of courses, thanks to the growing digital knowledge commons and the rise of freely available Open Educational Resources (OER). But, even if we leave aside issues of information literacy and information overload for now, a note of pedagogical caution is necessary here. While collaborative construction of knowledge, discussion of learning and community mentoring are quite possible online (think: contributing to Wikipedia), the reality more often involves simple transmission of bite-sized content (think: looking up a fact in Wikipedia). This may be a very useful kind of learning, but without structure or guidance it may amount to a very limited kind of education. Still, with these caveats, independent learning is a democratising supplement to institutional learning; and in contexts where there are few institutions, teachers or even information sources, it may be radically empowering. In either case, it dramatically enhances students' autonomy and opens up lifelong learning possibilities.

In the above scenarios, the learners are mobile to varying extents during the process of learning, yet the learning experience remains largely the same, wherever it's accessed. These users are not yet making much use of their settings to generate their own learning contexts or content. But when moving around the classroom or schoolyard, there are possibilities for drawing the context itself into the learning. And independent learning is very often inspired by contextual factors – as we use our phones to check details of places we're visiting or confirm facts we're discussing – and thus begins to shade into just-in-time learning, where the learning experience itself takes on a degree of mobility. M-learning at the next level can be a markedly different phenomenon from m-learning at other levels and, because it more fully exploits the affordances of mobile devices, can also be markedly different from e-learning.

When the learning experience is mobile

In some scenarios, not only are the devices and the learners mobile, but so too is the *learning experience*, as learners shift between contexts that feed directly into their unfolding learning. Here, the principle of mobility applies to the devices, the learners *and* the learning experience:

☑ devices   ☑ learners   ☑ learning experience

In the classroom or the schoolyard, as well as on excursions and outings, mobile devices support situated learning, as students receive or seek information from online sources, peers and mentors to inform their interactions with their contexts, and as they use their devices to make and share multimedia records of their contextualised learning experiences. In other words, they're turning real-world contexts into learning contexts at the point where their local experiences intersect with their global communications channels, and where their personal experiences intersect with their social networks. Students' situated learning – captured, reorganised, and (re-)presented as user-generated content – can be shared across digital networks, where it may be reused as learning material by other students (Comas-Quinn et al., 2009; Kukulska-Hulme, 2010b). This is web 2.0 gone truly mobile. We can see this in the iPads for Access project (see Case Study 2), where teachers are now considering how best to recycle and build on the user-generated multimedia content created by students around the school. Indeed, the Brazilian project demonstrates how a single mobile tool, in this case the iPad, can sometimes be used by largely immobile learners; sometimes by partially mobile learners; and sometimes as part of a mobile learning experience where students generate their own learning content. In fact, the production of user-generated content, often within user-generated contexts, characterises a number of recent MALL initiatives. It forms the basis of the European SIMOLA project (see Case Study 1), which provides a framework within which learners have built a multimodal lexicon of contextualised language use, complete with comments, tags and ratings. It can be seen, too, in dedicated intercultural initiatives like the Spanish mobile blogging project at the Open University in the UK (see Vignette 11).

It's been suggested that mobile devices promote a shift from traditional *just-in-case* to newer *just-in-time* learning (Traxler, 2007; Woodill, 2011). The essence of this kind of learning is its relevance in terms of *when* (right now!), but also *where, who, what* and *why*, combined with brevity: not too little information, but certainly not too much. It's closely related to the idea of performance support, notably in a workplace learning situation, but its applications go well beyond this. Technologically, it's simpler to deliver just-in-time learning in pull mode; in the European MASELTOV project (see Case Study 13), a Turkish immigrant to Vienna who doesn't understand a German sign, for example, might activate the text lens software on her smartphone and scan it to obtain an instantaneous translation. It's more complex, but increasingly possible, to deliver this kind of learning in push mode; when the same Turkish immigrant visits an Austrian doctor, a recommender system can automatically send her a set of relevant German language expressions through her location-aware smartphone. AR technology, which underpins MASELTOV, as well as the Mentira Spanish learning game in the USA (see Case Study 8) and the Singaporean Heritage Trails where students can practise English and Chinese (see Case Study 14), can effectively scaffold students' (co-)creation of learning contexts and learning content, supporting them in turning all kinds of interactions in the real world into learning interactions. In all of these scenarios, transfer distance – that is, the difficulty of transferring learning to real-world situations and applying it – is minimised, if not eliminated, because learning is already taking place in a real-world setting (Klopfer, 2008; Quinn, 2012).

Just-in-time learning raises its own questions. Is systematic just-in-case learning a necessary complement to – or precursor of – personalised just-in-time learning? Do we need an overarching just-in-case structure to ensure episodic just-in-time learning doesn't become superficial and fragmented? Do we need to differentiate performance support from learning, with each individual applying filters which facilitate performance (just-in-time), learning (just-in-case), or both together (Quinn, 2013)? Should learning tools always support us, or should they challenge us too (Stodd, 2012) – and is that possible without a just-in-case element? We'll take up these kinds of questions in the next chapter, when we look at the attacks on formal education in recent years. For now, it's worth noting that the Brazilian iPads for Access project is linked to a formal curriculum at a language school, the US Mentira project is linked to a formal curriculum at a university, the Singaporean Heritage Trails have been developed in conjunction with the Ministry of Education (MOE) and are linked to the national curriculum, and the SIMOLA project has been integrated by teachers into a variety of formal educational courses. The MASELTOV project navigates this tricky territory by building links between its pull and push functions and learners' ongoing language lessons, as well as including monitoring and mentoring options. Perhaps a hybrid of just-in-case and just-in-time learning is the way of the future.

Crucially, not only are the devices and the learners mobile in all these scenarios, but so too are the learning experiences. The *affordances* of mobile technologies for linking the local and the global, the episodic and the extended, and the personal and the social, are present to some extent at all levels of m-learning but greatest at this third level, which, consequently, is also the level where m-learning differs most from e-learning, and MALL from CALL. Conversely, the *affordability* of m-learning is lowest at this level. It's no accident that the AR projects outlined above are led out of Albuquerque, Singapore and Vienna. M-learning is always a product of a particular interplay of affordability and affordances in a particular context. A clear example of this within the context of a single country is seen in the contrast between the Pearson/Nokia Mobiledu project and the British Council/Nokia Life Learn English project (see Case Studies 6 & 9), both running in China and each seeking to exploit the potential of mobile language learning to the greatest extent possible with its respective target audience. While the latter project is limited to sending richly formatted text messages (using SMS as the bearer) to a demographic which only has access to lower end handsets, the former was able to offer multimedia apps and interactive content to a wealthier demographic with higher end feature phones and smartphones.

The larger context, then, plays an important role in shaping our approach to m-learning, and in determining the extent to which we can draw on the various affordances of mobile technologies. It's not a case of better or worse uses of m-learning, but of how the affordability, affordances and context combine to determine the space of what is possible.

Where to from here?

But just how large is the space of what is possible? From a global perspective, will mobile technologies change language and literacy learning a little, or a lot? These questions, which implicitly run through all the chapters to come, underpin Agnes Kukulska-Hulme's comments (see Vignette 1 below). It may well be – as foreshadowed in this chapter – that we can identify ways to operate effectively at the intersection of the affordability and affordances of mobile technologies. It may be that as a result – as suggested in Kukulska-Hulme's comments – mobile learning could change everything. Is this a journey we're ready to take?

Vignette 1   Shiny technology masks seismic change

Agnes Kukulska-Hulme, The Open University, UK

On the one hand, mobile learning changes nothing. Learning content is simply delivered to smartphones and tablets and accessed at learners' convenience. Podcasts and mobile apps replace some traditional resources, but they essentially imitate familiar learning materials. More people gain access to language learning, but they still struggle to express themselves in a foreign language and to understand others. Mobile language learning is mainly an adjunct to, or an extension of, existing educational practice. It is a small, incremental change, hardly worth a mention. Learners occasionally stumble upon seemingly useful mobile resources that they download to their phones and tablets, and they are quite content with that. Teachers' awareness of new resources and tools is growing, but it has no real impact on their practice.

On the other hand, mobile learning changes everything. Language learning is opened up to millions of people who are variously disadvantaged. Language learners lead the way, finally able to influence what they would like to learn, with whom and how. Situated language use is captured and communication experiences are shared as they happen. Learners record language samples and use portable tools to monitor and analyse foreign language use across space and time. If someone cannot or will not learn a new language, their personal device acts as their interpreter or it speaks as they type. Immediate translation and cumulative data analysis are available as part of a repertoire of services provided by linguistically informed, portable educational tools. Language learning materials and curricula are transformed. Language learning keeps on changing, as new conversational styles evolve when people speak to devices and to robots attending to their needs. We are nearly there. Is it a welcome direction of travel?

▶ Further reading: Kukulska-Hulme (2010a, 2010b, 2013b).

M-learning and MALL are relatively young fields that still lack strong theoretical foundations. As we theorise m-learning, it's vital to keep a close eye on real-world examples where m-learning, and more specifically MALL, is making a difference. Vignettes like the one above are distributed through the book, each reflecting the insights of an educator or educators with intimate knowledge of a particular mobile learning context, and often multiple mobile learning contexts. Case studies, too, are interwoven throughout the chapters that follow: some of the language and literacy projects described are small, some large; some are local, some international; some are commercial, some not-for-profit; some are from the developed world, but many more are initiatives from developing regions, which tend to be very much underreported if reported at all. Unsurprisingly, China and India loom large, with their multitudinous language learning populations. But many other countries are represented here too. Casting the net widely will, it is hoped, help us to view MALL not just as an offshoot of Western pedagogies and practices, but as a global endeavour with many different inflections in many different parts of the world. Between them, the vignettes and the case studies can help expand our sense of the potential of m-learning, while ensuring that our theoretical understandings remain grounded in practical experience as we explore what is possible in widely varying contexts.

These contexts may be cultural and linguistic, of course, but they are also political, economic and social. And in each context, there are certain agendas which are more or less prominent in driving m-learning and MALL. It is to these that we now turn.

2
Agendas for Mobile Learning

As mobile technologies flourish around us, it's important to pause and ask ourselves: why should (or shouldn't) we be using these tools in education? What do they achieve? Whose interests do they serve? These questions go to the heart of what we think education is, or could be.

Is this picture familiar? Uniformed students sit silently in fixed rows, hands raised, waiting to be chosen to respond to a question from the teacher. Or they sit with their heads down, reading set texts and penning their answers, as they memorise facts for regurgitation in high-stakes tests. Most of us know this stereotype. Most of us have experienced some version of it at some time. But this 20th century model of education, with its genesis in the late 19th century, is outdated, say critics (Dikkers, 2011; Leadbeater, 2008). Such a model is more about industrial efficiency than educational effectiveness (Quinn, 2012); is of ever decreasing value in preparing for life in post-industrial, networked societies (Dudeney et al., 2013); and, for various reasons, fails to cater to large numbers of people, young and old, around the world. Digital technologies, it is suggested, may offer a way forward.

We can identify at least three major agendas, related to the above concerns, which underpin the promotion of digital technologies in education: *transforming teaching and learning; developing 21st century skills; and promoting social justice* (cf. Warschauer, 2011). All three apply to m-learning as much as, if not more than, to e-learning in general. While the three agendas sometimes mesh together, at other times they may be partially in conflict. We should be wary, then, of claims that introducing digital tools will lead to direct educational benefits in any simple way. New technologies function within complex cultural, social, political, economic and educational ecologies (Selwyn, 2011, 2013; Warschauer, 2011), and whatever benefits they bring can only emerge from within these complex ecosystems.

First agenda: Transforming teaching & learning

For many educators, digital technologies open up space for introducing new pedagogies and reworking old ones, with educational approaches, methods, curricula, syllabi and lesson plans being reimagined in light of the affordances of new tools. Like new technologies in general, mobile devices can support a whole spectrum of pedagogical approaches, starting with traditional transmission and behaviourist approaches (Kukulska-Hulme & Shield, 2008; Naismith et al., 2006; Oakley et al., 2012). However, as in the broader e-learning research, there is an emerging consensus in the m-learning research that the affordances of mobile technologies are especially suited to promoting approaches like *constructivism* and, explicitly or implicitly, *social constructivism* (e.g., Cochrane, 2014; Dikkers, 2011; Melhuish & Falloon, 2010). Many MALL studies come to the same conclusion (e.g., Comas-Quinn et al., 2009; Petersen et al., 2009).

Social constructivism, whose origins lie in the work of the Russian psychologist Lev Vygotsky (1978), is based on the idea that individual learners actively construct their understanding through their experiences and their interactions with others, as they integrate new knowledge with their existing knowledge base. It fits better than transmission or behaviourist approaches with what we know about how people learn. Nowadays there are many versions and interpretations of constructivism (Levy & Stockwell, 2006) but there is broad agreement that learning should be active and exploratory; social and collaborative; discussion-oriented and reflective; authentic and contextualised; and above all, student-centred. The role of teachers is not to command and lecture but to orchestrate and guide. The affordances of mobile devices – their ability to promote learning which is locally situated but globally linked, initially episodic but ultimately extended, and highly personalised but socially embedded – mean that m-learning fits neatly with this kind of approach, especially, though not only, when the learning experiences themselves are mobile. Indeed, their affordances are powerful enough that mobile technologies may even function as something of a Trojan horse (JISC, n.d.) for introducing new pedagogical possibilities into resistant teaching and learning environments.

In many ways social constructivism is a subtle pedagogy that takes the focus off teachers and teaching – though it demands that educators adopt a complex structuring and guiding role – and places it on learners and learning. Naturally, when classrooms become learner-centred, when students become active, and when teachers become guides – in short, when education shifts from push mode to pull mode (Leigh Bassendowski & Petrucka, 2013) – structures of authority are also transformed. There is a move away from hierarchical power relations to more open collaboration between teachers and students, with both being positioned as members of wider networks that stretch far beyond the classroom walls. The relative equality and freedom of students, coupled with digital technologies, increases their agency to take control of their education and to complement formal with informal learning as they generate their own contexts and content. In some cases, experienced learners may choose to leave behind qualified teachers and formal classrooms altogether as they independently pursue their goals, a choice facilitated by the wealth of digital resources and informal learning opportunities available. Whether this is an ideal option is a question we'll return to below.

Of course, social constructivism doesn't stand alone as the sole contemporary educational approach. In the m-learning literature, commonly referenced elaborations of and complements to constructivism include Seymour Papert's *constructionism*, with its emphasis on learning-by-making (Harel & Papert, 1991); Jean Lave and Etienne Wenger's (1991) *situated learning*, which focuses on construction of knowledge through participation in communities of practice; George Siemens' *connectivism* which, drawing on the concept of distributed cognition, emphasises learning through navigating and building connections within social and digital networks (Siemens & Tittenberger, 2009); Yrjö Engeström's *activity theory* model, which offers a way of understanding the complexity of learning mediated by artefacts, including mobile tools (Engeström et al., 1999); and Diana Laurillard's (2012) *conversational framework*, which codifies design principles for technology-enhanced, including mobile-enhanced, learning. Constructivism and related approaches are often realised through *inquiry-based learning*, *problem-based learning, project-based learning* and *task-based learning*. The underpinning principles are seen not only as part of effective pedagogy, but as part of effective preparation for 21st century life, as students become adept both at constructing individual knowledge and at contributing to collective intelligence in authentic, complex, networked settings. The motivational benefits of these empowering approaches dovetail with the motivational benefits of empowering technologies.

A deliberate approach to the transformation of teaching and learning can be seen in Ruben Puentedura's (2011) well-known SAMR model (see Figure 2.1). Most teachers who work with new technologies, suggests Puentedura (2012), will begin on the lower levels of *substitution*

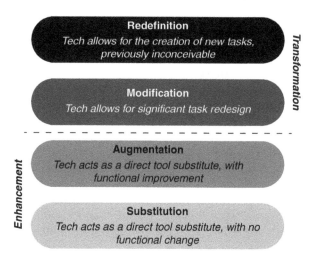

Figure 2.1 The SAMR model.
Source: Puentedura (2011), reproduced by permission.

(e.g., asking students to use an e-book instead of a paper book, where there may be efficiency gains but no learning gains) or *augmentation* (e.g., asking students to export their e-book annotations as an integrated file, giving them a coherent overview of their notes as the basis for an essay, and resulting in small learning gains). Changes on these levels result at most in *enhancement* of learning, but not *transformation,* which requires either task *modification* (e.g., students sharing their integrated notes and incorporating them into essays posted on a blog for feedback by classmates, leading to real improvement of their writing and thus significant learning gains) or task *redefinition* (e.g., students responding not through essays but through digital videos, which can go through a cycle of feedback and editing before being shared online with a wider public, potentially leading to dramatic learning gains). It's apparent that for Puentedura, transformation essentially involves a shift in a social constructivist direction, where students can actively co-construct understanding while building their 21st century skills, as discussed below.

Critical questions about transforming teaching & learning

Despite the hype, there is limited evidence that teaching with technology improves learning more than teaching without technology – though there is little evidence it does any harm, either. This idea is neatly captured in Thomas Russell's (2010) *No Significant Difference* phenomenon, based on studies of technology in education stretching back to the 1920s. That said, recent studies focusing on digital tools in particular have found small improvements when they're used, especially in blended approaches (ibid.; US Dept of Education, 2010). Setting aside the question of what is measured – are we teaching digital skills but assessing print skills? are we preparing students for 21st century jobs but testing 20th century knowledge? – the improvements observed may be due less to the technology per se than to the chance seized by enthusiastic teachers to rework courses and reconfigure classrooms in line with the technology's affordances (Blake, 2008; Burden et al., 2012; Livingstone, 2012). In short, it's more about the pedagogy than the technology (DEECD, n.d.; Pegrum, 2009). Ultimately, it's possible to build barricades against the Trojan horse; it's possible to constrain the affordances of new tools; it's possible to use them to simply make existing approaches more efficient, as on Puentedura's substitution level; and it's even possible to draft them into old content transmission and behaviourist pedagogies. But teachers who are willing to reimagine their classrooms in light of the affordances of their new tools may well find their pedagogies becoming more constructivist, their classes more learner-centred, and their students more engaged – as in Puentedura's view of digital technologies, used appropriately by teachers, transforming learning, or as experienced by the teachers in the Brazilian iPads project (see Case Study 2) who have successfully shifted their mindsets on their new tools.

However, that doesn't mean constructivism is the whole answer. Laurillard (2012) suggests that for all their differences, the major 20th century pedagogical approaches are not entirely incompatible. In practice, different approaches do slot together. Classroom teachers, even when they work in a broadly constructivist mode, don't shut out transmission or behaviourist approaches; very few language classes operate entirely without grammar tutorials or vocabulary drills, for instance. Students who work independently frequently include, and even privilege, transmitted content and behaviourist apps within their learning palette. But the limitations of constructivism are perhaps most evident outside the West. The potential benefits of new technologies will only be realised if they are used with sensitivity to local contexts, and those contexts may not yet be culturally, socially or educationally ready for constructivism and related approaches. This can be seen in learners' positive evaluations of their passive roles in the Learn English SMS project in Sudan (see Case Study 4), or investigators' realisation of the need to align mobile games with traditional educational approaches in the MILLEE project in India (see Case Study 7). There is certainly an argument to be made for engaging in learner training, and indeed teacher training, and sharing what we have found out so far in our research about effective teaching and learning practices – involving communicative, social constructivist and other sociocultural approaches to language education (see Chapters 4 & 7) – but we must proceed slowly, sensitively, and responsively.

Successful projects, like successful classrooms, typically combine a pragmatic attitude to blending pedagogies with a sensitivity to contextual readiness for those pedagogies. Some, like the European MASELTOV project (see Case Study 13), work certain elements of traditional behaviourist pedagogy into a broadly constructivist framework. Others, like the SIMOLA project (see Case Study 1 below), demonstrate the value of student-centred, situated, collaborative language learning in an appropriate cultural, social and educational context. Interestingly, among the project's multicultural cohorts, those students who were less used to active roles found this approach demanding. But SIMOLA ultimately serves as a proof of concept, showing that it is possible to integrate mobile tools and social networking functionality in the service of social constructivist educational goals, provided that the context – in terms of *where, when* and *who* – is right. For many of SIMOLA's students, the time was clearly ripe for this kind of approach, as it may well be for more students in more contexts in the future.

Case Study 1   Situated mobile learning in Europe (SIMOLA Project)

Figure 2.2   Lingobee app. © SIMOLA, reproduced by permission.

Case Study 1 (Continued)

Project:	SIMOLA (Situated Mobile Language Learning).
Languages:	English, Norwegian, Italian, Dutch, Lithuanian, Hungarian & Japanese.
Focus:	Capturing & sharing everyday language & cultural content.
Level:	All levels.
Format:	Android app, *Lingobee,* for collaborative language learning, with an accompanying website.
Hardware:	Some users supplied their own devices in a BYOD model, but Android devices needed to use the app were loaned to those who didn't have appropriate technology. Any web-enabled devices could be used to access the website.
Key partners:	European Commission (funding provider); University of Brighton, UK (lead partner & developer of app & website); StudyGroup; ROC van Amsterdam, Netherlands; University of Molise, Italy; Baltic Education Technology Institute, Lithuania; Norwegian University of Science & Technology; Hungarian e-University Network; Tokyo University of Agriculture & Technology, Japan (Lingobee was trialled by the participating educational institutions).
Timeline:	2010–2012. The Lingobee app & website are still available & in use.
Location:	UK, Norway, Italy, Netherlands, Lithuania, Hungary & Japan. Because the resources are publicly available, they have also been used in a number of other countries.
Participants:	The project was designed for students in the EU Erasmus programme & adult migrants in the EU Grundtvig programme. During the evaluation period, which ran from October 2011–October 2012, there were 800 registered users of the app as well as 9,500 unique visitors to the website, generating over 50,000 page views.
Funding model:	The project was funded through the European Commission's Lifelong Learning Programme. Users supplied their own devices or were loaned Android devices. The app is freely downloadable from the website (simola.org/lingobee).

The Lingobee app and website involve crowdsourcing situated linguistic and cultural content from target language contexts. Users are invited to upload examples of language, such as a contextualised word or phrase, which they see or hear in everyday life and want to capture. Content may be shared with other users, who can also be asked for further information about it. Individuals can filter content by language or user groups, create favourites lists, and construct a multimedia glossary of language that is relevant to them. Building on social networking principles, individuals can add to or modify definitions, comment on them, tag them, and rate or flag them. While conceived initially for advanced learners, the multimedia aspect of Lingobee means it lends itself to all levels, with less proficient learners able to simply upload a picture, for example. The language selected by users runs the full gamut from slang to highly formal lexis. In many cases, the cultural contexts for language use are strongly foregrounded. In practice, the distinction between language- and culture-related content is often blurred, for instance in names of local personalities, events and places; idioms and common sayings; or expressions such as 'Bank Holiday' or 'Free House' in the UK.

With no set guidelines on how to introduce learners to Lingobee, or how to use it inside or outside the classroom, teachers participating in the project developed their own ways of presenting it and encouraging learners to use it. The app was well used where teachers were able to integrate it into a course and actively promote it. It was less well used in contexts where it was voluntary. Digitally literate students found it easy to use, but it was sometimes viewed as just one more app among so many others. Despite a general familiarity with recording everyday experiences and sharing them through social media, there was still the need to acquire the habit of doing this with a language learning focus. Some students expressed a desire for a more proactive app that would motivate them with regular reminders or alarms. Other students, who were more used to passive learner roles, struggled with the proactive role which the app thrust on them.

Overall, the user uptake, going beyond the seven partner countries and continuing beyond the project dates, suggests that this is a concept that has come of age. Future plans, depending on time and funding, include developing a cross-platform web app to open up the project to a wider range of users; promoting the use of Lingobee as an informal learning tool for advanced students outside formal education; and even extending the concept into other educational domains where there is a need to connect in-class with out-of-class learning.

Case Study 1   (Continued)

The key interviewees about this project were Lyn Pemberton (School of Computing, Engineering & Mathematics, University of Brighton), Marcus Winter (School of Computing, Engineering & Mathematics, University of Brighton) and Sobah Abbas Petersen (Dept of Computer & Information Science, Norwegian University of Science & Technology, Trondheim). For further information, see the *SIMOLA* website (simola.org), the *Lingobee* webpage (simola.org/lingobee), the *Lingobee* blog (lingobee.wordpress.com), the *LingoBee* Facebook page (www.facebook.com/lingobee.eu), or follow @LingoBee on Twitter.

A variation on the first agenda: Dismantling formal education

We hear from time to time that the days of formal education are over. We hear that many, most, or all educational institutions will collapse in coming years as people begin to forge their own pathways through global learning options. We hear that teachers are no longer necessary, with students learning either from distant celebrity professors or through interaction in peer networks. At their extreme, arguments about the need to *transform teaching and learning* turn into arguments about the need to dispense altogether with formal education.

It's true that there are currently issues around the informal–formal divide (Johnson et al., 2012; Pettit & Kukulska-Hulme, 2011). In our era, '[f]ormal education systems dedicated to delivering learning at specific locations and at specified times are less and less well-aligned to the needs and behaviour of our societies' (Traxler, 2012, p.3). Informal learning, which is now more possible and more powerful than ever thanks to widely accessible mobile technologies, increases the autonomy and agency of learners vis-à-vis institutions and teachers (Kukulska-Hulme, 2013b; Traxler, 2010). At one end of the scale, there are casual if focused interactions on social media platforms. At the other end, there are MOOCs offered through platforms like Coursera, edX and Udacity (see also Vignette 12) which, at their best, are carefully designed to maximise student engagement with content, other students, and sometimes tutors. It's time for classroom walls to become more permeable to m-technologies and m-learning, and for formal structures of teaching and learning to open up to informal educational experiences.

But this doesn't mean we should simply jettison the tradition of structured, guided, just-in-case learning in favour of personal, spontaneous, just-in-time learning. As Mark Warschauer (2011) observes in respect of school classrooms, 'good learning with technology stems from good teaching. And good teaching sometimes involves being a guide, but often involves much more than that' (p.74). Yes, there are advantages to more learner-centred education, but there is a need for structuring and mentoring of learning if it is not to become fragmented and trivialised (Kukulska-Hulme, 2010b; Traxler, 2010). Yes, user-generated content and contexts are more viable than previously, but many inexperienced learners gravitate towards pedagogically traditional materials and need guided exposure to alternatives if their activity choices are to go beyond content transmission or drilling (Kukulska-Hulme, 2013b). And yes, there are some situations where fully independent learning may be the only option, but this places a premium on educators' involvement in the effective pedagogical design of available materials (as in the best MOOCs). In fact, it's well-known that a shift towards greater learner autonomy can be challenging and disconcerting for many students (Comas-Quinn & Mardomingo, 2012; Stockwell, 2013a) and requires careful learner training, with the gradual removal of scaffolding.

Both formal and informal learning must have their place, as they always have done, but the expansion of informal learning options makes it more urgent to forge 'a dialogue between two worlds of education' (Sharples et al., 2010, p.97). Significantly, m-learning not only fosters informal, web 2.0-style learning, but also offers novel ways to 'help[] ensure that learning which happens inside and outside classrooms is mutually supportive' (UNESCO, 2013c, p.21). The SIMOLA project (see Case Study 1) permits learner-directed, networked learning, for instance, but has been integrated into formal courses by many teachers. We can draw lessons from projects like SIMOLA as we explore ways of bridging the informal–formal divide, perhaps through apps like Lingobee, or perhaps through PLNs and PLEs (see Chapter 4) or other as-yet-unimagined platforms. The rise of mobile technologies and digital networking options doesn't mean the demise of classrooms; but in time it may mean the demise of those classrooms which fail to open up to mobile technologies and digital networks and to evolve in a student-centred direction.

Second agenda: Developing 21st century skills

In the developed world in particular, digital communications are very much woven into the fabric of contemporary personal, social and working lives. They're at the core of a set of so-called *21st century skills*, which amongst other things include creativity and innovation, critical thinking and problem-solving, collaboration and teamwork, autonomy and flexibility, and lifelong learning, all bundled together with digital literacies (Dudeney et al., 2013; ISTE, 2012; Mishra & Kereluik, 2011; NCTE, 2013; P21, n.d.). While 21st century skills are crucial everywhere, this notion seems to have found a deep resonance in Asia, where it features frequently in discussions of how to complement existing highly effective education systems, which often produce superior performance on standardised examinations, with an emphasis on independence, creativity and innovation (Chan et al., 2006; Barber et al., 2012; So, 2012). The affordances of mobile devices can integrate with and support the development of such attributes.

Many educators emphasise the importance of 21st century skills for individuals' personal agency, helping them to lead fulfilling personal and social lives, and enabling them to participate as engaged citizens in national or international conversations (Dudeney et al., 2013; Pegrum, 2009). Many politicians and policymakers emphasise the importance of the same kinds of skills for the economic empowerment of individuals as well as the economic competitiveness of nations (Buchanan, 2011; Moyle, 2010), a move that is broadly in line with a *human capital* model (ibid.; Selwyn, 2013). There is tension here; but not necessarily a contradiction. Arguably, 21st century skills can support personal and political empowerment on the one hand, and economic performance on the other. Moreover, many of these skills align with the principles underpinning social constructivist, learner-centred classrooms, and may be fostered through the use of e- and m-technologies (Moyle, 2010; Quinn, 2012).

The upshot is that governments the world over are promoting 21st century skills at all levels of education. In developed countries, 21st century skills and digital competencies are becoming embedded in mainstream school curricula, often from an early age (Belshaw, 2011; Selwyn, 2011), while numerous programmes are underway to reach underserved sections of the population. Initiatives in the developing world often begin introducing 21st century skills, including digital literacies, at the same time basic education itself is spreading for the first time to many sections of the population. Such approaches fit neatly with a social justice agenda, as discussed below.

Critical questions about developing 21st century skills

Some educators are in fact troubled by the underlying tension in the use of educational technologies to develop 21st century skills like creative and innovative thinking, which can serve identity development and global citizenship purposes on the one hand, and utilitarian economic agendas on the other (Moyle, 2010). What's more, the very tools being used to promote 21st century skills and new literacies, like mobile phones and mobile software, are deeply implicated in the consumerist marketplace (Castells et al., 2007; Merchant, 2012; Traxler, 2010). Globally, educational opportunities are increasingly inseparable from marketing opportunities, with technology companies making considerable inroads into educational institutions in some countries, and taking it upon themselves to promote 21st century skills via organisations like the corporate-backed Partnership for 21st Century Skills (P21) (Moyle, 2010; Selwyn, 2013).

Given the potentially ambiguous implications of these tools and the skills taught through them, as well as the wider economic realities in which they are embedded, educators have no choice but to adopt a critical stance. This doesn't mean that economic agendas or multinational corporations have no place in education: after all, employability is a key educational outcome; and corporate expertise may have much to contribute to understandings of new technologies, just as corporate funding has much to contribute to facilitating development of new skills, sometimes under the auspices of social responsibility programmes. But it does mean that it's important to question anew in every context whether mobile technologies are being used to promote empowerment and equality rather than (merely) serving economic or corporate imperatives. For educators, it is important to develop a *critical mobile literacy*. This offers a lens through which to focus on finding a balance among competing interests and to help students open up spaces for growth amid the multiple discourses clamouring for their (and all of our) attention (see Chapter 6).

In fact it's clear that all learners, but perhaps language learners in particular, need to acquire a range of digital literacies to complement their traditional language and literacy competencies, and a range of 21st century skills to allow them to communicate and collaborate effectively. Without these literacies and these skills, their language learning will be impoverished. New literacies and new skills, after all, don't only improve the chance of self-realisation through economic opportunity – though they must surely include this – but increase the richness of personal and social lives, and make it easier to acquire a voice in local, national and international conversations.

A number of successful initiatives show that language, literacy and 21st century skills can be taught simultaneously to great effect. In Australia, teachers in remote schools are employing XO laptops to increase Indigenous students' engagement in literacy learning at the same time they are beginning to develop their digital skills (see Case Study 12). In Singapore, AR Heritage Trails designed with input from the MOE interweave inquiry-based learning, language and literacy practice, and 21st century skills, including digital literacies (see Case Study 14). In Brazil, the Casa Thomas Jefferson iPads for Access initiative set out from the start to integrate English language and digital literacy learning opportunities for socioeconomically disadvantaged youth (see Case Study 2 below). The success of the Brazilian approach can be seen in students' growing independence and creativity, as evidenced in the English-medium, digitally enabled work they have been empowered to produce, and which can now be publicly viewed online.

Case Study 2   Mobile empowerment in Brazil (iPads for Access Project)

Figure 2.3   Teacher training on iPads. © Carla Arena/Casa Thomas Jefferson, Brasília, reproduced by permission.

Project: iPads for Access.
Language: English.
Focus: Language & digital literacy learning.
Level: Basic English for Access students; all levels of English for non-Access students.

Format:	Teacher-selected iOS apps, with teacher trainers encouraging a focus on productive & generic apps.
Hardware:	Two class sets of iPads were purchased for Access students & one set for non-Access students, totalling 43 devices in 2012, rising to 203 devices in 2013 with the purchase of extra class sets for non-Access students. Additionally, teachers & non-Access students have used BYOD devices.
Key partners:	US Embassy/US State Dept (initial provider of funding for one set of iPads for Access students); Casa Thomas Jefferson [CTJ] (provider of infrastructure, teacher training & funding for additional sets of iPads).
Timeline:	2012 – ongoing.
Location:	Brasília, Brazil.
Participants:	The project was initially designed to benefit low-income students with good school grades who were selected to participate in a 2-year US State Dept Access programme for English learning; 48 young teens were enrolled in 2012, rising to 104 in 2013. Other students among the 17,000 enrolled at CTJ, aged from 4–80 years, have also benefited from the use of class sets of iPads. CTJ has offered its 250 teachers training as well as setting up a partnership with a local store to provide them with discounted prices on their own Apple mobile technology purchases, with a view to encouraging them to adopt a BYOD approach in their classes.
Funding model:	A class set of 23 iPads, funded by the US State Dept, was provided for Access students & used with non-Access students as well. Extra sets of iPads for Access & non-Access students were provided by CTJ. Teachers have purchased their own mobile technologies at discount prices. A move towards a broader BYOD model for teachers & students has been encouraged.

CTJ, a binational US–Brazilian English language teaching centre in Brasília, won a competitive grant to purchase a set of iPads for talented students from low-income backgrounds participating in the US State Department Access programme, with a second set of iPads funded by CTJ. Because these students attend only one day a week, the class sets are used during the rest of the week by students in some of CTJ's many other classes,

Case Study 2   (Continued)

along with extra sets purchased specifically for non-Access students. Following initial training of three teachers by the Consultants-E, an extensive internal teacher training and mentoring programme was established. It was designed, firstly, to encourage the pedagogically appropriate use of the class sets of iPads and, secondly, to promote the use of other mobile digital technologies under the auspices of a BYOD model, given that many of CTJ's regular students already own suitable devices. Teachers have been able to purchase Apple devices at discounted prices thanks to a partnership established by CTJ with a local store, and they have been encouraged to explore ways of incorporating not only their own devices but students' devices into their lessons.

Key challenges, similar to those reported in many other educational projects, included infrastructural issues (notably the need for adequate wifi bandwidth) and logistical issues (such as how to prepare, manage, store and secure the devices). Trainers found that some teachers were reticent to use new technologies, and that others needed encouragement to use productive, generic apps rather than relying on language-specific behaviourist drills and quizzes. Most importantly of all, trainers identified the need for a change of mindset among teachers, who have to be prepared to relinquish some centralised control as students begin to work more independently and creatively on personal devices. Extensive teacher training and support has helped to effect this change, resulting in growing 'pockets of success' where classroom pedagogy is becoming increasingly learner-centred thanks, at least in part, to the mediation of new technologies. Time has also been spent on the training of managers, to develop their digital literacies and secure their support for the iPads initiative.

The key successes of the programme to date have been opening up the opportunity for Access students to learn English in tandem with digital literacies; beginning to shift teachers' views of a BYOD approach and the integration of digital devices into their pedagogy; and concomitantly promoting an ongoing shift towards learner-centred, technology-mediated classes where students have much greater freedom to move around as they find their own ways and places to produce language. While students sometimes work individually on the iPads, they often move around the classroom to engage in pair work, group work and provide each other with peer support, and sometimes they work outside the classroom to take photos and make recordings around the school. With some 80% of CTJ teachers now using their own smartphones or tablets, there is a solid base on which to build in the next round of teacher training, which will focus on further pedagogical integration of mobile technologies into lesson planning, and ways to more extensively reuse and remix the user-generated digital content students have begun to create.

The key interviewee about this project was Carla Arena (Head of the Educational Technology & Digital Communication Dept, CTJ, Brasília, Brazil). For further information, see the teacher blogs *Collablogatorium* (collablogatorium.blogspot.com.br/search/label/mlearning) and *M that Learning!* (mthatlearning.blogspot.com.br). For examples of student work created using iPads, see the *CTJ Blog* (thomasonline.org.br/mlearning).

A variation on the second agenda: Setting the digital natives free

Discourses which draw on Marc Prensky's (2012b) notion of 'digital natives' and Don Tapscott's (2009) notion of 'the net generation' are usually based on the assumption that young people have already intuitively developed many of the skills and dispositions necessary to use digital technologies effectively in 21st century contexts. In an echo of wider attacks on formal education, it's sometimes claimed that schools just need to get out of the way and stop holding back the digital natives. The problem with this assumption is that digital natives simply don't exist, at least not as they're imagined in these discourses. A growing body of research roundly debunks the notion of a homogenous, technically able generation of young people (Bennett et al., 2008; Hague & Williamson, 2009; Hargittai, 2010).

Still, the door remains open to what we might call a *weak nativist* perspective, which suggests that many young people have developed certain digital habits that, if harnessed appropriately, give teachers a base on which to build and foster 21st century literacies. In this view, many students are *tech-comfy*, that is, adept at using new technologies for social and entertainment purposes, but need guidance on becoming *tech-savvy*, that is, skilled in using the same technologies for academic and professional purposes, and able to view these technologies with a critical eye. Teachers need to make provisions for upskilling less digitally fluent students, while guiding all students in making the shift from tech-comfy to tech-savvy use of digital tools (see Vignette 13). This need for learner training in turn raises issues of teacher training (see

Chapter 7), but it's clear that educators should not simply be ceding the floor to students' assumed abilities, and instead should be helping them broaden and deepen their existing skillbase in educationally appropriate ways.

Third agenda: Promoting social justice

Broadly speaking, *social justice* is about bringing the social and educational – and economic and political – development benefits of digital technologies to underserved populations. The main focus is typically on the affordability rather than the affordances of mobile tools, though the latter are far from irrelevant. For many people who live in remote areas, impoverished conditions or crisis zones, who belong to mobile or nomadic communities, or who are culturally or socially marginalised, mobile devices may lead to *new educational opportunities* which otherwise would not exist or would be difficult to access (GSMA, 2010a; UNESCO, 2013c; West, 2012b). Sometimes, the affordances of the devices may also provide *better educational opportunities* in the form of more effective pedagogy (implicitly, a learner-centred approach with a constructivist flavour, where teacher and student relationships are democratically reconfigured) and more applicable skills (implicitly, 21st century skills and literacies) (Vosloo, 2012). The affordances of the devices can play a role, too, in reaching those who are disengaged educationally and socially (Kukulska-Hulme, 2012; Oakley et al., 2012), including indigenous peoples who may feel alienated by mainstream educational systems and computer-based e-learning (Wallace, 2013) and who may prefer to capture their self-expression in multimodal formats (ibid.; Zelezny-Green, 2013a).

From a human capital perspective, development opportunities benefit both individuals and wider society, leading to greater economic productivity, political stability and social cohesion (Selwyn, 2013; Tyers, 2012). In a typical statement of social justice goals, the English in Action (EIA) project in Bangladesh (see Case Study 16) described itself thus:

> The Programme's goal is to contribute to the economic growth of the country by providing communicative English language as a tool for better access to the world economy. The purpose of EIA is to significantly increase the number of people who are able to communicate in English, to levels that enable them to participate fully in economic and social activities and opportunities.
>
> (EIA, 2013; text subsequently revised)

While digital social justice agendas underpin some initiatives in developed countries, they are most clearly in evidence in *Information and Communication(s) Technologies for Development (ICT4D)* or *Mobile(s) for Development (M4D)* projects in developing regions, of which the EIA project is one example. Such projects are often viewed as aiding progress towards a series of interlinked goals, all with target achievement dates of 2015:

- the six UNESCO *Education for All (EFA) Goals* (UNESCO, n.d., a);
- the eight UN *Millennium Development Goals (MDGs)*, with educational projects often focusing on Goal 2 of achieving universal primary education (UN, n.d.);
- the numerous indicative targets set by the UN-backed *World Summit on the Information Society (WSIS)*, which feed into the MDGs by aiming to improve global ICT connectivity and access (WSIS, 2013);
- the four *Broadband Targets for 2015* developed by the UN-backed Broadband Commission for Digital Development, which also feed into the MDGs by aiming to improve global broadband access (Broadband Commission for Digital Development, n.d.).

The recently released *UNESCO Policy Guidelines for Mobile Learning*, aimed at policymakers around the world, promote these goals (UNESCO, 2013c). M-learning can play a major role in developing regions, which are typically 'book-poor but mobile device-rich' (UNESCO, 2013b). With some 775 million illiterate adults in the world in 2010 (UNESCO, 2012), many mobile initiatives have a strong focus on literacy, some covering local languages (such as Urdu in Pakistan or Khmer in Cambodia; see Case Studies 3 & 5) and others focusing on English as a language of international development. In addition to supporting traditional literacy and numeracy, many initiatives also promote digital literacies, thus helping to combat a digital divide that is as much about skills and uses of technology as it is about access (Warschauer, 2011).

Digital social justice initiatives are buoyed by other recent developments, including the availability of open source software ranging from the Android operating system to the Firefox browser, and the rise of OER – as in fact advocated by UNESCO (2013c) – ranging from MIT's OpenCourseWare and the OU's OpenLearn to the wealth of materials freely available through iTunes U, the Khan Academy, TED and even YouTube. There's also the growing popularity of MOOCs, whose original aim of making high quality education freely available has at least an implicit social justice element. mMOOCs go a step further, potentially opening up education to an even more diverse set of learners. In addition, in many developing world contexts where educational infrastructure is limited, mobile devices can play an important role in the administration and organisation of teaching (UNESCO, 2013c; West, 2012a).

One major plank of the social justice agenda is the improvement of women's and girls' literacy, in line with the EFA Goals and MDGs, notably EFA Goal 5 and MDG 3, which focus on gender equality (GSMA, 2010b; UNESCO, 2013b; Zelezny-Green, 2013b). With women making up two-thirds of the world's illiterate adults, UNESCO (n.d., b) launched the Mobile Phone Literacy project in 2011. It aims to identify the most effective ways to reinforce and improve the skills of newly literate women, to provide them with critical information in areas like human rights, health, nutrition and agriculture, and to do so sustainably on a large scale. Due to report in 2013, it has studied successful initiatives from around the world, including the Pakistani Post-literacy project, the Indian MILLEE project and the Nokia Life service which, amongst many other initiatives, supports the Chinese Learn English project (see Case Studies 3, 7 & 9).

Yet the relationship between mobile technologies and gender equality is complex (Tacchi et al., 2012). Some initiatives, like the Pakistani Post-literacy project, the Afghan Institute of Learning's Mobile Literacy initiative which was inspired by it (Yacoobi, 2013), and the Afghan Great Idea project (see Case Study 17), were set up to address the gender divide from the outset. In other contexts, such as the Bangladeshi EIA project (see Case Study 16), ongoing research has led to new insights about the gender divide and new strategies for tackling it, such as establishing girls' ICT clubs. Reflecting on both the Bangladeshi and Pakistani projects, Alexandra Tyers (see Vignette 2 below) shows that despite some ambiguity around the impact of mobile technologies on gender equality, there is hope for positive change in this area.

Vignette 2   The gender digital divide

Alexandra Tyers, British Council, Bangladesh

The relationship between mobile learning, transformation and gender issues is not, in my experience, straightforward. In my longitudinal study on women learning English through information and communication technologies (ICTs) in

Bangladesh, as part of the English in Action project, I found that mobile phones had the power to transform learning for women. This was mostly through enabling them to overcome the higher barriers they faced to participation in education; that is, barriers to choosing how and when to learn.

Interestingly, mobiles were perceived by the female participants not as learning tools in their own right, but as tools that could create access to other ICTs like computers which were seen as more educationally valid. Generally, however, my research showed that learning through mobiles can and does enhance women's capabilities and their perceptions of their life choices – though learning with computers does that too.

At the same time, there is a growing body of literature from around the developing world that points towards mobile phones potentially reinforcing gendered stereotypes. Although they may create access by bringing learning to women in their own homes, they also reinforce the gender divide by keeping women in the domestic sphere and not challenging social norms, such as a lack of safe public spaces for women to learn in Bangladesh. This may however change in the future – this can be seen in the setting up of ICT clubs for girls in Bangladesh [see Case Study 16], while a recent UNESCO mobile literacy project in Pakistan [see Case Study 3] had the unexpected effect of allowing the adolescent girls more freedom of movement, since they and their parents felt more secure knowing they were contactable at all times.

▶ Further reading: Tyers (2012).

Critical questions about promoting social justice

Some commentators advise taking a cautious approach to social justice and international development agendas. Neil Selywn (2013) contends that education is tightly enmeshed with processes of globalisation, and promotes the political and economic agendas of the developed world by integrating formerly marginalised countries and their citizens into the global knowledge economy. The involvement of corporate interests in ICT4D and M4D has led to unease about the promotion of 'digital capitalism' (Sreekumar & Rivera-Sánchez, 2008, p.160) and the commodification of education, already noted in respect of 21st century

Case Study 3   Building literacy in Pakistan (Mobile-Based Post-Literacy Programme)

Figure 2.4   Participants in Pakistan's post-literacy programme. © Ichiro Miyazawa/ UNESCO, reproduced by permission.

Project:	Mobile-Based Post-Literacy Programme.
Language:	Urdu.
Focus:	Follow-up practice & information access after Urdu literacy programme, combined with basic digital literacy development.
Level:	Elementary, designed for semi-literate students.
Format:	SMS messages to reinforce literacy learning & disseminate educational information, complemented by three books (two Urdu, one basic maths) &, from Phase II onwards, a feature phone app, *eTaleem*, containing Urdu literacy & maths lessons.
Hardware:	Participants are supplied with Nokia feature phones & books.
Key partners:	UNESCO (funding provider, designer & co-ordinator); Punjab Department of Literacy & Non-Formal Basic

	Education, Lahore, National Commission for Human Development, Islamabad, Bunyad Foundation, Lahore, & Dhaka Ahsania Mission, Islamabad (content providers & managers of learning centres); Nokia (mobile manufacturer & app developer); Mobilink (mobile network operator & SIM card provider); Federal Ministry of Education & Training, Islamabad (supporter of Upscaling phase).
Timeline:	2008 – ongoing, with the following phases: 2008–2009: Pilot; 2010: Phase II; 2012: Phase III; 2013 onwards: Upscaling.
Location:	Punjab, Khyber Pakhtunkhwa & Sindh Provinces & Federally Administered Tribal Areas (FATA), Pakistan.
Participants:	The learners are predominantly rural women aged approx. 15–30 years. In the Pilot Phase there were 250 learners in Punjab; in Phase II there were 1250 learners in Punjab; in Phase III there were 1750 learners in Punjab & Khyber Pakhtunkhwa. In 2013, the project is being scaled up in co-operation with government departments; by mid-2013, there were already 2,000 learners in Punjab, Sindh & FATA, including 500 rural males in FATA.
Funding model:	The project is funded through the UNESCO Regional Development Fund. Nokia mobile phones are supplied to participants, SIM cards are provided by Mobilink & SMS costs are covered, with phones becoming the property of learners after the programme. Learners from Bunyad centres who wish to continue receiving messages are asked to contribute PKR 300 (approx. US $3) for a year. The app is freely downloadable (unesco.org.pk/education/etaleem.html).

Pakistan has one of the lowest literacy rates and one of the highest literacy gender gaps in the world; for males over 15 the literacy rate is around 69% and for females it is 40% (but see Case Study 17 for a comparison with neighbouring Afghanistan). The main aim of this intervention is to help maintain the skills and sustain the learning of women who attend introductory literacy courses (though the most recent phase has also begun to cater for male learners in tribal areas). It takes the form of a six-month programme involving an initial two months of face-to-face classes, where participants

Case Study 3   (Continued)

firstly learn how to read, use pens and write, before receiving mobile phones, which are then used over four months for receiving and sending SMS messages. The SMS messages are not a standalone strategy, since they work in tandem with the use of books and, more recently, an app, but they are a core part of the programme. More than 800 texts are sent to female learners on educational themes including the importance of literacy, health and hygiene, mother and child care, recipes, agriculture, religion, daily news, the political participation of women, how to vote, the right to education, and a culture of peace, as well as beauty tips, jokes and riddles. When they receive messages, participants read them aloud and copy them into their notebooks, as well as responding to them. They communicate frequently with other learners and a teacher, attend a community literacy centre several times a week to work with the teacher, and take a regular monitoring exam.

The programme faced a number of challenges at the outset, and proceeded despite some opposition to female education. It was necessary to convince communities and families to accept adolescent girls having mobile phones, which was achieved with the help of the local, well-respected NGO Bunyad. As in a number of other projects, this illustrates the importance of co-operation between IGOs like UNESCO, NGOs like Bunyad, government departments, and corporations like Nokia and Mobilink. It is precisely this kind of larger partnership which is permitting even greater expansion of the programme from 2013 onwards. On a more technical level, typing in Urdu, which uses Arabic script, was found to be a challenge, as was the SMS limit of 70 characters (which applies to many languages with non-Roman alphabets as a result of the encoding process).

From the start of the pilot programme, consistent general improvement in literacy skills was evident in the regular exams taken by participants. Dramatic improvement was evident in pre- and post-evaluations conducted in later phases. The value of the basic digital literacy skills established through mobile phone use became clear as some girls moved on to using computers within the space of around eight months. It was found that girls shared their lessons with their mothers and sisters, sometimes even bringing family members with them to the literacy centres, and thus expanding the reach of the programme in informal ways. There is an enhancement of the sense of ownership when participants elect to pay to continue learning beyond the first six months, as well as an enhancement of both girls' and parents' sense of security which comes from knowing that the girls are carrying a mobile phone with them at all times.

The key interviewees about this project were Ichiro Miyazawa (UNESCO, Bangkok) and Fakhar Uddin (UNESCO, Islamabad), with additional input from Shaheen Attiq-ur-Rahman (Vice Chairperson, Bunyad, Lahore). For further information, see the video reports in Urdu and English on the UNESCO Islamabad *Mobile-Based Literacy Programme* webpage (www.unesco.org.pk/education/mlp.html). See also Bunyad (n.d.); Miyazawa (2009); So (2012); and UNESCO (2013a).

skills. Concern has been expressed over a vein of technological determinism which implies that the spread of new technologies will automatically produce modernisation and growth (Servaes, 2011; Sreekumar & Rivera-Sánchez, 2008), linked to a concern that growth is viewed from an overly narrow perspective focused on economic outcomes, with inadequate attention paid to more intangible cultural, social or personal outcomes (Tacchi et al., 2012; Unwin, 2009a, 2009b).

Perhaps the main failing of a narrow economic focus is the neglect of the wider cultural and social ecology of technology uses and impacts. After all, there are risks in importing both technology and pedagogy. New technologies may bring the cultural values of their creators crashing into unsuspecting local communities (Pegrum, 2009; Servaes, 2011), imposing 'the pedagogies of *outsiders*' (Traxler, 2013a, p.4; italics in original) on sometimes fragile learning cultures. On the other hand, educational technologies are rarely transposed from one culture to another without some distortion or hybridisation of their anticipated effects (Traxler, 2013b). Indeed, sometimes digital tools may come to reinforce existing local undemocratic power structures, including socioeconomic hierarchies (Gulati, 2008; Sreekumar & Rivera-Sánchez, 2008; Unwin, 2009a) and gender divides (Gulati, 2008; Tacchi et al., 2012; see also Vignette 2), and shore up traditional didactic pedagogical approaches (Selwyn, 2013; Traxler, 2013b). Thus, in some views and some contexts, new technologies may disrupt local cultures to create new consumers who buy into global markets, technologies and pedagogies. In other views and other contexts, new technologies may not disrupt local cultures and their entrenched inequalities enough. In short, educational technologies exist in a complex and uncertain relationship with social justice.

Yet it's apparent that m-learning can be effective in opening up educational, social and economic possibilities in the developing world, and for poorly served populations in the developed world, provided that it is based on a deep understanding of the cultural ecology into which new technologies and pedagogies are being introduced. This entails drawing on local expertise and insights and, more than this, giving the intended beneficiaries a say in how to realise the possibilities and a chance to contribute to their realisation. While external researchers and educators can offer valuable new perspectives and scaffold new understandings, and while external political, corporate and civil society organisations can offer resources and funding, there's no doubt that in order to avoid some of the dangers outlined above, 'the point of departure must be the community' (Servaes, 2011, p.221; cf. Unwin, 2009a).

Many of today's most successful projects strike a fine balance between global and local agendas, understandings, and participation. The Brazilian iPad deployment (see Case Study 2) has been based largely on local expertise complemented by an initial buy-in of external teacher training expertise, and supported by a combination of initial external funding with ongoing internal funding and technology acquisition arrangements. Notwithstanding a socioeconomic divide between project staff and Access students, this allows a nuanced approach to local learning needs. The Mobigam pilot project, based in India (see Case Study 15), has an explicit focus on coming to understand the local cultural ecology through observation as well as interactions between foreign and local staff. Researchers are exploring patterns of digital inclusion and exclusion, and considering how mobile devices may impact these patterns, before beginning to develop concrete language teaching plans. Already the original focus on English is shifting to a contextually sensitive focus on multiple languages, codeswitching and 'translanguaging'.

Large ICT4D and M4D projects, like the Pakistani Post-literacy project, the Bangladeshi EIA project and the Afghan Great Idea project (see Case Studies 3, 16 & 17), often involve complex multisector constellations of global and local organisations and actors. Intergovernmental organisations (IGOs), non-governmental organisations (NGOs), government bodies, educational institutions, content providers, device manufacturers, software developers and mobile network operators come together to build capacity, generally with a view to scalability and sustainability under local control (Vosloo, 2012; West, 2012b). Such state–corporate–civil society constellations go some way to balancing political, commercial, developmental and educational interests, with local input – exemplified in the Great Idea project's 'co-creation' workshops – ensuring fitness for the context. Meanwhile, an initiative like the Post-literacy project in Pakistan shows just how much it is possible to accomplish in a development project, in terms of teaching traditional language and literacy skills (in this case in Urdu) alongside basic digital literacy (which serves as an introduction to 21st century skills), while simultaneously addressing the gender digital divide.

A variation on the third agenda: Catering for special needs

It is true that, as we often hear, mobile technologies have the potential to increase educational access not only for those who are socioeconomically disadvantaged or socially disengaged, but more specifically for those with disabilities or special needs (Kukulska-Hulme, 2012; Unwin, 2009a). It is all the more true when hardware, software and digital materials are designed in line with accessibility, usability and universal design guidelines (Rainger, 2005; Roberts, 2013; Vosloo, 2012). With some 80% of all disabled people living in the developing world, where only about 2–3% of disabled children are in school (GSMA, 2010a), even basic mobile devices can contribute to social justice initiatives by making educational material more accessible to this population. In Uganda, for example, the Cambridge to Africa Network has set up an innovative SMS system allowing deaf students to access learning materials and communicate with peers (UNESCO, 2013c).

In the developed world, the technological opportunities are expanding rapidly on smart devices. Students with visual impairments or dyslexia can benefit from resizing and reformatting text; from natural user interfaces, which offer input options like voice and gesture recognition; and from new output options, like text-to-speech conversion and haptic (touch-based) feedback (Johnson et al., 2012; Kukulska-Hulme, 2010b; Pegrum et al., 2013). People with hearing impairments may benefit from text messaging (Vosloo, 2012), while sign language users can make use of video messaging (Ring & LaMarche, 2012). The iPad, with its intuitive interface and immediate sensory feedback, has been found to improve the classroom communication of autistic students (Johnson et al., 2012), while multimodal texts created on iPads and laptops have been used to support the literacy learning of autistic children (Oakley et al., 2013). In fact, the combination of touch sensitivity with visual and auditory features seems to hold some promise for supporting the learning of students with a whole range of special needs, with smart devices potentially fostering these learners' engagement, academic and communication skills, and social interaction (Campigotto et al., 2013; Kagohara et al., 2013).

A transitional stage

It's conceivable that e-learning may eventually turn out to be a transitional stage on the road to m-learning, which builds on e-learning but adds affordability and affordances which make it more powerful. But it's also possible that both e-learning and m-learning are transitional stages on the road to u-learning, that is, ubiquitous learning which takes place with multiple, integrated devices across a variety of interwoven real and virtual contexts, and where the devices eventually fade into the background so that we rarely think of them as distinct, or distinctive, tools. It was and is useful to set e-learning and m-learning apart from other kinds of learning, and to analyse them as discrete fields, but this is a temporary situation. The day will come when we'll drop our prefixes – the e's, the m's and even the u's – as technologically enhanced learning comes to be seen as 'just learning' (Kukulska-Hulme, 2010a, p.184). But until that day arrives, we still need to look closely, and separately, at m-learning.

All three agendas underpinning mobile learning can, singly or in combination, produce educational and social benefits. But given the complex ecologies in which mobile tools are used, the benefits are rarely entirely certain. As we've seen, there are critical questions we can and should ask about each agenda. But there are many more questions we still need to ask, not to undermine m-learning, but to identify its strengths as well as guarding against its potential pitfalls. We'll ask many of these questions as we go on to examine mobile learning, and MALL specifically, from a variety of angles. What kinds of language learning are actually possible with mobile tools (Chapters 4 & 5)? How can learners develop the digital literacies they need to process content, communicate effectively, and interact with culturally different others (Chapter 6)? And how do we ensure that teachers, learners and policymakers are ready to capitalise on the full potential of m-learning and MALL (Chapter 7)?

But before we get to these larger questions, we need to take a closer look at the technologies themselves. In the next chapter, we'll turn to questions of hardware, connectivity, and software, exploring their significance for the kinds of learning enabled by mobile devices, and examining the limitations they impose on us.

3
The Technological Ecosystem

Mobile devices are increasingly part of a multiscreen ecosystem. This ecosystem comprises mobile devices like smartphones and tablets; borderline mobile/portable devices like notebooks and laptops; and fixed devices ranging from desktop computers to television screens and interactive whiteboards. In the developed world, where many people own several devices, it's up to each of us as individuals to work out the right niche for mobile technologies in the stream of information and communication flowing across and between our multiple screens. In other words, mobile devices don't replace but rather supplement our other digital technologies (Hylén, 2012; Pettit & Kukulska-Hulme, 2011). In fact, different mobile devices can also complement each other, as pointed out by Mike Levy (see Vignette 3 below) in his survey of tools used in a technologies and language learning course in Australia.

In the developing world, there's a pressing need to find the most accessible digital interface, which is often a mobile phone screen, but may sometimes be a screen on a laptop or other device. Naturally, a given mobile device doesn't only supplement other digital tools (whether mobile or not) but also analogue tools, which is important in the developing world – and also in evidence in the developed world. A combined digital and analogue approach is seen for instance in the complementary use of phones and books in the Pakistani Post-literacy project (see Case Study 3), but equally in the technology choices made by Levy's university students in Australia.

Vignette 3   Profiling the mobility-technology divide

Mike Levy, The University of Queensland, Australia

There is a tendency to talk about mobile learning as if the term stands for one unitary way of thinking about technologies, mobility and learning. This is far from the case. In a recent survey with my students in a course on new technologies and language learning, I found that three mobile technologies were in regular use – the phone, the tablet and the laptop computer. Each of these technologies is 'mobile' in different ways, of course. Further, we found two or more of these technologies were used regularly for particular tasks, with varying profiles. For our group, reading the news was primarily conducted via the laptop (90%), with the phone a strong second (59%). With reading a book, the profile changed, with the laptop (59%) and the phone (31%) representing the newer technologies and the hard copy book (62%) the old; of course, the traditional book is a good example of a mobile technology and it is still the leading modality – just. When accessing online dictionaries for language learning, again the laptop (92%) and the phone (79%) dominated, while traditional paper-based dictionary use had almost disappeared. These results represent just one example. The contribution of each mobile technology shifts over time, giving each individual user a particular profile.

The spread of mobile technology types now available on the market is intriguing. In some ways, it is as if technology designers are experimenting with the customer as they invite us to implicitly evaluate designs through our product choices. Variables in play include screen size, virtual or material keyboards, touchscreens, and so forth. Whatever the final result, the user is empowered with the range of technologies they have at their disposal, at least in the developed world. Technology is meant to be emancipatory, to do yourself what has been formerly done by others. In language learning, our own research is showing personal technologies are being used increasingly inside the classroom as well as outside, for example in consulting a mobile phone dictionary to look up a new word when it arises in class.

Vignette 3   (Continued)

The age of the truly emancipated student is upon us. The field is mobile not only in terms of the capabilities of the technologies in use, but in the speed with which the landscape is changing.

▶ Further reading: Levy (2009); Steel & Levy (2013).

In order to function, *mobile hardware* depends on either an intermittent hardwired internet connection (say, via a desktop computer) or, more commonly nowadays, regular wireless *connectivity* through telephone or wifi networks. It also depends on the *software* installed which, in the case of smart devices, includes the *platform* (or operating system) and the *apps* (or applications) which have been downloaded. The possibilities for learning in general, and for language learning in particular, are simultaneously enabled and constrained by any given constellation of hardware, connectivity and software. Our devices mediate our use of language through the types of input they accept, the types of manipulation they support, and the types of output they allow. In this way, they set the parameters of the language we can use and learn through them.

Mobile hardware

Depending on your perspective, the original mobile learning technologies might be toys (Gray et al., 2009) or books (see Vignettes 3 & 5) or radios (Ho & Thukral, 2009). But even if we just focus on digital technologies, the category includes many devices beyond those that first spring to mind, such as the British Council's radio/MP3 'Lifeplayers', powered by wind-up handles and solar power, which are currently being rolled out in Ethiopia. Of course, there's some debate over exactly what counts as a mobile digital device. As already mentioned, a good guide is Puentedura's rule of thumb that mobile devices can be used at Point A, Point B and everywhere in between. Or, as Klopfer (2011) puts it, '[m]obility requires the ability to casually use a device on the go – without sitting down' (Kindle location 19). Laptops are generally seen as portable rather than mobile (ibid.; Rushby, 2012), though exceptions are often made for smaller laptops, including notebooks and netbooks (generic terms referring to smaller and sometimes less powerful laptops) and XO laptops (see Case Study 12), as well as the traditional tablet PCs which preceded today's tablets; all of these may sometimes be used more like mobile devices.

Among the more obvious mobile devices are *personal digital assistants (PDAs)*, an older generation of information management devices which typically have mobile phone, media player and web access capabilities. More specific functionality is seen in *digital media players*, notably MP3 players like Apple's iPod, which can play audio and video. It should be noted that the iPod Touch, which evolved from the iPod, shares a lot of its much wider range of functionality with smartphones, apart from the ability to make phone calls. *E-readers*, like Amazon's Kindle, Barnes & Noble's Nook or Sony's Reader, are dedicated to downloading and reading e-books. Other single-function mobile devices with educational applications include *digital voice recorders, compact digital cameras, electronic dictionaries* and *satellite navigation (sat nav) systems* (which can develop listening skills!). Some people would include *smartpens* (or *digital pens*) and even *USB drives* (also known as *flash drives* or *thumb drives*) as mobile tools. More complex devices include *clickers* (known more formally as *audience* or *personal response systems*), which can be used to aggregate student responses, and *handheld games consoles,* like the Nintendo Dual Screen (DS) and the Sony PlayStation Portable (PSP) or PS Vita.

But, for all the educational potential of these devices, it's important not to slip into the use of technology for technology's sake. The affordances of mobile tools must be exploited in the context of a broader, pedagogically informed approach. Indeed, technology doesn't always lead to the educational benefits we might hope for or imagine, as Lisa Merschel notes (see Vignette 4 below) when she looks back on one of the first internationally publicised iPod trials, which took place at Duke University in the USA.

Vignette 4   On the bleeding edge

Lisa Merschel, Duke University, USA

In the fall semester of 2004, all Duke University freshmen were given iPods. As a professor of a Spanish language course, I was approached and encouraged to incorporate iPods in my teaching. My students used them in class that semester to listen to audio clips that normally they'd listen to on a computer. To practice pronunciation, they listened to audio flashcards. Using a small microphone, they recorded a variety of homework activities and uploaded them to Blackboard.

Vignette 4 (Continued)

It turned out, however, that iPods for language learning were of limited use. The publicity seems to have been more of an attraction. National and international media descended upon Duke to see how the faculty were using the technology. The BBC wanted to film my class. An American morning show invited me to appear as a guest. *The New York Times* called. I had lunch with the owner of a professional football team who was interested in deploying iPods for language learning. The iPod was such an innovative product at the time that people were naturally interested in understanding its potential. But in the end, for academic purposes, it turned out to be a glorified player, recorder and storage device.

In the wake of this media scrutiny I realised that the hysteria surrounding the iPod giveaway and the 'starry-eyed' view of the device were outweighing sound pedagogical application. I'm eager to work on projects with colleagues, but am wary of intense promotion of any one technology or approach. I love 'play' and am very curious about emerging mobile technologies and their applications, but the enormous publicity and lack of clear pedagogical purpose surrounding the iPod project have made me hesitant to just dive in and say 'let's see what happens' as I did in 2004.

▶ Further reading: Carlson (2004).

It seems preferable, then, not to get hooked on any one piece of hardware, especially a single-function device. There is considerably greater pedagogical potential in multifunctional devices, of the kind that are now becoming widespread. In fact, most of the devices discussed above are declining in popularity due to the convergence of their individual functions in two particular multi-purpose devices, namely *smartphones* and *tablets* (which are frequently accompanied by peripheral hardware like earphones, headphones or external microphones). E-reader sales, for instance, appear to have peaked in 2011 (Yarow, 2012); although e-book reading continues to grow dramatically (Rainie & Duggan, 2012), it's increasingly taking place on other devices. Recent reports show falling sales of digital media players and compact digital cameras (Hall, 2012), while other victims of device convergence include PDAs, digital voice recorders, electronic dictionaries, sat nav systems and even watches (smartwatches notwithstanding). Handheld games consoles,

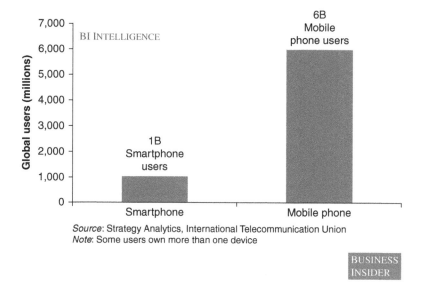

Figure 3.1 Estimated global smartphone vs total mobile phone users, 2012. © Business Insider Intelligence, https://intelligence.businessinsider.com, reproduced by permission.

Note: These figures represent subscriptions rather than unique users.

which nowadays can support web browsing and apps, may also be under threat, with games having emerged as the most popular app category on smartphones and tablets (see Figure 4.5). Smartphones and tablets, it seems, are the devices to keep an eye on.

Pre-smart devices

It's more accurate, however, to say that the devices to watch are mobile phones in general (including smartphones, of course) and tablets. The world over, mobile phones are providing more and more people with a gateway into the digital era (see Chapter 1) but, as of 2012, over 80% of mobile phone subscriptions in the world were *not* for smartphones (see Figure 3.1). The World Bank proposes two categories of non-smart mobile phones (see Figure 3.2). *Basic phones* have voice telephony and SMS as their main functions. *Feature phones* (written as one word or two) typically add Multimedia Messaging Service (MMS) functionality as well as a still camera and MP3 music player, have some internet access, and may be able to run some apps.

More commonly, basic and feature phones are grouped together in a single *feature phones* category, as in this book, though it's useful to

Device	Capabilities	Device	Capabilities
Basic mobile phone	*Network services, including*: Voice telephony and voice mail SMS (short message service) USSD (unstructured supplementary service data) SMS-based services, such as mobile money USSD services, such as instant messaging	Smartphone	*As Featurephone plus*: Video camera Web browser GPS (global positioning system) 3G+ internet access Mobile operating "platform" (such as iOS, Android, Blackberry) Ability to download and manage applications VoIP (Voice over Internet Protocol) Mobile TV (if available) Removable memory card
Featurephone	*As basic mobile phone plus*: Multimedia Messaging Service (MMS) Still picture camera MP3 music player 2.5G data access	Tablet	*As smartphone plus*: Front and rear-facing video cameras (for video calls) Larger screen and memory capability Faster processor, enabling video playback Touchscreen with virtual keyboard USB (universal serial bus) port

Note: The list of capabilities is not exhaustive, and not all devices have all features.

Figure 3.2 Mobile devices and their capabilities.
Source: World Bank (2012) under CC BY 3.0 licence.

remember that it covers a wide spectrum of functionality. The pejorative term 'dumbphones', which is sometimes applied to this category, or to the subcategory of basic phones, is in many ways unfair. SMS, for example, may have considerable impact when used to deliver chunked content, facilitate revision, provide automated feedback, or support networking, as seen in projects from Pakistan through Sudan and Libya to China and Indonesia (see Case Studies 3, 4, 9 & 18). What's more, there's a grey area where overlapping functionality makes it difficult to distinguish the growing number of high-end feature phones from low-end smartphones. Thus, rather than viewing these as 'dumb' devices, we might be better to see them as 'pre-smart' tools which are gradually evolving in a smart direction.

Smart devices

Smartphones and tablets, as we've seen, have vacuumed up the functionality of multiple older or more narrowly focused devices, including voice calls, SMS and MMS in the case of smartphones, and multimedia recording and display or playback in the case of both smartphones and tablets. Running on dedicated mobile operating systems (OS), smart devices are capable of constant internet connectivity, which allows users to browse the web and download specialised apps which in many cases can then function independently of an internet connection. When net access is available, they allow multimedia communication through Voice over Internet Protocol (VoIP) services, IM or social networking apps, and facilitate the sharing of text, photos, videos and audio through these channels in addition to numerous other social media platforms. Moreover, the advantages of such devices are very much enhanced by a rapidly expanding range of input and output options (Quinn, 2012; Woodill, 2011), where the evolving hardware intersects with evolving software.

When it comes to *input mechanisms*, traditional physical features like buttons or trackpads, and virtual features like onscreen keyboards (whose lack of tactile feedback makes them slower to use than physical keyboards, pending future developments in personalised keyboarding), are being complemented and even superseded by new possibilities. The overall trend is away from a graphical user interface (operated via a mouse or trackpad and to some extent a keyboard) and towards a natural user interface (operated for example via touch, gesture and voice) (Johnson et al., 2012; Meeker, 2012). In this way, smart devices are becoming more closely aligned with our everyday actions, making them more intuitive for inexperienced users.

Touch input includes swiping or pinching on touchscreens, which feature in most of today's smart devices, while *shaking, turning* or *tilting* of devices can be sensed by an accelerometer. *Gestural input* includes moving the hands or body without the need to physically touch a surface. *Voice recognition* of language spoken into an inbuilt microphone, and automatic typing or translation of spoken text, erodes the need to type – or even translate! Similarly, *optical character recognition (OCR)* of text scanned with an inbuilt camera allows it to be typed or translated (as with the text lens service in Case Study 13). More broadly, *scanning* of quick response (QR) codes can launch media files or websites; scanning of AR markers can produce annotated displays of the real world; and scanning of objects can allow their identification (as with Google Goggles, which also recognises and translates text). In recent advances, *eye tracking* through a forward-facing camera can reveal when you're looking at the screen (and pause a video when you look away). Such developments will inevitably impact on the language we produce – or don't produce – when interacting with smart devices, or using them to interact with our wider environment.

And then there are more *automated input mechanisms*. Smart devices are *geoaware*, or *location-aware*, which is the basis of their context sensitivity. They recognise where they are and which direction they're pointing or moving in, usually thanks to the combined presence of a Global Positioning System (GPS) receiver, compass, gyroscope and accelerometer. They may also be able to pick up signals from Bluetooth or Radio Frequency Identification (RFID) tags (as distinct from optical tags like QR codes which require manual scanning). Tagging permits 'ambient findability' (Morville cited in Woodill, 2011, Kindle location 1916), that is, 'the labeling of the environment so that it speaks directly to us through our mobile devices' (ibid., Kindle location 1917). This promotes a shift towards AR, and again changes the nature of our linguistic interactions with our devices and our surroundings.

The spectrum of *output mechanisms* is expanding too, which also has consequences for language use. Firstly, output may be *visual,* ranging from written text on a screen or images projected on a wall through to text and images layered over an AR camera view. Meanwhile, work is underway on developing holographic displays. Secondly, output may be *auditory,* such as spoken text heard through speakers or headphones, including audio translations of spoken, written (scanned) or typed text. Thirdly, output may be *haptic,* that is, tactile, based on movement such as the vibration of a phone. All of the above input and output mechanisms are complemented by *multimedia recording capabilities,* with keyboards, cameras and microphones allowing learning moments to be captured, and *multimedia sharing capabilities* allowing captured records to be distributed across telecommunications and wifi networks.

Mobile is no longer just a 'choice' for education; nor are smart devices. It won't be long before internet access around the globe is primarily via mobile tools. Smart mobile devices are already selling much faster than PCs (see Figure 3.3). What's more, in the first quarter of 2013, smartphones outsold feature phones globally for the first time (IDC, 2013). Given that feature phones will continue to open up educational opportunities for underresourced populations for many years to come, we need to maintain a broad focus on all mobile phones, while recognising that smartphones and tablets will become far more dominant in the future.

In 2012 Samsung overtook Nokia to become the world's largest mobile phone manufacturer, with both companies making feature phones

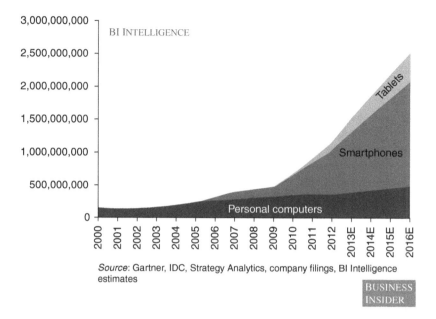

3,000,000,000
2,500,000,000
2,000,000,000
1,500,000,000
1,000,000,000
500,000,000
0

BI INTELLIGENCE

Tablets

Smartphones

Personal computers

2000 2001 2002 2003 2004 2005 2006 2007 2008 2009 2010 2011 2012 2013E 2014E 2015E 2016E

Source: Gartner, IDC, Strategy Analytics, company filings, BI Intelligence estimates

BUSINESS INSIDER

Figure 3.3 Global internet device shipments 2000–2016 (partial forecast). © Business Insider Intelligence, https://intelligence.businessinsider.com, reproduced by permission.
Note: Figures from 2013 onwards are estimates.

as well as smartphones. Other well-known smartphone manufacturers, some of whom also make feature phones and many of whom make tablets, are Apple, BlackBerry (formerly RIM), HTC, LG, Motorola and Sony, with increasingly dominant Chinese manufacturers including Huawei, Lenovo, TCL and ZTE. With the exception of Apple and BlackBerry, who use their own OS, these manufacturers use a mixture of platforms, such as Google's open source Android and Microsoft's Windows Phone. With smartphone penetration already at over 50% of the mobile market in the USA and many European countries, growth is shifting to emerging markets like China, which has overtaken the USA as the leading smartphone market (Cocotas, 2013). Significantly, although smartphones constituted fewer than 20% of all mobile handsets in 2012, they were already generating 92% of mobile handset traffic around the world (Cisco, 2013).

While tablets still have a far smaller market share than smartphones (see Figure 3.3), sales are ramping up quickly vis-à-vis PCs (Meeker & Wu, 2013). The best-known tablets include Apple's iPad, Samsung's Galaxy Tab, Amazon's Kindle Fire, ASUS's Eee Pad, Google's Nexus, and Microsoft's Surface. Like smartphones, tablets run on mobile OS: Android is the most common (used in Eee Pad, Galaxy Tab, Kindle Fire and Nexus tablets), with Apple's iOS in second place (though it's used only on the iPad). Although they cannot make phone calls, tablets share most of the functionality of smartphones, including their input mechanisms (notably touchscreens) and output mechanisms, recording and playback options, and the availability of internet access and downloadable apps. The main difference is a larger screen, which improves consumption of text (allowing tablets to serve as e-book or e-textbook readers) and video (allowing tablets to play a role in flipped classroom models, where content is often delivered in video format). Their size also renders content manipulation and creation more feasible, as well as facilitating group work and collaboration (see Chapter 1). It's for these reasons that, as the 2013 *Horizon Report* (Higher Education edition) observes, '[t]ablet computing has carved its own niche in education' (Johnson et al., 2013, p.4).

Convergence, divergence & new directions

Individually, smartphones and tablets already represent a convergence of separate devices, but smartphones and tablets themselves may be converging in the form of large phones, or small tablets, referred to by the portmanteau term *phablets*. It's unlikely, though, that we'll see uniform screen sizes any time soon: rather, a variety of smart devices will be integrated into our multi-device ecologies, with differently sized screens used simultaneously and often in synchrony to achieve specific purposes.

The biggest screens (and projections of screens) are getting bigger. New options are opened up by *microprojectors* (or *pico projectors*), which can project a display from a mobile phone, tablet or digital camera onto any flat surface, with the newest projectors having inbuilt memory that allows them to function as standalone devices. Other screens are becoming independently mobile. Today's *robots*, 'a type of anthropomorphized media' existing at the intersection of information technology and robotics (Han, 2012, p.1), usually incorporate some kind of display screen technology. They're already starting to teach language in Japanese, South Korean and Taiwanese schools (ibid.; Khanna & Khanna, 2012). After CALL and MALL, we may see the development of RALL, or Robot-Assisted Language Learning (Han, 2012).

At the same time, the smallest screens are getting smaller. In time they'll effectively disappear altogether, as pervasive computing becomes integrated into our everyday environments, objects and clothing. In the immediate future, *flexible glass* will make our mobile devices far more malleable, and we'll see *flexible displays* wrapped around furniture or woven into clothes (Johnson et al., 2013). Indeed, today's big news in hardware development is *wearable computing*. We're seeing the arrival of *smartwatches*, which may pair via Bluetooth to a smartphone or may be standalone devices, with users able to see incoming message notifications, access online content, and monitor health and fitness levels. Another key development is *smart glasses*, again paired via Bluetooth to a smartphone or functioning as standalone devices. In the Google Glass prototype, a tiny screen above one eye (which appears very large to the viewer) can be controlled by voice, touch or movement, can display directions, search the web, take photos or videos, show video chats with friends, and can even translate spoken text into another language. Samuel Joseph and Maria Uther (2009) imagine that augmented reality glasses will one day allow language learners to view 'virtual post-it notes and graffiti' (p.25) in their real-world surroundings. But even smart glasses are likely to be a transitional stage on the way to smart contact lenses (Carmigniani & Furht, 2011; Chen, 2011), which physicist Michio Kaku (2011) envisages as being able to present us with subtitled translations of everyday spoken conversation by mid-century. New kinds of translation technology are already under development (*The Economist*, 2013) and will impact far more than today's translators on the nature of language learning – though, as Trude Heift points out (see Vignette 6), this doesn't mean there won't be a role for language teachers!

Meanwhile, research is proceeding apace in emerging areas like brain-computer interface (BCI) (or brain-machine interface, i.e., BMI) technology and neurogaming, which entail the brain directly communicating with and controlling external devices. Work is underway on a brainphone, for example, which uses brainwaves as input to produce text and audio output (the latter using a human speech generator) as well as to allow device control and web navigation (Trivedi, 2013). Designed in the first instance for disabled users, the applications for all users – and the implications for language use and learning – are potentially dramatic. As computers continue to shrink, they may well end up inside the body (*The Economist*, 2012), bringing to fruition the sci-fi-like dreams of many tech entrepreneurs, like Google's co-founder, Sergey Brin, who a number of years ago envisioned 'a little version of Google that you just plug into your brain' (cited in Carr, 2008, p.213). This is part of the ongoing process of 'our conscious intrusion into the evolutionary process' (Khanna & Khanna, 2012, Kindle location 80). If voice, touch and gestural input are already changing our linguistic interactions with our devices, what further changes will these new developments bring? What will it mean when language production retreats into the realm of our thoughts? For now, these must remain open questions.

If there's one clear message in this ongoing technological develop-ment, it's that we should avoid tying ourselves to using any one device, platform, or system (Stead, 2013) – whether that means particular media players in Spanish teaching in the USA (see Vignette 4), or particular media players in English teaching in Bangladesh (see Case Study 16). In fact, the Bangladeshi EIA project is a good example of an initiative whose success is partly due to its ability to move beyond the limitations of specific devices or delivery channels. As our tools continue to evolve, this is a lesson we all need to take on board. As Graham Stead (2013) recommends: 'Focus your energy on enabling, not containing'.

BYOD & BYOT

In some cases, mobile devices are rolled out by national governments, as in Thailand's One Tablet Per Child (OTPC) programme or Turkey's *Fırsatları Artırma ve Teknolojiyi İyileştirme Hareketi* (FATİH, or Movement of Enhancing Opportunities and Improving Technology) programme. Sometimes they're supplied by state governments, as in the iPads for Learning trial in Victoria, Australia. Sometimes they're supplied by insti-tutions, like the iPads at Casa Thomas Jefferson in Brazil (see Case Study 2) or the iPods at Duke University in the USA (see Vignette 4). Sometimes they're supplied within the parameters of projects, like the iPods, iPod Touches and Nokia mobiles used at different stages of EIA in Bangladesh (see Case Study 16). In some cases students have access to class sets; in others they are loaned devices; in still others they are given them. But given the financial burden of supplying and upgrading hard-ware, even with the support of grants and other external funding, and given that more and more people possess their own devices or are will-ing to invest in them, there's now a move towards more sustainable BYOD – sometimes also called Bring Your Own Technology (BYOT) – models (Fritschi & Wolf, 2012b; Hylén, 2012; Vosloo, 2012). In fact, people do not always 'bring' their technology with them, in the sense of carrying it with them to an educational institution – an idea which reflects the historical origins of these terms – but BYOD and BYOT have developed into blanket terms to cover all situations where end users supply their own technology.

BYOD models are often found in Europe and the USA (see Case Stud-ies 11 & 13). When formal institutional learning is involved, provision is usually also made to loan devices to learners who lack appropriate hardware, like Android devices in the European SIMOLA project or iPod Touches in the US Mentira project (see Case Studies 1 & 8). BYOD is also very much in evidence in a number of developing world projects in Africa, China, India and Indonesia (see Case Studies 4, 6, 9, 10 & 18), and EIA in Bangladesh is shifting this way in its next phase. In other hybrid models, some technology is supplied, but participants are encouraged to supplement it with their own devices, as with the subsidised Apple products in the Brazilian iPads project (see Case Study 2) or the potential use of personal mobile devices in the Cambodian Smart4Kids project and the Afghan Great Idea project (see Case Studies 5 & 17).

Sometimes a distinction is made between a BYOD model, in which students are asked to purchase and bring a specific device, or one of a small range of devices preselected by an institution, and a BYOT model, in which students can bring any device they choose (Dudeney et al., 2013). While the term BYOD is used in a generic way in this book, it's sometimes useful to remember this potential distinction. BYOD and BYOT present shared challenges, like the need for robust wifi networks, as well as individual challenges; a BYOD approach is naturally subject to hardware- and software-specific limitations, but a BYOT approach raises questions about compatibility, comparability, and equity of student access. Whatever the challenges, though, there's little doubt that we're beginning to see a global shift in the direction of BYOD, and chiefly the version sometimes known as BYOT.

Mobile connectivity

Accessible and affordable networks, in the form of *mobile telephone networks* or *wifi networks,* are important in making the most of mobile hardware. There are, however, some innovative workarounds – involving *hardwired connections* or *Secure Digital (SD) memory cards* – employed in developing regions.

Since the beginning of mobile telecommunications, a new generation of wireless mobile telephone technology has been developed every ten years or so. In 1979, a first generation (1G) analogue network was launched in Japan, with Scandinavia following in 1981. In the 1990s, these networks were superseded by 2G digital networks, most commonly based on the Global System for Mobile (GSM) Communications standard established by the European Telecommunications Standards Institute (ETSI). Significantly, 2G networks introduced data services like SMS, which allows the exchange of text messages of up to 160 characters in languages which use the Roman alphabet. Later 2.5G networks made it possible to access the internet through Wireless Application Protocol (WAP) sites, optimised for low capacity mobile devices, and MMS emerged as a fusion of SMS and WAP.

By the end of 2011, as noted earlier, 90% of the world's population lived in areas covered by 2G networks, including in transitional 2.5G versions. These networks are heavily used in the developing world; in 2012, it was reported that 62% of African subscriptions were on 2G networks, with 27% on 2.5G networks, and the remainder on 3G networks (Gallen, 2012; note that the first percentage is a correction to the original article). This shows the importance of educational interventions which are compatible with 2G networks, and indeed with feature phones that can only access 2G networks even when 3G networks are available. Examples include the British Council's SMS projects in North Africa (see Case Study 4 below), or the technologically more complex British Council/Nokia Life Learn English project in China, where richly formatted text is carried by SMS (see Case Study 9). These initiatives show that despite its tight technological constraints, SMS can be highly effective in bringing language learning to large numbers of people who otherwise would lack this opportunity.

Case Study 4   Mobile messaging in Sudan & Libya (Learn English SMS Projects)

Figure 3.4 Promotion for Learn English SMS project in Libya. © British Council, Tripoli, reproduced by permission.

Project(s):	Learn English SMS.
Language:	English.
Focus:	Vocabulary, grammar & study tips.
Level:	Three levels (elementary, intermediate & advanced).
Format:	SMS messages containing vocabulary, grammar & study tips, with quiz questions available in pull mode in Sudan.
Hardware:	The SMS services are delivered to users' own feature phones in a BYOD model.
Key partners:	British Council (content provider); Sudani & Zain (mobile network operators in Sudan); Libyana & Al Madar (mobile network operators in Libya); local service providers (liaison with mobile network operators).
Timeline:	2009 – ongoing (Sudan); 2013 – ongoing (Libya).
Location:	Sudan & Libya.
Participants:	In both Sudan & Libya, participants are largely young people, often students or professionals. In Sudan, there are around 65,000 subscribers per month; in its first month of existence in Libya, the service had already attracted 20,000 subscribers.
Funding model:	Users supply their own devices. Subscribers in Sudan pay 12 piasta (SDG 0.12, or approx. US 3¢) per message; subscribers in Libya pay LYD 3 (approx. US $2.40) per month. The aim is partial to full cost recovery.

Repurposing content originally developed for Thailand, the Sudanese and Libyan Learn English SMS projects operate in push mode, delivering regular messages – four per week in Sudan and five per week in Libya – containing vocabulary (a word or phrase with an English explanation and example), a grammar point (with an example of use) or a study tip. In Sudan, an additional pull option allows users to request quiz questions and receive automated feedback on their responses, but this is not possible in Libya due to the limitations of the available technology. In both countries, the services have captured pent-up demand for English learning among young people.

In contexts where geography or security issues limit movement – with staff in Libya, for example, presently being unable to operate outside Tripoli – mobile technologies offer a way to reach a larger number of people. While more technologically sophisticated markets might demand more sophisticated educational services, SMS is ideally suited to the current technological and economic context of North Africa. Key challenges in projects

Case Study 4   (Continued)

like these include working with local operators in each country – which makes a regional approach difficult – and the cost of promoting the services, though in the Sudanese project a successful partnership was developed with a local network operator, Sudani, who promoted the service by sending bulk SMS messages free of charge.

Evaluation can be a challenge in many projects, but in this case, the same operator was willing to share subscribers' phone numbers, so that they could be called directly and asked for feedback on the educational benefits of the service. Subscribers indicated that they liked receiving short messages regularly, found the content relevant, and appreciated the simplicity of the system. Strikingly, respondents specifically reported liking their relatively passive role as learners. This suggests some caution may be needed in attempting to directly transfer contemporary Western active learning models to other cultural contexts, even when the spread of more affordable technologies and networks eventually makes such models realisable. Cultural issues can surface on many levels in such projects. When the Sudanese project was set up, the vocabulary originally used in Thailand was vetted for its compatibility with local sensitivities, with references to pigs and pork being removed, for instance. The Sudanese and Libyan projects nevertheless demonstrate that, when due attention is paid to context and culture, some synergies are achievable across international language learning initiatives.

The key interviewees about this project were Ben Gray (ELT Manager, British Council, Tripoli, Libya) and Neil Ballantyne (Mobile Learning Manager, British Council), with additional input from Yomna ElMeshad (Regional Mobile Learning Manager, British Council, Cairo). For further information, see Ballantyne & Tyers (2012).

The next major step came in the early 2000s with the launch of 3G networks, which introduced improved data transmission capability. 3G networks conform to the ITU International Mobile Telecommunications-2000 (IMT-2000) specifications for reliability and data transmission speed (specifically, peak rates of 0.2 Megabits per second, or Mbps). The first commercial launch of a 3G network occurred in Japan in 2001. By the end of 2011, some 45% of the world's population lived in areas covered by 3G networks. Improvements in speed occurred in later transitional versions, 3.5G and 3.75G.

4G networks are now emerging. These should conform to the International Mobile Telecommunications-Advanced (IMT-Advanced) specifications for reliability and speed (peak rates of one Gigabit per second, or Gbps, when stationary, and 100 Mbps when highly mobile, e.g., in a car), again established by the ITU. The initial versions of the two commercially released 4G systems, the Worldwide Interoperability for Microwave Access (WiMAX) standard first available in South Korea in 2006, and the Long Term Evolution (LTE) standard first available in Scandinavia in 2009, did not quite meet IMT-Advanced specifications but are seen as forerunners of full 4G. Newer versions of the standards, WiMAX 2 and LTE Advanced, should eventually meet the IMT-Advanced specifications. While there has been loose speculation about 5G, there is currently no such set of specifications and they are likely to be the best part of a decade away.

4G networks, with LTE currently dominating, will continue to roll out for many years (see Figure 3.5). In 2012, 4G represented fewer than 1% of global connections but was already generating 14% of mobile data traffic; by 2017, these figures are predicted to reach 10% and 45% respectively (Cisco, 2013). Given that the use of mobile video and other high bandwidth applications increases markedly when users switch to 4G, there's little doubt that those who can afford 4G connectivity will be best able to exploit the affordances of mobile technologies.

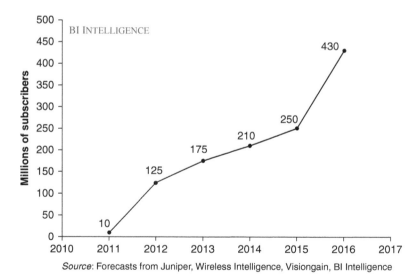

Source: Forecasts from Juniper, Wireless Intelligence, Visiongain, BI Intelligence

Figure 3.5 Global 4G LTE networks consumer base 2011–2016 (partial forecast). © Business Insider Intelligence, https://intelligence.businessinsider.com, reproduced by permission.
Note: Figures from 2012 onwards are estimates.

But for some time to come most of the world will remain on 2G or 3G networks – with the latter expected to represent 50% of connections by 2015 (ibid.) – so it's vital to pursue educational initiatives that work within the limitations of those networks, as well as exploring the alternative option of wifi.

Although the Institute of Electrical and Electronics Engineers (IEEE) established a global standard for hardwired ethernet networking, called *IEEE 802.3*, in the mid-1980s, it wasn't until the late 1990s that a similar standard for wireless networking, called *IEEE 802.11*, was hammered out. Recognising the value of a more user-friendly name, in 1999 a newly established industry-wide organisation, the Wireless Ethernet Compatibility Alliance (WECA), branded this standard 'Wi-Fi' (nowadays often written as 'wifi') and later renamed itself the Wi-Fi Alliance. While devices which conformed to an early standard, *802.11b*, delivered speeds of up to 11 Mbps, devices which conform to the current standard, *802.11n*, deliver up to 600 Mbps (Tanaza, 2012). A wifi access point, known as a *hotspot,* can be set up using a router linked to an internet service provider. With their limited range, hotspots are typically set up for local use in homes and businesses, though it's increasingly common that larger areas – for example, city centres – are blanketed with a series of overlapping access points. Another wireless technology, Bluetooth, may be used for short range data connections between devices that are relatively close together.

4G networks are faster and much more widely accessible than wifi but they are also becoming more expensive. Many users of smart devices switch to wifi whenever possible. This is important when using increasingly common *cloud computing* services, where software and data are accessed online rather than being stored on local devices. The cloud can overcome device memory limitations, reduce storage costs and facilitate sharing – but it requires constant connectivity. Having access to both 4G and wifi certainly offers the greatest technological freedom. This underlines the importance of public venues and educational institutions providing robust wifi, both for users on older networks as well as for those on 3G/4G telephone networks who must bear the cost of data usage. It's essential, too, for the many users of wifi-only tablets.

There are certain workarounds available when wireless telephone networks or wifi are inaccessible, unreliable or unaffordable. Mobile devices can also access the internet through a hardwired connection to a computer, allowing software and media files to be preloaded onto them, a technique used in the Mobiledu project in China (see Case Study 6). Another option is to use SD memory cards, which are commonly found in digital cameras and games consoles, to make multimedia content available on mobile phones (which generally require micro SD cards). This approach is seen in the EIA project in Bangladesh and the Great Idea project in Afghanistan (see Case Studies 16 & 17). While these may not be long-term substitutes for wireless connectivity, they allow multimedia content to be rolled out right now in locations which are still waiting for dependable and affordable wireless access.

Mobile software

Once we move beyond 2G and SMS into the realm of 3G/4G and smart devices, software choices become extremely important. Smart input and output mechanisms, examined earlier, depend very much on the interplay of hardware features with software capabilities. The latter derive from the functionality of specific mobile operating systems and the apps they support. In the absence of the kind of standardisation and interoperability we're used to on PCs and the internet, current tussles over mobile platforms, and the relationship of apps to the web, determine much of what is, and will be, educationally possible.

Battle of the platforms

The mobile OS (also known as platforms) which are used in smartphones and tablets are evolving rapidly, requiring users to frequently download updates. Their speed of development far exceeds that of desktop or laptop OS. This is obvious if we compare the rate of mobile OS releases (such as Apple's iPhone OS/iOS and Google's Android) with desktop OS releases (such as Apple's Mac OS and Microsoft's Windows) (see Figure 3.6). This reflects the current emphasis on development in the mobile space. There are numerous mobile OS, including BlackBerry, Symbian (used, notably, on older Nokia phones) and Windows Phone (used on newer Nokia phones), as well as home-grown OS reportedly under development in China, but Android dominates global sales, with iOS in second place (Cocotas, 2013). In fact, Android is not just the dominant *mobile* platform but the dominant *computing* platform on the planet by shipments, if not yet by installed base, with Windows in second place and iOS in third place (see Figure 3.7); this is due partly to Android's dominance in developing markets like China.

As an open source platform, which functions differently on different devices and is not always updated by users, Android faces a problem of fragmentation (Cocotas, 2013). Apple devices provide a more uniform and controlled experience, but this has its own limitations. For example,

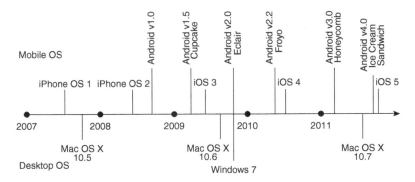

Figure 3.6   The speed of mobile vs desktop operating system development.
Source: Udell (2012), reproduced by permission.

iPhone and iPad users can't view Adobe Flash-based multimedia and interactive content (including a lot of e-learning material) due to Apple's decision not to support Flash on its iOS platform. Some recent mobile learning projects have been designed around Android devices (see Case Studies 1, 5, 10 & 13) and some around iOS devices (see Case Studies 2, 8 & 16). Some allow for a BYOD mixture or may eventually do so,

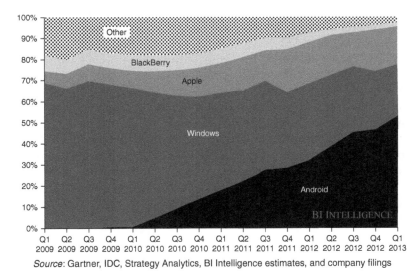

Figure 3.7   Global computing platform market share 2009–2013. © Business Insider Intelligence, https://intelligence.businessinsider.com, reproduced by permission.
Note: These figures represent quarterly shipments rather than installed base.

but the downside of increasing flexibility in this way may be the need to provide multiple apps or app versions.

Web vs apps

Although smart devices are equipped with general purpose web browsers that allow users to visit any website, whether optimised for mobile or not, users have gravitated towards the single-purpose functionality of apps. There are two main kinds available. A *mobile web app,* or simply *web app,* is usually written in HyperText Markup Language (HTML) 5 and runs in a browser on most mobile devices, regardless of the OS. Thus, although an icon may be installed on the device, the app runs on the web. However, time spent on smart devices is dominated by *native app* usage. A native app is designed for a specific OS, like Android, BlackBerry, iOS or Windows Phone, and must be downloaded to the device. It can make better use of the features of the hardware and platform, from cameras to GPS; has greater functionality when offline; and generally offers a faster, smoother experience than a web app. At the same time, hybrid apps, which are HTML5 web apps wrapped in a layer of native code to create native-like Android, iOS or other versions, are becoming more common, especially when a polished look and complex functionality are not necessary. Hybrid apps can be generated automatically from an HTML5 base using a cross-platform app builder, or for finer control can be hand-coded from the HTML5 base.

Whatever the process used, many project teams now feel compelled to bump up the flexibility and reach of their initiatives by offering several app versions. Some start with an HTML5 web app and then create native apps, as in the Nulu project which is now developing Android and iOS apps (see Case Study 11). Others start with a native app before considering developing a cross-platform web app, as in the SIMOLA project which began with an Android app (see Case Study 1). Meanwhile, the Singaporean Heritage Trails project encourages teachers to use a rapid authoring tool to generate their own trails, which can then be converted to Android or iOS apps as required for different school contexts (see Case Study 14). While we await greater interoperability of mobile systems, multiple app development may become a preferred strategy, perhaps especially in the developed world, with all the advantages (of native functionality on two or more devices) and disadvantages (of development costs) that this entails.

By the end of 2013, there are likely to be more than a million apps available to download, respectively, from Google Play (for Android) and the iTunes App Store (for iOS). Most are commercially produced. Some are free (usually supported by advertising); some work on a 'freemium' model (a portmanteau word composed of 'free' and 'premium', signalling that the basic app is free but users pay for increased functionality); and some are for sale (usually for no more than a few dollars). With so much choice available, apps are often seen as supporting the personalisation of our devices, our activities and our learning (Quinn, 2012). But there are dangers in the ongoing 'appification' of the web (Quitney Anderson & Rainie, 2012). In contrast to the open and interconnected spaces of the web, mobile OS and native apps are not interoperable. Apps may therefore function as walled gardens shut off from other apps, with their isolation compounded by the fact that the OS which support them are shut off from other OS. Most commercially available apps offer limited, preset customisation options and, in the case of iOS apps, are only available from iTunes after undergoing Apple's strict approvals process. Most significantly of all, perhaps, the vast majority of educational apps are pedagogically highly traditional, underpinned by information transmission or behaviourist drill-and-practice approaches (Oakley et al., 2012; UNESCO, 2013b). As Murray and Olcese (2011) put it in one of the earliest educational studies of the first generation iPad, most apps 'are woefully out of sync with modern theories of learning and skills student[s] will need to compete in the 21st century' (p.48).

Though *consumption apps* are somewhat removed from constructivist ambitions of transforming teaching and learning, they may play an ancillary role in contemporary classrooms, including flipped classrooms, and permit the kind of independent learning preferred by many students. Moreover, they may find resonance in varying cultural and educational settings around the world, and can facilitate study in contexts with limited educational resources, thus dovetailing with social justice agendas. When well-designed, even pedagogically traditional apps can reflect current understandings of appropriate content; can bring learning to life through multimodal presentations and interactivity; and, in the case of language learning, can provide authentic verbal and written material accompanied by reliable, system-generated feedback, offering learning opportunities which may be far superior to anything previously available in some settings.

As we've seen, making apps available for a variety of platforms maximises the flexibility and reach of a project, especially if provision is also made for the feature phones which dominate many developing contexts, with Android and iOS apps offering scope for growth as markets become more technologically sophisticated. But, as demonstrated by the Smart4Kids Khmer app (see Case Study 5 below), which is designed to

Case Study 5   App support in Cambodia (Khmer App Project)

Figure 3.8   Smart4Kids Khmer app. © et4d, reproduced by permission.

Project:	Smart4Kids Khmer App for TRAC (Total Reading Approach for Children).
Language:	Khmer (Cambodian).
Focus:	Reading (including phonics, letter recognition, word & story reading).
Level:	Grades 1 & 2 (with students aged 5–7).
Format:	Android app containing 31 units, each comprising an introductory lesson, three interactive games & a short story.
Hardware:	Participating schools will be supplied with Android phones or tablets, with a final decision on the device yet to be made. The app will be locally installed on devices.
Key partners:	USAID, World Vision & AusAID (funding providers); World Education & Kampuchean Action for Primary Education [KAPE] (NGOs responsible for the TRAC project, including content creation, testing, implementation & deployment); Education Technology for Development [et4d] (creator of Smart4Kids software & adapter of the software for the Android OS);

Case Study 5   (Continued)

	Media One (local NGO responsible for illustrations & audio); Ministry of Education, Youth & Sport (MoEYS), Cambodia (curriculum designer & provider of input on content).
Timeline:	2013 – ongoing. The project is beginning with a large-scale pilot.
Location:	Kampong Cham & Siem Reap Provinces, Cambodia.
Participants:	Initially there will be about 2,000 Grade 1 & 2 students participating from eight state primary schools, five of which are rural & three urban/semi-urban.
Funding model:	The project has been funded through a seeding grant from the All Children Reading Fund, financed by USAID & partner organisations including World Vision & AusAID. Devices will be supplied to participating schools. The app will be locally installed in schools & also available as a free download from Google Play.

Against a background of widespread parental illiteracy and poor student reading performance on national literacy tests, the MoEYS began to develop a new curriculum and textbooks in 2010. This involved a shift away from whole word recognition to a phonics approach, which was seen as more appropriate given the structure of the Khmer language and the complexity of the Khmer script. The Smart4Kids Khmer app has been developed under the auspices of the TRAC project set up by World Education in support of the MoEYS push to improve literacy levels. The development of the app began in January 2013 and, despite the challenges of developing a techno-logically complex app in a short timeframe, it is due to reach classrooms in September 2013. It is based on materials and activities modelled after the 'Big Five' focus areas recommended by the US National Institute of Child Health and Human Development – phonemic awareness, systematic phonics, vocabulary, fluency, and comprehension – and is simultaneously linked to the new MoEYS curriculum. Children are challenged to learn sounds and recognise new words as they play simple, interactive sound, word and memory games. World Education and KAPE will evaluate improvement in reading levels using Early Grade Reading Assessment (EGRA) tools.

The creation of educational software in the local language is new for Cambodia, and this is the first Khmer app ever made available for primary school students. While the technological and pedagogical design is globalised, the language and content are very much localised. A data simulator was built by et4d so that the local World Education team could focus on the content and test it online, without having to use the app itself. The involvement of a Khmer language team, combined with the enthusiasm, support and input of the MoEYS, has ensured the validity and relevance of the content, with all stories and settings tailored to students' lives, and the images reflecting local culture and settings.

While the app will not work on feature phones, over 20% of mobile subscriptions in Cambodia are already for smartphones, mainly Android devices, a figure which is set to increase in coming years, allowing more personalised use of the app. In the meantime, Android devices will be supplied to participating schools and students. The app developers see themselves as creating a product, the Smart4Kids app, which will be ready when developing nations or small language communities need it. The globalised approach to design, combined with a localised approach to language and content, will make it affordable to create materials for less widely spoken languages, potentially allowing every child, no matter what their location or language, to access interactive tools to support the acquisition of reading and literacy skills.

The key interviewee about this project was Isabelle Duston (CEO of et4d), with additional input from Willem van de Waal (International Reading Consultant, World Education). For further information, see the *Smart4Kids* website (www.smart4kids.com), the *et4d* website (www.et4d.com), World Education's *TRAC* webpage (www.worlded.org/WEIInternet/projects/ListProjects.cfm?dblProjDescID=12281), the *Smart4Kids* Facebook page (www.facebook.com/pages/Smart4Kids-LLC/131722593645313) or follow @S4KApps on Twitter. See also Global Partnership for Education (n.d.).

support a national Cambodian effort to improve reading skills, smart apps are already becoming more viable in some developing countries. While Android devices are being supplied in the pilot phase of this initiative, more than a fifth of mobile subscriptions in Cambodia are for smartphones, suggesting that the market is ripe for smart apps which can be used beyond the boundaries of m-learning projects and the equipment they supply. In coming years, other countries which currently lack technological support for local language learning may be able to capitalise on such developments.

Since the publication of Murray and Olcese's study of the iPad 1, more *productive apps* oriented towards creation and networking have become available (Pegrum et al., 2013). Unlike consumption apps which are generally subject-specific – aiming to teach a particular language, for example – many productive apps are *generic*. They might support digital storytelling or communicative networking in a general way, and, handled appropriately, can lend themselves to language learning or any other subject. Where appropriate hardware and connectivity are available, and where teachers and students are ready – or almost ready, with the support of teacher or learner training – such apps can be used to promote pedagogical transformation and 21st century skills agendas. This can be clearly seen in the Brazilian iPads project (see Case Study 2), where trainers have encouraged teachers to move away from consumption apps and towards productive apps as part of a broader shift towards more student-centred classrooms.

Web meets world

The future direction of internet development leads beyond the internet itself, and it's here that mobile devices truly come into their own as they challenge our sense of space and place (see Chapter 1). Mobile tools permit the web and the world to intersect, a phenomenon which has been dubbed 'Web Meets World' (O'Reilly & Battelle, 2009). The resulting *mixed reality* has two complementary aspects. The *internet of things* involves the digital communication of data collected or generated by real-world objects. *Augmented reality* involves dynamically overlaying contextually relevant digital information on a real-world environment. It's been suggested that such a broad, conceptual definition of AR is more productive than a technocentric definition linked to the annotated viewfinder displays most people associate with AR, since it draws our attention to the whole range of contemporary tools and approaches that create similar effects (FitzGerald et al., 2012; Wu et al., 2013).

Today's widespread *quick response* codes act as hardlinks from the real to the virtual, and may be seen as a 'manual' stage on the path to the development of more automated AR. These two-dimensional barcodes (see Figure 3.9) can be scanned using a freely downloadable QR code reader app and the camera on a mobile device. Invented by the Toyota subsidiary Denso Wave in 1994, they only became widely popular with the commercial spread of mobile devices capable of scanning them. The

Figure 3.9 QR code linking to E-language wiki. Generated with Kaywa, qrcode. kaywa.com.

codes are very robust and are found nowadays in books and magazines, on notice boards and billboards, on business cards and even on t-shirts! Once scanned, a QR code may open up a text file, a media file or a webpage, send an SMS, or load contact details onto a device. Near field communication (NFC) tags are another similar technology, though they are RFID rather than optical tags; they are not free of charge and don't yet work with all smartphones, but are able to be recoded. QR codes in education have been seen to 'increase the impact of mobile devices, to enhance flexibility of provision and also to advance the personalisation of learning' (Leone & Leo, 2011, p.338). QR codes can be attached to handouts to provide optional answer keys, scaffolded guidance, or extension exercises, thus giving students greater autonomy. Taking learning outside the classroom, QR or NFC tags distributed around a school or community can form the basis for problem-solving treasure hunts (Rivers, 2009) or vocabulary scavenger quests (JISC, 2012). Such activities, which often incorporate real-world linguistic interactions, can eventually lead to students developing their own QR/NFC challenges for peers, which can function much like simple AR games.

Augmented reality and *virtual reality* are part of a single continuum (see Figure 3.10). Virtual reality is mostly the province of fixed desktop or laptop computers: a user enters a virtual world (like Second Life) or a gaming environment (like World of Warcraft) which exists in a digital space on the other side of the monitor screen and, as observed by John Traxler (see Chapter 1), turns their back on the real world for the duration of their online experience. But we already know that location-aware mobile devices lead to a reintegration of the virtual and real. In AR, digital elements are overlaid on the real world without removing the user from it. And if reality is augmented with details that the user might otherwise not know or observe – or even perceive, as in the case of visual

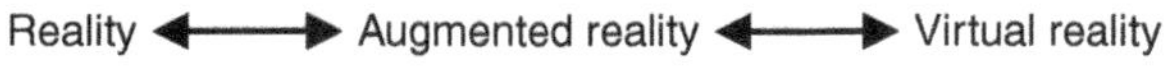

Reality ◄─────► Augmented reality ◄─────► Virtual reality

Figure 3.10   The mixed reality continuum. Adapted from: Milgram & Kishino (1994).

cues for hearing impaired users (Carmigniani & Furht, 2011), or audio and haptic cues for visually impaired users (ibid; FitzGerald et al., 2012) – then AR can actually increase a user's integration with the real world.

AR systems have a number of possible *input mechanisms*. Marker-based AR displays can be triggered by manually scanning visual markers, including QR codes. More flexible markerless AR displays may be based on image or object recognition. Additionally, GPS and other kinds of spatial positioning may determine location, as in geofencing, where information becomes accessible once a user crosses a virtual boundary drawn around an area in the real world. Combinations of these and other input mechanisms are likely to become more common, as in the Singaporean learning trails (see Case Study 14) which make use of image recognition, geofencing and Bluetooth technology. Using the broad definition of AR given above, there are many possible *output formats*, including geoaware maps or location-sensitive push notifications. However, the output format commonly associated with AR, and seen in key apps like Aurasma, Junaio, Layar and Wikitude, is digital content overlaid on a live display of the real world viewed through the camera of a mobile device (see Figure 3.11) or through wearable technology like smart glasses (as in Google Glass). Audio and haptic output, as noted earlier, are also possible.

AR isn't just a one-way street. Users can leave text, image, audio or video files attached to real-world locations for others to access and react to, in the process 'transform[ing] reality into a multi-modal social text' (FitzGerald et al., 2012, p.3). These annotations may be created on mainstream social networking platforms (like Facebook and Twitter) or newer geosocial platforms (like Foursquare and Yelp), or added directly into the AR software itself. Wikitude, as seen below, overlays public, commercial and personal content, including user-generated Wikipedia information, on its camera view of the real world. Emerging AR software enables users to interact with virtual objects and characters, while there are both desktop programmes (like buildAR) and mobile apps (like Aurasma; see also Vignette 10) that already make it possible for ordinary users to create their own simple AR displays, going well beyond more manual QR codes. However, because – like so much of the mobile universe – AR systems aren't yet interoperable, annotations or displays created with one

Figure 3.11 Augmented reality view of a London street through the Wikitude browser.
Source: Wikitude under CC BY-SA 2.0 licence, 2011, http://www.flickr.com/photos/wikitude/5706690186/, reproduced by permission.

app won't necessarily be visible in another. We can expect a lot more development, as well as more standardisation, in years to come.

Mobile AR has clear implications for situated learning: 'Students find connections between their lives and their education through the addition of a contextual layer' (Johnson et al., 2012, p.29). AR makes room, too, for embodied cognition (FitzGerald et al., 2012; Potter, 2011). It can underpin guided tours of campuses or towns, with connections to teachers or classmates only a click away on geosocial services. It can underpin geocaching, which essentially involves GPS-enabled treasure hunts. It can allow students to view objects or creatures that no longer exist, like demolished buildings or extinct animals. In mixed reality gaming, players can communicate with virtual others – who may never have existed! – superimposed on their view of reality. In the place-independent 'Alien Contact!' game developed within the Handheld Augmented Reality Project (HARP) at Harvard University, for instance, students' GPS-enabled devices presented them with relevant digital content, virtual characters, and literacy and maths puzzles as they moved around their school grounds, working collaboratively in teams to solve the mystery of why aliens had landed on earth (HARP, n.d.; Potter, 2011).

There is considerable potential for students to create user-generated contexts for language learning where their local real-world experiences intersect with their virtual global communications and connections via an AR interface, as Nik Peachey suggests (see Vignette 5 below). Language learners can even create their own AR stories or games for others to navigate and enjoy; a sophisticated example built with Augmented Reality for Interactive Storytelling (ARIS) open source software can be seen in the Visitas de la Colonia game that grew out of the Mentira Spanish language learning project in the USA (see Case Study 8). It's time for teachers to start introducing their students to the possibilities.

Vignette 5   The promise of augmented reality

Nik Peachey, Freelance Learning Technology Consultant & Teacher Trainer, UK

To really understand and exploit the full potential of how mobile devices can impact on language learning and literacy, and for that matter learning of any kind, we have to understand what is important about the recent shift. Mobile learning has been around for centuries; it used to be called books. For a good while now we have been able to carry round cameras. Even mobile phones, though relatively recent, aren't incredibly new.

What excites me about the more recent developments in m-learning is the ability of mobile devices to overlay our virtual world of information and media creation onto our real world of experience through augmented reality applications. This ability to make learning geographically and contextually specific to such a degree really holds huge potential for on-demand supported experiential learning that is directly relevant to each individual learner and which they can participate in creating. What I believe we really need to be doing now is helping our students to understand and exploit these resources so that they can develop as autonomous learners outside of the classroom.

▶ Further reading: Peachey (2011, 2012).

This mixed reality, with all its promise of u-learning, will soon be our everyday reality. But as Brian Chen (2011) notes, '[o]nce augmented reality is optimized, having 20/20 vision will no longer be sufficient: if we're not seeing data, we're not seeing' (p.200). There are implications for processing multimedia annotations (which necessitates multimodal literacy), evaluating and filtering content (information literacy), and sharing meaning through virtual connections (network literacy). How will we deal with an increasingly *customised reality* filled with personally tailored information and advertising (Sándor, 2012), or indeed a *deletive reality* where our smart lenses strip the real world of anything we don't want to see (Khanna & Khanna, 2012)? What will it mean to be 'real' in augmented reality? Digital literacies, clearly, will be at a premium (see Chapter 6). But as will be obvious by now, AR is not the only mobile development that may have trouble in store for us, and that will require us to hone our mobile literacy – above all our critical mobile literacy.

The trouble with mobile technologies

Mobile hardware, networks and software were generally not designed with education in mind. When they are repurposed, their limitations and risks are bound to become evident. Those we've touched on so far are just the tip of the iceberg. Mobile literacy must surely include an awareness and understanding of all these limitations and risks.

The *hardware* confronts teachers and learners with *limited screen sizes,* especially on feature phones, which are a challenge for extended reading; *limited input options* which, newer developments aside, are a challenge for composing extended text and, on smart devices, for multimodal creation and manipulation; *limited speed and capacity,* which is a challenge for working with multimodal and AR apps; *limited storage,* which is a challenge for saving large amounts of multimedia material; *limited export options,* particularly hardwired options, which are a challenge for sharing larger documents and artefacts; *limited battery life,* which is a minor challenge in the developed world but a major one for the 1.6 billion people living off the electricity grid (GSMA, 2010a); *limited environmental adaptability* to conditions like sunshine and rain, again a minor challenge in much of the developed world but potentially a major one elsewhere; and *limited robustness,* which is a considerable challenge in harsh conditions. Many of these issues both reflect and contribute to broader *design limitations:* mobile devices, including smart devices, were designed largely for consumption, or for simple kinds of creation and curation. Repurposing them for active, collaborative learning is far from impossible, but requires a thoughtful approach. As a result, in the developed world, iPads and other smart devices are often viewed as a supplement to more generative devices like laptops, especially at higher educational levels (Oakley et al., 2012).

The price tag attached to purchasing, repairing and upgrading hardware is a considerable barrier in many contexts. In the developing world, where the luxury of multiple devices is rare, teachers and learners may have to work within the limitations of affordable low-end technology, often provided through a combination of IGO, NGO, government, corporate and other project funding. On the other hand, thanks to the growing prominence of BYOD models in both the developing and developed world, teachers may soon find themselves dealing with a whole spectrum of devices with different affordances and limitations. These are tied ultimately to their affordability and therefore, perhaps especially in the developed world, highlight digital divides and raise thorny equity issues (Hylén, 2012; UNESCO, 2013c).

But when it comes to hardware, perhaps the greatest danger of all is the fallacious belief that it's possible or advisable or, worse still, inevitable that we should replace all our analogue tools with digital ones. Writing by hand is important for developing fine motor skills, for instance, and evidence is building that its embodied, sensorimotor aspects contribute in key ways to letter recognition and memorisation, and may impact on reading and writing skills (James & Engelhardt, 2012; Mangen & Velay, 2010). Whether and how our brains may adapt in time is an open question. For now, pencils, pens and paper must still have a place in any learning ecology.

Connectivity is problematic, too. In the developing world, mobile networks may be unreliable, slow and expensive, especially outside urban centres, with large areas covered only by 2G networks – hence the use of SD cards in projects from Bangladesh to Afghanistan (see Case Studies 16 & 17). But even in well-provisioned cities and institutions, limited bandwidth is an issue as developers, teachers and learners seek to exploit the full potential of their smart devices – whether through 3G/4G networks as on the Singaporean learning trails, or through wifi as in the Brazilian iPads project (see Case Studies 14 & 2). And while wifi can dramatically reduce data transmission costs for learners, it must be robust and secure, above all in BYOD contexts where multiple, potentially unknown devices are seeking to connect to the network.

And then there's *software*. The ongoing appification of the digital landscape – and of education – matters. It matters from a content point of view, with particular concerns over Apple's stringent controls and vetting processes (Chen, 2011; MacKinnon, 2012; Melhuish & Falloon, 2010). It matters from a pedagogical point of view, given the educationally reductive nature of many consumption apps. But productive apps can be problematic, too. Commercially available software in general constrains communicative options through templates and defaults which, for those lacking in code literacy, present absolute limits to digital self-expression (see Chapter 6). Mobile apps are often even more tightly locked down than desktop or laptop software, including for the code literate, who may have to resort to designing their own apps – which then may or may not be approved for distribution through platforms like iTunes or Google Play.

Much has been said about the need for adequate technological and pedagogical support for teachers and learners as they integrate new tools into their teaching and learning processes (Cochrane, 2014; Oakley et al., 2012; Pegrum et al., 2013). Certainly, this is vital. But, as the foregoing discussion has implied, the potential issues with mobile tools go well beyond both technology and pedagogy. It's also vital that educators start to think *critically*, and help their students to do the same – not just about hardware, connectivity and software, nor even just about the pedagogies they support, but about the broader cultural, social, political and economic ecologies in which they're embedded.

There are profound yet intangible *cultural questions* to be asked about the provenance of hardware and software, with their roots in a Western tradition of rationalism and individualism crossed with the libertarian, egalitarian ethos of Silicon Valley (Pegrum, 2009); and there are similar questions to be asked about the provenance of Western pedagogies (see Chapter 2). There are more concrete but no less pressing *commercial questions* to be asked about mobile devices as desirable, disposable consumer items which promote marketplace values (Merchant, 2012). They may also expose vulnerable populations to advertising of which they have little experience or critical understanding (Kukulska-Hulme, 2011). Meanwhile, mobile hardware remains tethered to manufacturers who can access and control it remotely (Zittrain, 2008), while social networking and social media platforms remain the proprietary terrain of service providers who may block data from being removed from their walled gardens, delete data within their walls, and even expel users altogether. At their limit, these commercial questions bleed into *ethical questions* over privacy and surveillance. There are issues around the commercial and political tracking of user data (Chen, 2011; Morozov, 2011) as well as, specifically, the educational tracking of student data (Chan et al., 2006; Pachler et al., 2010; Traxler, 2010). This has been explicitly flagged up as a challenge in the European MASELTOV project (see Case Study 13), which relies on location-aware devices. As the collapse of the traditional divide between public/private, and between work/leisure, is hastened by mobile devices and the changes they engender in our conceptions of space and time (Castells, 2010; Rainie & Wellman, 2012), students may find themselves unwilling inhabitants of a 24/7 learning landscape under constant surveillance (see Chapter 4). And that's before we even consider the risks students may face from strangers, peers, or their own missteps in permanent, pervasive networks (see Chapter 7).

Then there are *health and environmental questions*. While the World Health Organization's classification of mobile phones' electromagnetic fields as 'possibly carcinogenic' (WHO, 2011) represents a very cautious approach in view of limited evidence and an absence of long-term studies, further research is needed (National Cancer Institute, 2012). There's also a lack of research on the effects of digital screen time on health. However, lessons may be drawn from many years of research on children's television screen time, which demonstrates a litany of negative effects caused by too much exposure at too young an age: delayed language development; disturbed sleep; reduced time for more beneficial developmental activities; and obesity caused by lack of physical activity (Centre for Community Child Health, 2009; Chonchaiya & Pruksananonda, 2008). While digital screens are much more interactive, they may increase overall screen time, potentially amplifying negative effects. These concerns layer medical reasons on top of the pedagogical reasons for not yet dispensing with our analogue tools. As far as the broader population is concerned, optometrists have noted a high incidence of eyestrain and blurred vision among people who read extensively on screens (Jabr, 2013), while psychologists have observed a rise in cases of internet addiction (though, as a behavioural addiction, it is still controversial), an elevation of stress levels caused in part by information overload, and a proliferation of symptoms mirroring attention disorders and even autism (Dudeney et al., 2013; Pegrum, 2009).

The jury is still out on the deeper impact of new technologies on the brain (Greenfield, 2008; Small & Vorgan, 2008), but it does seem that a balanced approach to our devices is in order. Youth in the developed world in particular may benefit from being encouraged to think about why, when and how to switch off their screens; whether for their physical health, mental health, or to promote reflective thought and learning. One topic they might be urged to reflect on is the growing environmental catastrophe of e-waste dumps poisoning people and land in the developing world (Chan et al., 2006; Vosloo, 2012). The commercial, social and even educational pressure to regularly upgrade our mobile devices – which typically have a much shorter lifecycle than other sources of e-waste, like televisions and PCs – is putting enormous pressure on still inadequate governmental and corporate recycling initiatives to mitigate the ensuing damage to the planet.

It's clear that any conception of *mobile literacy* as a skillset underpinning the effective use of mobile tools must involve an element of *critical mobile literacy*, which pushes us to ask questions not only about our hardware, connectivity and software, but about the ecologies within which they're used. We'll have more to say about mobile literacy in Chapter 6, but first there are many more pedagogical questions to ask about m-learning and MALL, which we'll tackle over the next two chapters.

4
How to Teach Language with Mobile Devices

In this chapter, we'll look at a series of *how* questions, considering how language teaching has changed over the years in relation to CALL and MALL; how different kinds of MALL can be put into practice; and how MALL can be assessed. In the following chapter, we'll approach MALL from a different angle as we turn to *what* questions and consider what aspects of language – including mobile language – can be taught through mobile devices.

Where language teaching meets technology

Technologically mediated language teaching, whether in its CALL or MALL incarnations, is profoundly affected by theories and approaches which derive from studies of second language acquisition (SLA) and applied linguistics. The past half century has brought about dramatic changes, as Carla Meskill and Natasha Anthony (2010) point out:

> The historical shifts away from teaching language in the abstract to teaching language *in use* have been significant. Where language was once treated as a subject area, the substance of which was to be *talked about*, contemporary views see the goal of language instruction to be active, productive *use* of the new language.
>
> (Kindle location 429; italics in original)

As they go on to say: 'Contemporary language learning is...about productive, socially motivated language *use* as a route to mastery' (Kindle location 4586). It's possible to identify a progression over time through several major language teaching approaches and their CALL and MALL manifestations, leading towards today's views on how best to teach and learn language.

An older *behaviourist approach* can still be found in some parts of language teaching generally, as well as in so-called 'tutorial CALL' and 'tutorial MALL'. This gives rise to repetitive drilling of vocabulary, spelling, grammar and pronunciation, aiming at consolidation of foundational knowledge through flashcard exercises, quizzes or simple games. Many teachers agree that such activities have a place in the classroom, especially if they include a focus on meaning, and even more so outside the classroom in flipped models. However, these activities are pedagogically limited since they do not typically involve real comprehension or communication, so they cannot be the whole story of language learning (Dudeney et al., 2013).

The *communicative approach* arose as the result of a shift towards a cognitive perspective, as Noam Chomsky's work on language performance and language competence, and Dell Hymes' subsequent work on communicative competence, led to a much greater emphasis on communicative proficiency (Meskill & Anthony, 2010). Several interrelated points of emphasis emerging from cognitive and psycholinguistic research have proven to be of considerable significance and are often referenced in the literature on communicative CALL and MALL, sometimes singly but more often in combination (e.g., Blake, 2008; Nah et al., 2008; Reinders & Wattana, 2012). These include the need for:

- *comprehensible input* (Krashen, 1985), which involves language that is slightly beyond learners' current level but can still be comprehended, providing them with material for intake;
- *noticing* (Schmidt, 1990), which involves learners attending to, or having their attention drawn to, new elements of language like grammar or vocabulary, which can then become intake;
- *negotiation of meaning* in the process of interaction (Long, 1996), which assists with comprehensible input, provides negative feedback that helps learners notice gaps in their grammar, vocabulary and other areas, and encourages them to modify their language output;
- *comprehensible output* (Swain, 1985), which involves learners testing out new grammar, vocabulary and other aspects of language as they generate linguistic output.

This opens up space for the computer-mediated communication (CMC) tasks often associated with CALL and MALL. In CMC, learners can also begin to develop their pragmatic competence, that is, their ability to engage in socially and culturally appropriate discourse in given contexts. This focus on pragmatics has been very much heightened with the more recent shift to a sociocultural perspective in CALL and MALL, as discussed below.

A cognitive perspective, and specifically a psycholinguistic perspective, also underpins the steady ongoing development of *Intelligent CALL*, where interactive computer systems use Natural Language Processing (NLP) to parse students' natural language input, conducting detailed error analysis and providing individualised feedback (Heift & Schulze, 2007). This is a much more sophisticated version of tutorial CALL (Blake, 2008). It explodes the boundaries of traditional flashcard and quiz tasks by allowing language to be embedded in communicative contexts and by providing feedback which is explicit and individually tailored. In some ways ICALL represents a longstanding, language-specific iteration of the recently popular idea of applying learning analytics to big data generated by students. Significantly, it involves building learner models which enable the software to adapt to individual learners as well as, in the case of open learner models, making those models available to students (and teachers) as a kind of formative assessment, an approach with considerable pedagogical promise (Heift & Schulze, 2007). Moreover, as ICALL interfaces become more user-friendly, teachers and students with little programming knowledge will increasingly be able to create their own ICALL materials (ibid.).

In terms of hardware, ICALL was originally associated with desktop or laptop computing environments, but it is beginning to migrate to mobile devices as these become more powerful, as seen for instance in the Odysseas Greek Language Tutor iOS app from Simon Fraser University (n.d.). In terms of language content, ICALL was initially associated with parser-based analysis of written text, but more recently statistical methods have been applied to both written and oral language, including for speech recognition. Work is now underway on linking ICALL apps to location-aware and AR technologies, which will permit individualised feedback to be provided in real time in real-world contexts, with intelligent systems adapting not only to learners but to their changing linguistic environments. Indeed, just as we've seen a shift from CALL to MALL, it seems that we're now moving from the era of ICALL into the era of IMALL. In the near future, suggests Trude Heift (see Vignette 6 below), we'll see IMALL developments that seem to come straight out of science fiction. But while the impact on language use and language learning may be considerable, it's not yet quite time for language teachers to hang up their boots.

Vignette 6 The potential of IMALL

Trude Heift, Simon Fraser University, Canada

In the spring semester, 2013, I taught a class on linguistics and language teaching and, as part of the syllabus, I included a unit on ICALL. One of the in-class group assignments asked students to design what they considered to be the perfect language learning tool. Interestingly, there was a noticeable overlap in their ideas. Students agreed that the device should be portable, include speech recognition and simultaneous translation, and take into account different accents, speech acts, social contexts, etc. For instance, in the case of *The Holographic Language Partner*, students designed a holographic native speaker with whom one could interact in different settings chosen as if through a handheld remote control. The settings ranged from casual to formal and allowed the user to practice language with different speakers, ask questions, and obtain feedback, thus aiming at a very individualized language learning environment. Moreover, students suggested that people should wear a device that would simultaneously convert and translate their concepts into the target language. For instance, *The Learning Cap* would provide subtitles and translations, and a visual speech synthesizer as well as a self-correcting accent-filtering chip.

From a language processing perspective, the students' ideas are not at all removed from what is already underway with IMALL technology. Although not yet perfect, simultaneous translation devices are becoming closer at hand and, according to an article in *The Economist* earlier this year, Microsoft's contribution seems to be very promising. Their simultaneous translation tool is not only capable of displaying subtitles on a video screen and speaking in a computer-generated voice but, much more impressively, the translated speech shares the phonetic and prosodic characteristics of the speaker's voice. Naturally, the underlying technology is grounded in ICALL, both natural language processing as well as speech recognition and generation. It is intriguing that we are getting quite close to what was limited to the sci-fi devices of Captain Kirk and his crew just a few decades ago. However, for language students this implies that they need to learn how to use

---

Vignette 6   (Continued)

these devices and resources most effectively, and thus from a pedagogical perspective, our job as language teachers in helping them
develop this knowledge has hardly changed.

▶ Further reading: *The Economist* (2013); Heift & Schulze (2007).

Going beyond both behaviourist and communicative approaches, an
even newer *sociocultural approach* – or, more accurately perhaps, a *sociocultural perspective* – has recently come to the fore. Consequently, the
focus of language teaching is 'increasingly moving away from linguistic inputs and products' towards a greater emphasis on meaningful,
contextualised activity (Comas-Quinn & Mardomingo, 2012, p.49). The
sociocultural perspective encompasses a number of approaches, many
of which are more or less loosely related to the first approach in the list
below, namely social constructivism (see Chapter 2). Such approaches
are often referenced in the literature on sociocultural CALL and MALL,
sometimes individually, but frequently in groupings of two or three
(e.g., Comas-Quinn et al., 2009; Driver, 2012; Petersen et al., 2008). They
include:

- *a social constructivist approach* (Vygotsky, 1978), which focuses on
  learners actively constructing knowledge in interaction with other
  learners;
- *a situated approach* (Lave & Wenger, 1991), which focuses on learners
  co-constructing knowledge within a particular social context;
- *an embodied approach,* which takes into account the relationship
  between the mind, the body and the environment;
- *an informal learning approach,* which focuses on the kinds of incidental, tacit and situated learning that take place in everyday life;
- *a learner-centred approach,* which focuses on students' autonomy,
  agency and potentially their identity development, at which point
  this may blend into an identity approach;
- *an identity approach* (Norton, 2000), potentially a more politicised
  version of a learner-centred approach that views language learning
  through the lenses of poststructuralism, critical discourse analysis
  and critical pedagogy, as it focuses on students' development of
  agency and identity;

- *an intercultural (communicative) competence approach* (Byram, 1997) or *an intercultural literacy approach* (Dudeney et al., 2013), which focuses on students' interactions and negotiations with others from different linguistic and cultural backgrounds, potentially including the development of agency and identity in intercultural contexts;
- *an ecological approach* (Lam & Kramsch, 2003; van Lier, 2004) or *a complexity approach* (Larsen-Freeman & Cameron, 2008), which takes a holistic view of the complex, interconnected processes involved in language learning, and again includes a focus on learners' agency and identity.

In our current *postmethod* era (Kumaravadivelu, 2006), language teaching typically draws on an eclectic combination of older approaches and methods alongside newer ones, but with an emphasis on meaningful communication within a sociocultural framework. There is no contradiction here. In many ways sociocultural approaches are quite compatible with older communicative and interactionist ideas (Blake, 2008; Meskill & Anthony, 2010), and serve to extend communicative language learning in new directions. In fact, today's vastly increased possibilities for disseminating multimodal content through online networks, receiving and responding to feedback, and reworking and building on one's own and others' materials, allow the notion of CMC to be taken to a whole new level. Many sociocultural approaches involve learners in rich and diverse content creation activities, often within task- or project-based frameworks, and open up the scope for learners' user-generated content to be integrated into class materials and even shared publically online. Sociocultural approaches are compatible, too, with new generation ICALL and indeed IMALL, which will soon provide context-aware, socially sensitive support for learners' real-world construction of understanding. It is here that some of the most exciting MALL developments are currently occurring.

But sometimes learners expect pedagogical approaches to be more restrictive and their own roles to be less challenging. It was noted for example that Sudanese SMS subscribers expressed a preference for passive learner roles (see Case Study 4), while an exploration of mobile learning options in China identified users' preference for lightweight, entertaining content (see Case Study 6). Both of these findings would surely be echoed in many other contexts. Pedagogically, content delivery and drilling – ideally in entertaining formats – still have a place in language learning; culturally, they may seem familiar and appropriate; and they're far better than no language learning at all in settings with few other opportunities. At the same time, teacher trainers, teachers and/or educational designers who have more room to manoeuvre could begin to engage in teacher and/or learner training to flag up the limitations of these as standalone approaches, and share what we've come to understand about effective language learning practice over many decades; this would include the need for active and interactive language use (from a communicative perspective) and the benefits of considering social, contextual and identity elements (from a sociocultural perspective).

Naturally, personal factors, like age, interests, language levels and needs, and even digital skills and attitudes, also impact on learners' preferences. For some students, digital learning may have *psychological benefits*. In online learning generally, it's important to establish a community where learners can practise language safely as they develop both their language skills and their new language identities (Meskill & Anthony, 2010). Those who are shy or belong to minorities may find it less threatening to participate in private or semi-private CMC or respond anonymously to online polls. There are also intrinsic *motivational benefits* often attributed to mobile learning which, novelty effects aside, seem to be connected with personalised ownership of the technology and the ability to use it to network locally and globally. Of course, digital networks open up opportunities for independent, personalised exploration of linguistic and cultural contexts and communities, with positive online experiences potentially serving to increase what Norton (2000) would call students' *investment* in language learning and identity building.

Going to the 4 MALLs

In 2006, George Chinnery wrote about language teachers and students 'Going to the MALL'. But, as already foreshadowed by the wide range of mobile projects covered in his article, there's more than one kind of MALL we can visit. At least four different kinds stand out, although they do interconnect. In her seminal overview of CALL, Garrett (2009) distinguishes between tutorial CALL, authentic-materials-engagement CALL, and communication CALL. Adapting these categories for MALL, adding an extra one, and rearranging them on a scale of rising (inter-)activity, we might identify *MALL for content* (covering graded as well as authentic content); *MALL for tutorials; MALL for creation* (an additional category); and *MALL for communication*.

As we explore these MALLs one by one, we'll see that increasing levels of interactivity are broadly indicative of increasing levels of pedagogical sophistication and increasing potential for transforming teaching and learning. The overall trajectory is from a behaviourist through a communicative towards a sociocultural paradigm, with a strong emphasis on agency and identity emerging in MALL for creation and communication, though it is not uncommon for multiple paradigms to be interwoven in a given language learning activity. The lower the level of the MALL, the greater the need to integrate other kinds of activities with it; the higher the level, the more comprehensive and freestanding the activities may be, though there are still benefits in a blended mode which combines the advantages of face-to-face and digital learning.

MALL for content

The technologically easiest and pedagogically simplest use of new technologies – whether we're talking about e-learning or m-learning, CALL or MALL, web-based or app-based learning – is for content consumption. Content delivery, as Diaz (2010) puts it, is 'the low-hanging fruit' of m-learning. It does however allow for self-determined, self-paced, autonomous learning. Language content can provide input, ideally comprehensible input, in the form of reading or listening texts. These may be graded for learners or may consist of more challenging authentic material, and they may be supported and made more comprehensible by inbuilt glossaries, standalone dictionaries or web-based concordances. Depending on the language being learned, there could be a vast amount of material available, or very little. In the case of English, material might be in a standard variety (as is most likely with graded materials) or a series of World Englishes (as is the case with authentic materials); the same principle applies to other widely spoken languages.

Compared to desktop or laptop devices, mobile devices present a number of challenges in making use of such content. Differences in OS mean that not all apps, audio or video formats can be accessed on all smart devices: Apple's iBooks can be read only on iOS devices; Flash videos can be played almost anywhere else. When it comes to reading, it's well-established that we read differently online than offline, whatever the digital device (see Chapter 5), but mobile phones add the obstacle of reduced reading fields. As usability expert Jakob Nielsen (2011) puts it: 'it's much harder to understand complicated information when you're reading through a peephole'. Constantly scrolling through screens takes time and diverts attention away from the text itself, as well as making it hard to obtain or maintain an overview of the shape and structure of a text (Jabr, 2013), and thereby undermining skimming (Sussex, 2012).

One approach is to promote *short-form reading*, which often has a lexical (or grammatical) rather than a reading focus per se, as seen in the British Council's SMS projects in North Africa or the British Council/ Nokia Life Learn English project in China (see Case Studies 4 & 9), with the latter obliged to work within a message limit of only 49 characters. When the focus is more on reading skills development, as in Nulu's Spanish and English news stories (see Case Study 11), texts are kept succinct and broken up under subheadings, a good illustration of the principle of chunking. In a more general context, Wikipedia Mobile (m.wikipedia.org) – accessible free of charge through Wikipedia Zero in many developing countries – shows how text can be chunked for mobile devices. Similarly, episodic mobile phone novels, which originated in Japan but have spread widely, and which are delivered by SMS in short chapters, are well-adapted to these devices.

But *long-form reading* is also possible. E-books and e-magazines are growing in popularity. Though they're often read on tablets in the developed world, they can also be read on phones. The enormous success of the Yoza project for South African teens, which provides English, Afrikaans and Xhosa mobile phone stories, plays and poetry free of charge along with commenting and voting features, demonstrates that small screens are not an insurmountable obstacle and constitute a good option in a book-poor, mobile-rich context (GSMA, 2010a; Isaacs, 2012b). By the end of 2012, there had been 575,000 readings of Yoza content by 200,000 visitors (Vosloo, 2013). Similarly, the Worldreader Mobile project, a complement to the original Worldreader e-reader project, distributes an app for feature and Android phones which gives users access to a library containing thousands of novels and stories. It's hoped that by the end of 2013, the app will be installed on 10 million phones, mostly in Africa and Asia (Worldreader, 2012). Steve Vosloo (2013) has even suggested that the '[m]obile phone is the e-reader of Africa' (see also Vignette 9).

But it's not only an e-reader for Africa, of course. In an exploration of different language learning options in the Mobiledu project in China (see Case Study 6 below), it became apparent that there was demand for both content MALL (in the form of e-books and e-magazines, for example, though it should be noted that these were interactive) and tutorial MALL (in the form of multimodal quizzes and exam preparation apps). In time, it may be possible to encourage some users to explore further, complementing their use of pedagogically traditional apps with

Case Study 6   Exploring mobile options in China (Mobiledu Project)

Figure 4.1   Mobiledu service in China. © Pearson, reproduced by permission.

Project:	Mobiledu (Mobile Education).
Language:	English.
Focus:	Exploring a range of approaches to providing English language & other learning materials.
Level:	Various (including adult learners & children).
Format:	Various, including e-books & e-magazines, mini-courses with quizzes, exam preparation apps & translation apps.
Hardware:	Users supplied their own Nokia feature phones or smartphones in a BYOD model. Some materials were preloaded onto users' devices at the point of sale; some were later downloaded or subscribed to on Nokia & other devices.
Key partners:	Pearson [including Pearson Education, Penguin & the *Financial Times*] (content provider); Nokia (mobile manufacturer); China Mobile (mobile network operator).
Timeline:	2009–2012.
Location:	China.

Case Study 6   (Continued)

Participants: There were various types of learners, notably teenagers, students & young professionals. There were several million users, though exact overall figures are not available.

Funding model: The development of the Mobiledu service was funded by Pearson & Nokia. Users supplied their own devices. Paid value-added materials were obtained by users at the point of sale or subsequently downloaded or subscribed to; free samples were also available.

This project, which targeted a more urban, affluent slice of the same market as the Learn English project (see Case Study 9), involved an exploration of a range of content types and product models for mobile learning in China, with a focus on English language learning. Content ranged from interactive e-books, e-magazines and visual dictionaries, through mini-courses with audio files and quizzes, to apps offering preparation for high-stakes exams and translation apps based on voice recognition. Product models included preloading content onto Nokia devices at the point of sale, where hardwired connections enabled the use of larger files with more sophisticated media and functionality; and users downloading materials or apps, or subscribing to services, over telephone or wifi networks.

The issues encountered led to valuable lessons. Firstly, as seen in other large-scale mobile projects, dealing with the regulatory environment and logistical issues in different countries can often be a challenge. In the Mobiledu project, this was found to be the case in China, with its evolving regulations and the requirement to work with local partners. Secondly, again as in other projects, it became apparent that detailed mobile trends in China – for example, the popularity of e-books and e-magazines – were partially country-specific and a complex consequence of culture, telecommunications networks and their charging models, and available devices shaping users' behaviour.

Thirdly, with mobile learning still at an early stage, it was found that there is some disjuncture between users' stated desire for mobile learning and the kinds of materials they actually buy into, with the latter often being 'lightweight' – that is, pedagogically simple and entertainment-oriented. The situation is complicated by the lack of a central platform where mobile users can easily find out about pedagogically sequenced offerings which might serve their needs better than repeated one-off app purchases. This is partly due to the complicated mobile marketplace where device manufacturers, app stores and network operators are promoting a variety of different and competing business models.

Echoing another theme which surfaced in other projects, evaluation was not straightforward. Overall numbers were encouraging but end user data was held by the network operator, and so detailed evidence of use of the materials was difficult to obtain. This made trends hard to spot although, as mentioned above, it was noted that e-books and e-magazines quickly became popular in China, and that young professionals appeared to constitute an important target market.

While demand for mobile learning applications in the developed world is starting to emerge in institutions (schools and colleges), demand in the developing world is driven more directly by end consumers, especially in places where growing consumer hunger for learning languages – notably English – has not yet been matched by educational opportunities. Although this project was wound up in 2012, many important lessons were learned, and explorations of mobile language learning possibilities are continuing in both developing and developed countries.

The key interviewee about this project was Adam Black (Chief Learning Technologies Officer, Pearson ELT).

more current materials. In the meantime, it's clear that for millions of largely young and educated users, Mobiledu opened up a smorgasbord of new possibilities for independent language learning.

E-books and e-magazines can offer numerous textual enhancements, some of them in evidence in the Mobiledu project. The list of possibilities includes glossaries or dictionaries; search functions; resizing, reformatting and read-aloud options, which are very valuable for those with special needs; multimedia materials; interactivity, which is prominent in storybooks for young learners; inbuilt quizzes; annotation tools; and collaborative sharing or discussion channels. Of course, the more of these functions that are present and used, the more we find ourselves moving away from content MALL towards tutorial, creation or communication MALL. Indeed, it is not uncommon to find creation or communication elements layered around content, which can be seen in both the Yoza project, as discussed above, and the Nulu project, as discussed below. Reading content is often just a starting point.

As noted earlier, content MALL also encompasses listening materials. Significantly, the very name *podcasting*, derived from 'iPod', advertises its link with mobile technology. While a podcast is technically speaking a syndicated audio file – part of a series which can be subscribed to using podcatcher software like iTunes – the term is more commonly used nowadays to mean any digital audio file accessible online. In many ways, listening materials transfer less problematically than reading materials from analogue formats (think: cassettes) and older digital formats (think: CDs) to mobile devices. Mobility lends itself to listening, since we can play spoken text or music through headphones while on the move. As with reading, there's an argument to be made for chunked texts to facilitate listening in noisy, distracting surroundings. But researchers have repeatedly found that students prefer to listen to podcasts and complete associated exercises on fixed computers at home (Chan et al., 2011; Rosell-Aguilar, 2009). One strong possibility is that, unless material is highly granular, it's easier to concentrate at home, which is even more important if there are handouts to look at or exercises to complete. This speaks to the value of a multiscreen ecosystem where, if feasible, students have the option to choose their preferred hardware.

There are plenty of 'existing resources' out there, as per Rosell-Aguilar's taxonomy of language podcasting (see Figure 4.2), some in the form of authentic materials like radio shows or public talks, others designed as courses or supporting materials for learners. Students can engage with these at their own convenience. Many are offered as

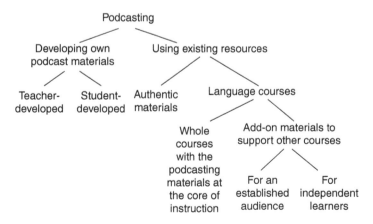

Figure 4.2 Taxonomy of uses of podcasting for language learning.
Source: Rosell-Aguilar (2007), reproduced by permission.

OER by educational institutions, including via proprietary platforms like iTunes U. As briefly indicated above, dedicated educational podcasts may have accompanying materials such as transcripts, word lists or exercises, which can provide scaffolding and expand the range of possible learning. In a German language learning project at the National University of Singapore, for example, podcasts supported by handouts went well beyond providing listening practice, extending to include grammar, vocabulary, learning strategies and cultural content, complemented by speaking and other exercises (Chan et al., 2011). Over 94% of students agreed or strongly agreed that the podcasts were useful, indicating their particular appreciation of the listening, grammar and cultural components. This shows that podcasts can be used to develop far more than listening skills, with the inclusion of a variety of exercises introducing elements of tutorial, creation or communication MALL. Podcasts may also play a role in flipped classrooms, where content delivery, perhaps accompanied by quizzes, takes place outside the classroom. Beyond this, podcasts may provide instructions as part of real-world tours and tasks, and can even be delivered as audio commentary triggered in specific locations on geoaware devices.

Vodcasting is the video equivalent of podcasting. Like a podcast, a vodcast is technically speaking a syndicated video file, but the term is commonly used to refer to any online video, and sometimes to the grey area of image-enhanced podcasts (such as slideshows with voiceovers) which exist somewhere between podcasting and vodcasting. Having long been popular on YouTube and various other platforms, video is turning into a runaway success story of the mobile era. It's currently showing such explosive growth (see Figure 4.3) that it is predicted to account for more than 66% of global mobile data traffic by 2017 (Cisco, 2013), with smart devices on 4G networks being a primary driver. In other words, there's plenty of authentic video material which students can watch and listen to. Promising work is also underway on tailored and graded language learning videos, such as those in the British Council's Jobseekers project in India (see Case Study 10). Like other mobile materials, videos benefit from chunking, a point to keep in mind as ever more videos are produced in flipped approaches and for independent study contexts.

The introduction of multimodal content, or multimedia material, holds some of the greatest potential and greatest danger for digital learning. Research in social semiotics and literacy has shown the importance of helping students develop *multimodal literacy*, the skillset involved in integrating meaning across multiple modes of

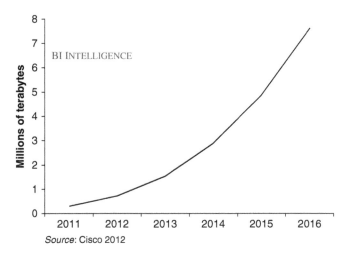

Figure 4.3   Global mobile video traffic 2011–2016 (partial forecast). © Business Insider Intelligence,   https://intelligence.businessinsider.com,   reproduced by permission.
Note: Figures from 2012 onwards are estimates.

representation and communication, which is vital when they attempt to decode authentic multimedia texts (a point we'll return to in Chapter 6). At the same time, research in psychology has led to the development of theories which begin to explain the value and limitations of *multimodal instruction,* that is, the use of multimedia material specifically to serve educational purposes.

Our current understanding of multimedia instruction is perhaps best crystallised in Richard Mayer's (2009) cognitive theory of multimedia learning, which draws on Paivio's (2007) dual coding theory, Baddeley's (1998) working memory model, and Sweller's cognitive load theory (Clark et al., 2006). It is based on the concepts of dual channels (humans have dual channels for visual/pictorial and auditory/verbal processing, complicated by the fact that written text is processed visually before moving to the auditory/verbal channel), limited capacity (each channel has limited capacity), and active processing (there is a need to carry out active cognitive processing in order to learn). Multimedia materials accessed through dual channels can be highly beneficial for learning if students are able to develop coherent verbal and visual representations in their minds, and integrate them with each other and with their prior learning. However, a high cognitive load may impair this process, perhaps partly caused by a confusing design or irrelevant material that distracts from the learning, or by overloading the visual channel with redundant printed text (where the text competes with imagery, leading to split attention and contravening Mayer's 'redundancy principle'). Guiding principles to reduce cognitive load and help to focus and motivate students include: removing extraneous content, signalling key material, avoiding redundant captions, presenting content in user-paced segments, pre-teaching key items, accompanying pictures (whether still or moving) with spoken rather than written words, adopting a personalised style – and, yes, using words and pictures rather than words alone, because this gives learners the chance to build both verbal and visual mental models and connect them, thus reinforcing learning. Generally speaking, we can say that good multimedia design is more important for lower level learners and higher complexity material, though it is important to note that there are also individual learner differences.

When it comes to language learning, there are advantages in multimedia materials: videos or animations can contextualise spoken text, offering visual support and insights into pragmatics – as seen in the Indian Jobseekers project (see Case Study 10) – as well as building broader social and cultural understanding. There's some evidence of the value of captions (in the target language) or subtitles (in learners' first language) which, in an important exception to the redundancy principle mentioned above, may serve to support language learners' limited comprehension (Clark & Mayer, 2011; Sydorenko, 2010). In other words, rather than unnecessarily cluttering the visual channel, captions and subtitles help turn spoken language into comprehensible input. Thus, when it comes to listening, captioned or subtitled videos may support both listening comprehension and vocabulary acquisition (Fallahkhair et al., 2007; Hsu, Hwang, Chang & Chang, 2013; Sydorenko, 2010). Similarly, when it comes to the reading of written texts, multimedia annotations or glosses – i.e., text with images or videos – may support vocabulary acquisition (Chun, 2006; Heift & Chapelle, 2012) and reading comprehension (ibid.), though evidence of the latter is less clear (Chun, 2006). In the case of video material, captions or subtitles may also benefit reading comprehension (Fallahkhair et al., 2007; Hsu, Hwang, Chang & Chang, 2013). One point that has become apparent, echoing work in the wider field of multimodal instruction, is that the value of multimedia materials depends on individual language learners' working memories, cognitive styles and levels, with a risk that under certain circumstances a multimedia approach may be distracting, or may cause too high a cognitive load if learners are processing verbal and visual information at the same time (Chun, 2006). It's clear that much more research is needed in this area. Ideally, however, adaptive systems might offer a variety of multimedia materials to suit different purposes as well as individual differences (ibid.; Joseph & Uther, 2009) – a task for ICALL and IMALL. Beyond this, of course, students can be invited to create their own multimedia content – illustrated texts, podcasts, vodcasts or combinations of these – though that leads us away from content MALL and into the realm of creation and communication MALL.

MALL for tutorials

In tutorial MALL, behaviourist exercises may be grafted onto content MALL, or may take the form of freestanding pronunciation, letter formation, vocabulary or grammar drills, quizzes and games. These can be made available through SMS, the web or apps, and may be delivered in any mode or multimodal combination. Podcasts, for example, are often used in a behaviourist manner (Rosell-Aguilar, 2009) as they lend themselves to audio flashcards and audio drilling. They've been used to train pronunciation (see Vignette 4), vocabulary (Borgia, 2009) and grammar (Rosell-Aguilar, 2007). Teachers may sometimes opt to include elements of tutorial MALL in a flipped model, asking students to complete low level consolidation exercises at home so as to release class time for more communicative or socioculturally informed activities. Of course, tutorial MALL, like content MALL, lends itself to autonomous learning outside the bounds of formal courses or classrooms, where students can work at their own pace and according to their own needs. Without a doubt the greatest promise lies in IMALL, where software currently under development will provide tailored feedback on the building blocks of learners' oral or written language production, very likely linked to recommendations for practice. But as IMALL applications become integrated into context-aware devices and begin to offer feedback on everyday language use, and flag up practice opportunities in everyday life, we'll find ourselves moving well beyond the limits of typical tutorial MALL.

In the meantime, traditional behaviourist activities have a place in establishing and reinforcing foundational language knowledge; they correspond to many learners' expectations and wishes; and they don't necessarily require users to possess high-end technology. These factors are evident in the tutorial MALL exercises which, along with e-books and e-magazines, were widely used in the Mobiledu project (see Case Study 6). The same factors are differently realised but equally in evidence in the MILLEE project's creation of effective game designs in India (see Case Study 7 below). For some educators, there's a

Case Study 7   Playing mobile games in India (MILLEE Project)

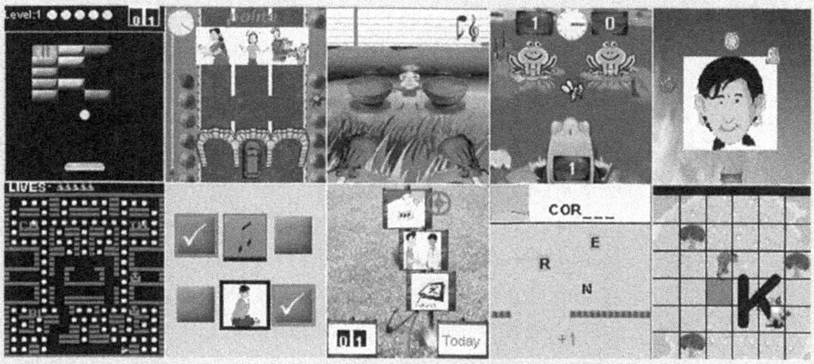

Figure 4.4   MILLEE Pilot III games. © Matthew Kam & team, reproduced by permission.

Project: MILLEE (Mobile & Immersive Learning for Literacy in Emerging Economies).

Language: English.

Focus: Vocabulary, grammar & spelling in Pilot I; vocabulary support in Pilot II; vocabulary & reading subskills in Pilot III.

Level: Primary & lower secondary school (with students aged 7–14).

Format: App containing educational games covering a semester's content in Pilot I; app containing educational games covering 180 word families in Pilot II; app containing ten games focusing on major predictors of success in reading comprehension (e.g., vocabulary, spelling, phonological awareness & word decoding), linked to the state government syllabus & supplemented by a remedial curriculum, in Pilot III.

Hardware: Motorola Razr V3m feature phones (Pilots I & II) & Nokia 3110c feature phones (Pilot III) were preloaded with apps & loaned to users.

Key partners: MacArthur Foundation, Microsoft, National Science Foundation, Nokia, Qualcomm & Verizon (funding providers); Suraksha & Study Hall Educational Foundation (local NGOs involved in facilitating community access & providing cultural guidance). Further local support in India

Case Study 7   (Continued)

was provided by undergraduate student programmers & pilot teams; village communities (Pilot II); & school communities (Pilots I & III). The work was carried out when its project director, Matthew Kam, was at the University of California, Berkeley, USA (Pilots I & II) & Carnegie Mellon University, USA (Pilot III).

Timeline: 2004–2012, with the following phases: 2004–2005: exploratory studies; 2006–2007: game prototype testing; 2008: Pilot I (one semester); 2009: Pilot II (one semester); 2011–2012: Pilot III (two semesters).

Location: Uttar Pradesh, northern India, & Hyderabad, Andhra Pradesh, southern India.

Participants: Pilot I involved 27 children aged 7–14 in an after-school programme in a village in Uttar Pradesh; Pilot II involved 18 children aged 10–14 in two villages in Uttar Pradesh; Pilot III involved 250 Grade 5 children in four low-fee private schools in Hyderabad, Andhra Pradesh. All were literate to some extent in their own language & were learning English as an additional language.

Funding model: The project was funded by a combination of public & private organisations, including the MacArthur Foundation, Microsoft, the National Science Foundation, Nokia, Qualcomm & Verizon. Phones were loaned to participants during the relevant project phases.

The MILLEE project explored the value of English language games played on mobile devices by both rural and urban slum children in India. Games were designed based on patterns abstracted from bestselling language learning software and successful videogames. An app containing the games was preloaded onto the feature phones lent to children during each of the three major pilot studies (with numerous formative studies having taken place before these three summative studies). In Pilot I, focused on vocabulary, grammar and spelling games, students showed statistically significant improvement from pre- to post-tests of spelling ability. In Pilot II, focused on a set of word family games, data logging, interviews and observations revealed that village children voluntarily played the games and learned around three words a week in their own time. In Pilot III, focused on games supporting components of reading comprehension, four schools were loaned phones which could be used by students to play games at the discretion of teachers. Observations and data logging revealed that the games were used for limited periods, with teachers focusing instead on teaching to high-stakes exams, and schools unwilling to risk students taking the phones home. There was general, statistically significant improvement from pre- to post-tests in two simpler competencies, but not in a third, more complex competency, possibly reflecting the limited time spent on the games.

In addition to addressing logistical and infrastructural issues – including a lack of reliable access to electricity – the project faced numerous social and educational challenges. It took local contexts into careful consideration: in Pilots I and II, for example, the help of village community leaders was enlisted to lend credibility to the project when it was rolled out. It was here that the full impact of local cultural practices on mobile learning became clear, with caste and gender contributing to distinct differences in game use. Upper-caste boys, for example, could play the games while supervising lower-caste boys hired to work in the fields, with the latter only being able to play the games when they reached home. The lower-caste boys could play the games at home after dinner, but their sisters needed to wash the dishes before they were allowed to play. Lower-caste girls, for their part, could play the games while grazing goats during the day. By contrast, upper-caste girls had to stay home since it was socially inappropriate for them to be outdoors and, in fact, it is likely that upper-caste girls had less time than lower-caste girls to play since mothers gave tacit approval for their sons to monopolise the phones at home.

While the project was initially conceived with constructivist and constructionist meaning-making approaches in mind, it was soon realised that, with a lack of skilled adult facilitators and with students lacking foundational knowledge in English literacy, it was necessary to go back to more traditional educational approaches in the games. In testing prototype games, it was also found that rural children in particular struggled to make sense of the rules in Western videogames, on which the initial game prototypes were based. This led the researchers to analyse the traditional village games which rural Indian children play every day, in order to determine game design guidelines which would be better suited to the local context. This dramatically improved the usability of the games for village children. Finally, it was necessary to carefully explain to teachers

Case Study 7   (Continued)

and parents that the games were educational, and from an instructional design point of view it was found to be more effective to tone down fantasy settings and orient the design of some screens towards teacher-centred, blackboard-dominated approaches that Indian children readily associate with school.

With the teachers in Pilot III under pressure to prepare students for high-stakes exams and unfamiliar with how to implement the differentiated teaching made possible by the technology, and with the schools insisting on keeping the devices on school grounds, the full learning potential of the games was not exploited. More training, not only of teachers but of school leaders and managers, would be necessary to make more of this potential. A BYOD model, where apps are loaded onto parents' own phones, could make it easier for students to use the games outside school.

The project team believes that mobile devices can make a real difference to underserved populations, given that school teachers no longer act as gatekeepers to the learning or the technology (as they do with computer labs). The insights gained from this project have already informed other projects, with the game design approach being applied to traditional Chinese games, for instance. But there remains a need, more broadly, for further funded research with a strong evaluative framework in order to determine how best to design and deploy mobile learning with sensitivity to local educational contexts, and how to ensure that projects are scalable and sustainable.

The key interviewee about this project was Matthew Kam (Senior Technology Strategist for Education, International Development, Evaluation and Research Program, American Institutes for Research, Washington DC, USA). For further information on the MILLEE project, see Kam (2013). For further information on a similar approach to Chinese games, see Tian et al. (2010).

certain stigma attached to 'drill-and-kill' activities dressed up as games (Klopfer, 2008; Quinn, 2012). But while there are advantages in complex multiplayer games (which sit better with communication MALL), simple games designed on behaviourist principles to support, say, vocabulary acquisition, grammar consolidation, or the development of reading skills – as seen earlier in the Smart4Kids Khmer app (see Case Study 5) – have a role in language learning. They may also mimic communicative language use in their content and form, providing system-generated feedback in the absence of feedback from human interlocutors. What's more, they may find an easier reception in non-Western contexts than more pedagogically sophisticated games underpinned by constructivist or constructionist approaches. Whatever the longer term possibilities for changing mindsets and preparing the ground for new pedagogies through teacher and learner training, serving immediate needs in a contextually sensitive manner sometimes demands a more overtly conventional approach.

After a long, iterative development process, the MILLEE project was able to produce games that reflected local gaming patterns, met cultural expectations of conventional classroom settings, and taught foundational knowledge through suitably traditional approaches. The fact that this development process has been successfully reproduced in a different cultural context, namely China, speaks to its efficacy. Yet, as has been found in gaming projects the world over, it was still necessary to specifically promote the educational value of games to teachers and parents.

While content and tutorial MALL both have their place – technologically, pedagogically and culturally – it's certainly beneficial to complement them, if not necessarily supersede them, with creation and communication activities. That brings us to the entrance of our next MALL.

MALL for creation

With MALL for creation and MALL for communication, we witness a breakthrough into more fully communicative and sociocultural territory. But technologically, creation and communication MALL generally require newer hardware, better connectivity and faster software, making them harder to implement outside the developed world. Pedagogically, creation and communication MALL presuppose that teachers and students can see beyond content and drills to appreciate the value of knowledge construction and collaborative networking, which may require both teacher and learner training in the developing and developed world alike. Organisationally, creation and communication MALL don't support independent or automated learning, or large-scale implementation, as easily as content or tutorial MALL. Creation MALL tends to require teacher guidance and feedback in a constructivist or constructionist process, though a project like SIMOLA (see Case Study 1) may offer a way forward, largely by building in a strong communication element. Communication MALL benefits from teacherly presence too, but the harnessing of decentralised communication networks in projects like SIMOLA and Nulu (see Case Study 11) holds promise for crowdsourcing feedback. While an untrained crowd can't equal the mentoring skills of an experienced teacher, it can help learning to scale. When teachers are present, this may help alleviate the workload pressures that follow from a vastly increased volume of student language production; and in the absence of teachers, it can ensure students still receive human as well as automated input, though careful design and structuring are needed to ensure that students are interacting effectively with each other and with wider networks. In short, the creation and communication potential of MALL is very real, but not always very easily realised.

At the simplest level of creation, students might take screenshots of letters they've traced or characters they've written, record podcasts of their pronunciation, or respond to SMS questions, and review any of the above, but none of this goes very far beyond tutorial CALL. On the other hand, comprehensible output can be foregrounded if students are asked to demonstrate their growing linguistic, sociolinguistic or intercultural competence by producing (and editing and revising) written texts in different genres, ranging from personal blog entries to polished narratives in e-book formats. Similarly, they might record (and review and rerecord) audio texts as podcasts in the format of speeches or radio shows; instructors could even give feedback in podcast format (Abdous et al., 2009). Many of these lend themselves to sharing with peers or wider audiences, thus beginning to edge into communication MALL.

A collaborative aspect could be introduced, with students jointly writing and editing texts or acting out interviews or radio plays. Alternatively, they could engage with each other's blogs (perhaps using one of the many blogging apps like Blogger or WordPress) or provide feedback on each other's wiki pages (though wiki apps are uncommon, some web services offer a degree of mobile optimisation) in a process writing approach, thus introducing a further element of communication. Moreover, as long as multimedia elements are not allowed to become a distraction or a way of bypassing language learning (Ware, 2008; Warschauer & Liaw, 2013), students can be guided in the development of multimodal literacy as they embed their language production in vodcasts or digital stories. This user-generated content can then be shared and even repurposed to support others' learning. Taking creation MALL to its limit, and integrating language production not only with multimodal literacy but also code literacy (see Chapter 6), students could be guided in using app-building software to create their own apps through which to showcase their work and invite others to learn from them. Communication, of course, plays a crucial role here.

Although CALL has certain advantages over MALL when it comes to multimodal creation, with full keyboards and large screens on laptop or desktop computers being preferable for extended text entry and multimedia editing (Bjerede & Bondi, n.d.; Sussex, 2012), mobile devices have two major advantages of their own. The first is the availability of growing numbers of generic digital storytelling and e-book apps for smart devices. While these may limit students' creativity by imposing templates, and while they may sometimes limit sharing due to incompatible formats, they make it easy to focus on language and multimodal literacy (rather than the technology itself) as materials are simply assembled and combined within pre-existing frameworks; this is especially valuable for young learners (see Vignette 10). The second advantage is the ability to create records in situ. Kukulska-Hulme and Bull (2009), for instance, recommend that learners use mobile devices to unobtrusively capture and annotate linguistic samples in target language contexts, thus promoting their 'noticing' of language. Dedicated apps like Lingobee (see Case Study 1), along with more generic mobile blogging and social media platforms, make it easy to share and respond to records of everyday language encounters or indeed everyday social and cultural experiences (see Vignette 11). Students' annotated language samples or cultural observations constitute yet more user-generated content, this time created within user-generated contexts in everyday life, that can serve as learning material for other students.

Creating and sharing digital artefacts – including multimodal 'identity texts' (Cummins cited in Warschauer & Liaw, 2013, p.5) in the form of digital stories – can help learners develop a sense of authorship and agency. Mobile devices in particular, which can be carried everywhere with us, can become 'tools for constructing a chronicling of the self', suggest Ros i Solé et al. (2010, p.40). When students use mobile technologies to facilitate and record their own language use in day-to-day life, and subsequently share it with teachers or peers, they may find themselves beginning to 'reflect and engage with their own language learning selves in significant ways' in the process of establishing a target language identity:

> [M]obile technology could be seen as the prosthesis that allows learners to depart from models of language learning based on machine-like metaphors of input-output, and instead adopt a social practices approach, in which the learner uses a variety of locations to enact and rehearse a personal *voice*.
>
> (Ros i Solé et al., 2010, p.51; italics in original)

In many of the above examples, but most especially here, it's clear that to maximise the potential of MALL for creation, what is created should also be communicated – mirroring contemporary trends in social media sharing – which means that creation MALL and communication MALL are inevitably tightly bound up together.

MALL for communication

Sometimes MALL for communication involves learners interacting with teachers, peers or other target language speakers, potentially supporting negotiation of meaning (from a communicative perspective) and identity exploration (from a sociocultural perspective). Sometimes it involves learners interacting with a wider audience, which can motivate better performance, heighten a focus on communicative purpose, put a premium on sociocultural competence, and bolster the range and depth of feedback received. Communication MALL most often builds on creation MALL but may also draw in elements of more traditional content and tutorial MALL. While it benefits from teacherly presence and personal attention, well-structured communication MALL can also scale if it's appropriately situated within decentralised networks where everyone becomes both a teacher and a learner.

Reading can become an interactive process when text-based or multimodal questions and annotations are shared and compared among learners. In fact, as e-texts become the norm, we may need to rethink the whole pedagogy of books (Smith & Kukulska-Hulme, 2012), which are arguably shifting away from being vehicles for delivering content or quizzes and becoming hubs for discussion and collaboration. *Writing* can become an interactive process when learners' mobile blog entries are commented on, their e-books are reviewed, or their multimodal artefacts are remixed. Beyond this, there's a whole series of dedicated communication channels, from simple SMS or MMS through synchronous VoIP or IM to asynchronous audio or written discussion boards, which can be employed in the service of linguistic interaction.

Digital polling is a newly popular technique which allows audiences to respond to a presenter's questions and see their aggregated results displayed in real time on a screen. Pricey clicker hardware has now been superseded by free or cheap websites and apps (like PollDaddy or Poll Everywhere), with learners using mobile devices to respond through the sites or apps themselves, or to send SMS messages or tweets. Polls can function as simple tutorial quizzes to check student understanding and help teachers recalibrate lessons as necessary; they can gather student questions or feedback, allowing teachers to better respond to students' perceived needs and wishes; and they can serve as a platform for teacher–student and/or student–student interaction, which may be especially valuable in large classes. In one study of upper level learners of English at Shanghai Jiaotong University in China, where in any given class around 200 students attended face-to-face and 30 online, an instant polling feature was introduced within a purpose-built mobile learning system (Wang et al., 2009). This enabled instructors to elicit student feedback and adjust their teaching accordingly, while a text messaging feature allowed them to receive individual responses, comments or questions from students. On the basis of survey and log data, the researchers concluded that the use of mobile devices 'for promoting interactivity in a traditionally culturally didactic learning environment' succeeded in changing 'students from passive learners to active participants' (ibid., p.693).

Social media websites and apps draw many of the above communicational possibilities together, typically combining synchronous and asynchronous channels, facilitating sharing of textual updates and multimedia artefacts, preserving records of conversations and interactions, offering numerous feedback options and even supporting polling. The confluence of the mobile and the social (see Chapter 1) finds its ultimate realisation in social networking services like Facebook, as well as microblogging services like Twitter, media sharing platforms like Flickr, Instagram and YouTube, and geosocial services like Foursquare and Yelp. On smart devices, the time spent on social networking apps is outstripped only by the time spent on gaming apps (see Figure 4.5). Mobile connectivity, says Lee Rainie (2012), allows '[p]ervasive, perpetual awareness of social networks', with major consequences for learning: '[s]ocial networks and social media become more important in people's learning strategies'. Generally, social networking platforms may constitute an important component of PLNs and PLEs.

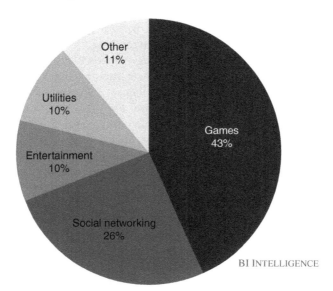

Source: Flurry Analytics, November 2012

Figure 4.5 Time spent globally on smart device apps (Android & iOS) by category, 2012. © Business Insider Intelligence, https://intelligence.business insider.com, reproduced by permission.

Specifically, they offer numerous language learning possibilities, though it may be necessary to convince a whole range of stakeholders of their value.

At their simplest, they can be used for target language communication. There are a number of dedicated language exchange services which connect learners with native speakers, such as the web-based Lang-8 (which involves the exchange of written journal entries), or the web-based xLingo and app-based HelloTalk (which facilitate multimodal chat). Facebook's communicational channels have been employed worldwide, from English classes in Saudi Arabia (Al-Shehri, 2011) to German classes in New Zealand (Leier, 2012). Naturally, much everyday usage of Facebook is multilingual, as users juggle global and local audiences and conversations, a phenomenon also in evidence on other social media sites like Flickr (Barton & Lee, 2012). This offers rich potential to practise codeswitching, develop pragmatic competence, and explore intercultural identities.

In the developed world in particular, there is a trend towards the twin, intertwined activities of *creation* and *curation* (Zickuhr, 2012):

it's possible to share our own creations, of the kind outlined under creation MALL, but it's equally possible to share others' creations, which are usually annotated, often tagged or rated, sometimes reframed and occasionally reworked. Curation is not simply a derivative activity based on others' creations, but may be highly creative in its organisation and representation of understanding, and may lead to new insights (Constantinides, 2013). What's more, a facility with language – and often multiple languages (Barton & Lee, 2012) – is just as essential to curation, including annotation and tagging, as it is to creation.

Given the enormous popularity of social networking and social media platforms, it's unsurprising that some of their core features are beginning to surface in major language learning projects. In the European SIMOLA project (see Case Study 1), the commenting, tagging, rating and flagging functions applied to language records mirror those on social media sites. In the US Nulu project (see Case Study 11), learners have the option to converse about readings in forums which parallel those on social networking sites. These initiatives cleverly leverage the power of learners' familiarity with social media to create rich communication options at the intersection of the mobile and the social, while simultaneously allowing intensive human interaction to scale.

Just like social networking, *gaming* is becoming more mobile, with games now accounting for 43% of user time spent on apps on smart devices (see Figure 4.5). These range from simple games which sit well with tutorial MALL to complex games which sit well with communication MALL. Over recent years there has been considerable educational interest in complex multiplayer games, which foreground contextualised negotiation of meaning and collaborative problem-solving, and can provide 'pedagogically rich, highly motivating learning environments' (Klopfer, 2008, Kindle location 22). Such games are fundamentally dependent on oral and/or written communication (both within and around the games) and multiple literacies; in fact, it's been suggested that in the context of massively multiplayer online games (MMOGs), gaming itself 'is a literacy practice' (Steinkuehler, 2007, p.204), and that there is a need for the development of gaming literacy (Dudeney et al., 2013). There are certainly many opportunities to use game characters, or avatars, to hone 'linguistic, sociocultural, and pragmatic competence' (Lotherington & Jenson, 2011, p.236) and experiment with 'projective identities' (Gee, 2003). As it becomes ever more common to use mobile devices to play complex games, educators should consider how to capitalise on the linguistic and motivational benefits of mobile gaming to enhance their students' learning and their own teaching, as Hayo Reinders recommends (see Vignette 7 below).

Vignette 7   The lessons of mobile gaming

Hayo Reinders, Anaheim University, USA

I think that in some ways our learners' experience of language and literacy development has already changed as a result of mobile technologies, but their learning less so. Partly this is because publishers, materials developers and even we as teachers and researchers are slow to recognise the changes that are taking place around us and the pedagogical impact they could potentially have. To give one specific example from my own research, when one of my PhD students, Sorada Wattana, and I adapted a commercial MMOG to help Thai students learn conversational English, initially on fixed devices but later on mobile devices as well, the students in our study made use of the game in ways that we had never anticipated, drawing on the resources and communicative purposes in the game well beyond what they had been asked to do. For example, students connected with players in other countries to find out how to solve the adventure game, in the process using English much more than they normally would have.

Most importantly, not only did the quantitative data we gathered show significant increases in the amount of target language production and a major shift in interaction patterns, our qualitative data also showed that the students had experienced the gameplay as a critically different way of learning – one that they felt more comfortable with, experienced less anxiety in, and felt more willing to take risks in. To us this showed that the game we used did not simply lead to some language gains (as important as this is), but also encouraged these students to engage more in the learning process. The mobile aspect allowed them to take the language out of the classroom and appropriate the learning process. Clearly, we had managed to connect with these learners and match the teaching environment with their learning experiences.

> The challenge for our profession is to investigate much more deeply how mobile games change the way learners learn, and critically examine if that should not change the way we as teachers teach.
>
> ► Further reading: Reinders & Wattana (2012).

While some mobile games are miniaturised versions of big screen games, more and more are tailored to the networked, context-sensitive devices on which they're played (Klopfer, 2008). Virtual reality games, which attempt to replicate the real world or generate new worlds, are gradually ceding prominence to mobile AR games, sometimes also known as *pervasive games,* though this is unsettled terminological terrain. Some, like 'Alien Contact!' (see Chapter 3), are place-independent, but most are place-dependent, like the US Mentira game (see Case Study 8 below). Such games retain all the advantages of global communication while placing a heightened emphasis on local situatedness, embodiment, and real-world authenticity. After all, as Eric Klopfer (2008) notes, 'nothing can provide a sense of reality like reality' (Kindle location 1339). As seen in Mentira, real-world encounters and conversations, which foster pragmatic competence and intercultural insights, can be incorporated into educational games, thus building bridges between informal learning and more abstract classroom learning. Intrinsic in-game feedback is complemented by extrinsic out-of-game feedback, while transfer distance, that old bugbear of education, is reduced when some learning is already taking place in the real world.

Like the European MASELTOV project (see Case Study 13), the Mentira project demonstrates the considerable language learning potential that exists at the intersection of gaming and AR. Nonetheless, it was found in the Mentira project – as in the Indian MILLEE project (see Case Study 7), with its pedagogically simpler games – that educational gaming requires a change of mindset in order for both teachers and students to recognise its potential. Interestingly, the success of Mentira has led to the development of a new game, Visitas de la Colonia, where students use the same gaming platform, ARIS, to build their own AR games, thus complementing their experience of communication MALL with a strong dose of creation MALL and, in the process, turning out user-generated content which benefits their Spanish-learning peers.

Case Study 8   Augmented reality gaming in the USA (Mentira Project)

Figure 4.6   Mentira app. © Chris Holden & Julie Sykes, reproduced by permission.

Project: Mentira.
Language: Spanish.
Focus: Integrated skills.
Level: Intermediate (second year of university).
Format: AR murder mystery game, built with Augmented Reality for Interactive Storytelling (ARIS) open source software (arisgames.org). Text-based & multimedia in-game materials are complemented by oral interactions in class & on location.
Hardware: ARIS games run on iOS devices. Around 75% of students use their own personal iPhones or iPod Touches in a BYOD model, with the remainder being loaned iPod Touches.

Key partners:	University of New Mexico [UNM] (research team & grant provider); University of Wisconsin-Madison (ARIS software developer); UNM Language Learning Centre (lender of iPod Touches to students who don't have their own devices).
Timeline:	2009 – ongoing.
Location:	Albuquerque, New Mexico, USA. The community contact phase occurs in the Spanish-speaking neighbourhood of Los Griegos.
Participants:	Each year, 200–300 second year Spanish learners at UNM take part in the Mentira game.
Funding model:	The project was initially funded through a Research Allocation Grant (RAC) from UNM. Users supply their own devices or are loaned iPod Touches.

Mentira (which means 'lie' in Spanish) is an AR game that carefully blends text and multimedia, and fact and fiction, to create a historical murder mystery. Students begin by engaging in simulated conversations with story characters as they seek clues about the identity of the murderer. Because no single player has access to all the clues, they must collaborate and share information with classmates. The story is set in a real local Spanish-speaking neighbourhood, Los Griegos, which students eventually visit in groups of three to five. They follow in-game instructions to locate key places and sometimes interact with local residents as they seek further clues. Students subsequently participate in a mock trial to determine the identity of the murderer, with the strength of the arguments they put forward being dependent on the evidence they have collected. Spanish is generally used within the game and is the primary language for all class discussions, within student teams, and on location in Los Griegos.

Mentira capitalises on the intersecting affordances of mobile devices, gaming and AR. As in other gaming and AR projects, the creators of Mentira have found that it requires a change of mindset on the part of staff and students, who need to appreciate that language learning is about more than grammar exercises, and that AR games are about more than fun. Indeed, Mentira has the potential to be transformative. Once students experience the local neighbourhood mediated by the AR game, they connect with both the language and the place in a different way. Spanish loses its abstractness and comes to be seen as part of a living, breathing culture in their back yard. Moreover, in dealing with contextualised and situated language,

Case Study 8   (Continued)

students are exposed to the pragmatics of its use in a way that is rare in traditional classrooms. And, because it is a game, they can fail without fear, simply trying again until they succeed. While the potential of Mentira is not always fully exploited by busy, time-poor students, they have generally proven receptive to the game; and language teachers have shown considerable interest in the underpinning concept of students practising language on location.

The development of Mentira is continuing in collaboration with the ARIS team at the University of Wisconsin-Madison, who originally developed the software, as more advanced features become available. The ultimate aim is for it to become a self-sustaining game which can be used without its creators, perhaps even in a place-independent version which can be employed in other locations. In 2012, building on the Mentira project but dramatically increasing the level of student input, a second game, Visitas de la Colonia, was piloted with 24 fourth year students of Spanish. Here, students work in teams to create AR games for each other using the ARIS software, which does not require programming knowledge. Each game takes the form of a guided tour of selected campus locations, and is designed for a historical colonial character, to whom students must explain the way that concepts like class and race have changed over time, using a combination of voice and images. This is a promising way of combining language and cultural learning in student-generated AR contexts.

The key interviewee about this project was Julie Sykes (Co-ordinator of Spanish as a Second Language Program, Dept of Spanish & Portuguese, UNM, Albuquerque, USA). Chris Holden (Honors College, UNM) is a co-creator and co-researcher on the project. For further information on Mentira, see the *Mentira* website (www.mentira.org) and Holden & Sykes (2011). For further information about Visitas de la Colonia, see the 'Visitas de la Colonia' post on the *Local Games Lab ABQ* blog (localgameslababq. wordpress.com/projects/span-431-visitas-de-la-colonia/).

Because mobile learning is so fluid, crystallising temporarily in multiple formats from drills to games, spilling from one platform onto others, flowing in multiple directions through networks, and often occurring on the fly, it becomes difficult for both teachers and learners to keep track of it. In the final section of this chapter, we'll consider some strategies for identifying, recording and evaluating the learning experiences – often multifaceted or amorphous – of the mobile era.

Capturing & assessing mobile language learning

When it comes to m-learning, a key challenge is to create stable spaces in which students can document their learning experiences and teachers can guide them (Melhuish & Falloon, 2010; Sharples et al., 2010). This is one reason for the growing prominence of PLNs and PLEs. A *PLN* is a broad, trusted network of human contacts (experts and peers) and material resources that can be drawn on for support and information as part of the process of lifelong learning (Couros, 2010; Richardson & Mancabelli, 2011). While interlinked with a PLN, a *PLE* is a temporary construct set up for the duration of a given course of study (Dudeney et al., 2013). It's a digital space – built for example on a blog, wiki, or aggregator platform – where a learner can connect to people and resources relevant to the course as well as capturing, organising and reflecting on relevant learning. An independent learner could also set up a PLE, related not to a course but to a particular current area of study.

Readily accessible through a personal mobile device, a PLE offers a place to begin building bridges between informal (local, episodic and personal) learning experiences and more formal learning, as well as obtaining feedback from teachers and peers. Over time, and ideally with teacherly mentoring, a student can develop a coherent, cumulative narrative of their learning journey to help them keep track of their progress, possibly with an eye to eventually presenting it for evaluation. At the end of a course, some work could be exported to an *e-portfolio* for assessment or public display – or, at the end of a period of independent study, for evaluation by a present or future employer – while the PLE itself might partly or wholly dissolve back into the learner's PLN.

Formative assessment

Formative assessment of learning is about providing ongoing feedback to help students identify strengths and weaknesses and improve performance. The digital records generated in the process of e-learning or m-learning provide a basis for detailed, informative feedback. Writing of CALL, Carla Meskill and Natasha Anthony (2010) note that 'running records of learner growth and development in the new language take assessment to a new and quite powerful level' (Kindle location 353). Such records are often incidentally and automatically created as part of e-learning, for example transcripts of online discussions, or can be easily set up, such as recordings of voice chat. When it comes to m-learning, real-world language learning experiences can be either automatically or manually captured by mobile devices. However they are generated, these records can be revisited by students, reviewed by teachers, and evaluated by both to map progress.

But the possibilities for manually evaluating digital records pale in comparison with the possibilities for automated processing not only of the kinds of records mentioned above, but of the full range of big data – that is, the copious information generated by students as they participate in learning experiences registered by digital systems, whether they're perusing content, responding to quizzes, creating multimedia artefacts or conversing with peers. This data underpins learning analytics, an area which is just beginning to be explored in education. Learning analytics software, which is designed to derive informative patterns and useful insights from big data, can, firstly, alert teachers to learners' strengths and weaknesses and identify at-risk students (Aljohani & Davis, 2012; Johnson et al., 2013). Secondly, not unlike ICALL software, it can provide students with differentiated feedback and customised learning materials:

> Learning analytics is envisioned as an effective, efficient way to assess student responses, provide immediate feedback, and make adjustments in content delivery and format. Those invested in the field of learning analytics see its potential to foster personalized learning environments that adapt to the learning behaviors of students.
>
> (Johnson et al., 2013, p.25)

A third possibility, already projected in some ICALL and IMALL initiatives, is for the emerging model of each student's learning to be presented to the student themselves as an open learner model (Kukulska-Hulme & Bull, 2009), perhaps in the form of a 'personal dashboard' (Aljohani & Davis, 2012). We see the beginnings of a move in this direction, for instance, in the My Chinese Language ubiquitOUs learning Days (MyCLOUD) project which has recently commenced in Singapore, where students of Chinese will have access to some statistics on their vocabulary usage in their personalised cloud-based lexicons and associated social and academic spaces, in order to help them monitor their progress (Wong et al., 2012). Giving learners access to a representation of their current state of understanding can promote reflection and formative self-assessment, as well as giving them greater agency in shaping their own language learning goals.

Mobile devices can contribute powerfully to big data and learning analytics because they are always with us. As Gary Woodill (2011) observes:

> specific individuals move through the world in a unique path. Because of the ability of mobile devices to track location, the trail of a learner can be recorded and used for both evaluation and feedback.
>
> (Kindle location 1240)

That means mobile devices can be continuously building logs of user learning at all times and in all places including, crucially, in user-generated real-world contexts (Aljohani & Davis, 2012). Of course, there are privacy issues with the constant surveillance of students (see Chapter 3) and few people may want to find themselves 'in a state of perpetual learning' (Pettit & Kukulska-Hulme, 2011, p.204), especially learning which is monitored. There has to be an 'off' switch. But the data gathered when the switch is 'on' will allow learning analysis of a depth and richness considerably greater than in e-learning or CALL, and barely imaginable in analogue learning.

Generally, the delivery of feedback is enhanced by new technologies, since it can be *instantaneous* (if automated) or at least *rapid* (if human); *differentiated*, that is, targeted to individual learners; *specific*, as effective feedback should be (an area where ICALL and IMALL hold great promise; see Heift & Schulze, 2007); and it can combine intrinsic and extrinsic elements. *Intrinsic feedback*, which is central to situated learning, is a natural consequence of performance and allows the learner to work out how to improve without teacher intervention (Laurillard, 2012). This can be seen for example in digital games, where a certain level of performance is necessary to accomplish in-game goals; but failure, which inevitably occurs from time to time, comes with no stigma – as noted in the Mentira project (see Case Study 8) – and an invitation to try again in light of new information or insights gained through the experience of failing. *Extrinsic feedback* consists of external evaluations of performance. It could be automated, ranging from simple verbal feedback in a tutorial game ('Wrong – try again!') to the kind of targeted, contextually and socioculturally aware guidance we might one day hope for in IMALL ('Your statement may be too direct – review the use of "would" for politeness before rephrasing your request for tickets!'). More often, extrinsic feedback comes from other people, most obviously teachers and peers, but it could be sourced from a wider collection of friends, colleagues, mentors, volunteers and other target language speakers in online communities (Chan et al., 2006; Kukulska-Hulme, 2013a). For instance, decentralised networks of target language learners and/or speakers are drawn into the feedback mechanisms in the Lingobee app, the conversations on the Nulu discussion boards, and the busuu component of the MASELTOV project (see Case Studies 1, 11 & 13). These networks represent a helpful complement to students' PLEs and a potential extension of their PLNs.

Summative assessment

The mismatch between m-learning and traditional summative assessment, which involves appraisal of achievement at the end of a course of study, has been widely noted (Comas-Quinn et al., 2009; Melhuish & Falloon, 2010; Traxler, 2010), and parallels evaluation issues in m-learning research projects. As Josie Taylor (2006) states in her report of a mobile evaluation workshop:

> Traditionally, evaluators might relate the success of a design to the success with which learners can achieve pre-identified learning outcomes. The nature of learning outcomes in the mobile age needs to be adaptive. For example, they may relate to the extent to which someone has assimilated information into their own experience and development, rather than how well they can reproduce knowledge in a pre-post questionnaire style study. (p.27)

As the model of the 'compliant, passive learner' grows less common, she goes on, students are 'becoming more independent, more assured, and consequently more unpredictable from an evaluation point of view' (ibid.). Obviously, the more local, episodic and personal the learning, the harder it is likely to be to assess or evaluate, making it all the more important that students take an active role in creating and collating digital records of their learning. A PLE can make space for such unpredictable and unsystematised learning – with students, perhaps, providing multimodal artefacts to demonstrate what they have learned about pragmatics, local culture or even collaboration during an AR game and, under the guidance of a teacher, weaving these into an analytical and reflective metacommentary on their own learning. But it's still hard to know how to handle such material when it comes to summative assessment.

One common approach is to ask students to export a selection of work from their PLEs to e-portfolios for assessment. Key questions for teachers include whether and how to assess the *process* and *products* of learning, and what is the most appropriate combination of *teacher assessment* (which supports authoritative evaluation and standardised marking), *peer assessment* (which, when appropriately scaffolded, supports evaluation of group processes and prepares students for self-assessment) and *self-assessment* (which again requires scaffolding but can support reflection and the development of autonomy) (Dudeney et al., 2013). But this remains an exploratory area, and there are many more questions to be asked. Can we really integrate informal learning into formal assessment without undermining either the learning or the assessment? How do we appraise progression in multimodal writing or game-based interactions? How do we develop rubrics (if in fact rubrics are not entirely too constricting) to evaluate curation and creation? How do we compare networked communication across student cohorts? How do we convert evaluations of personal and situated learning into impersonal and abstract marks and grades? And what does all this mean for accreditation and credentialling?

Of course, teachers can also require students to incorporate traditional linguistic assessments into their e-portfolios. It's not unreasonable to include a number of conventional tasks – quizzes on content MALL, or tutorial MALL exercises – in a supporting role, while retaining some teacher assessment of writing (say, a mobile blog) or speaking (say, an audio diary). In time, learning analytics will offer us more options. It may never give us the whole picture, and we should always ask what mathematical models of learning might leave out (boyd & Crawford, 2012; note that danah boyd does not capitalise her name). Nevertheless, it can provide a first, automated level of summative assessment, giving teachers a base on which to build a second layer of more manual analysis and commentary. NLP parsing of students' language production, in particular, could have an important role to play. Current initiatives like the MASELTOV project (see Case Study 13) are pushing at the limits of IMALL, seeking to deliver automated feedback on – and thus potentially assessment of – many elements of learners' language, captured in everyday settings, and going well beyond simple evaluations of lexis or syntax. Indeed, the emergent possibilities in IMALL may eventually make the task of assessment much easier, and may even lead us to some responses to the questions outlined above.

But perhaps the most pressing question of all is how to exploit the full spectrum of educational possibilities inherent in m-learning when we're constrained by traditional assessment regimes. In the MILLEE project in India (see Case Study 7), teachers who were under pressure to focus on high-stakes exam preparation felt unable to allocate much time to students' individualised learning through mobile games. In the EIA project in Bangladesh (see Case Study 16), high-stakes reading and writing exams have limited some teachers' willingness to make use of speaking and listening materials. In Australia, it has been noted that the collaborative and communicative skills developed by students working with iPads – that is, some of the so-called 21st century skills – are far removed from those tested in university entrance exams, leading to the danger of students and parents seeing such devices as a distraction at upper school levels (Pegrum et al., 2013).

In short, the potential of digital technologies to open up space for new skills, and new ways to practise old skills, is at odds with traditional assessment regimes, which have been re-energised by the global trend towards standardised national and international testing. A high-stakes focus on the traditional three Rs is not sufficient to prepare students for contemporary social lives, working contexts, or involved citizenship. There is a chance for enthusiastic teachers to help their students to do some things differently, and to do some things better, with mobile technologies. But that chance is very much constrained by the seeming immutability of today's testing regimes.

5
What Language to Teach with Mobile Devices

Mobile devices, as we've seen, may be drafted into the service of a variety of language learning approaches (from behaviourist through communicative to sociocultural approaches), linked to a series of MALL types (from content and tutorial to creation and communication MALL), and used to dish up a range of materials and activities (from e-books and grammar apps through to multimodal blogging and complex gaming). Having considered *how* language can be taught with mobile devices in the last chapter, we turn now to *what* aspects of language can be taught. In the process, we'll draw together numerous examples of successful MALL projects. But before considering what language to teach through technology, we need to consider how technology changes language itself.

When language goes mobile

The mobile medium isn't neutral. Mobile devices impact on the language we use (Baron, 2008, 2011; Kenning, 2007), with the resulting changes being a subset of the linguistic changes associated more broadly with digital technologies. In fact, it's been suggested that digital tools require us to extend the concept of communicative competence to cover new ways of communicating and interacting (Chapelle, 2009). Mobile devices inflect and amplify these changes in their own ways.

Textspeak, friend or foe?

Although the term 'netspeak' is sometimes used to refer to online language (Crystal, 2006), the term *textspeak,* which refers specifically to the language used on mobile phones, is more common nowadays, reflecting the fact that this linguistic phenomenon has become associated predominantly with mobile devices and SMS texting (as well as the rapidly spreading mobile IM apps that parallel texting). It's a heavily abbreviated and often playful form of language which serves to increase speed (with abbreviations being faster to type), decrease messaging costs (by keeping within the SMS character limit), avoid misunderstandings (by adding emotional context through abbreviations like 'lol' and emoticons like ☺), and signal in-group membership (via the use of certain slang). While voice recognition and other new input mechanisms may eventually reduce the need for textspeak, there's little doubt that a command of this kind of language is currently essential to everyday functioning in mobile environments, particularly in social channels involving synchronous communication.

It's an easy target in the political and media discourses around falling literacy standards, but attacks on textspeak turn out to be very misguided. A growing body of research demonstrates that there is a positive correlation between students' use of textspeak and their standard literacy skills (Kemp, 2011). Linguists suggest this is because you can only play with language rules, as is common in textspeak, if you already know what the rules are (Crystal, 2008, 2011; Plester et al., 2009). Research also shows that children and teenagers generally understand the distinction between textspeak and standard language (Crystal, 2008; Lenhart et al., 2008), which suggests that if they break the rules, they may well be doing so on purpose.

Given the importance of textspeak for mobile communication, and given its positive correlation with the development of standard language, teachers might adopt a codeswitching approach where they recognise the value of textspeak but offer guidance, as necessary, on when and where it's appropriate (Dudeney et al., 2013). Of course, it may be that educators need to rethink where the boundaries of appropriate language use lie: if most teen feedback on the Yoza stories (see Chapter 4) is in textspeak, this could reflect the development of mobile literacy skills suited to the medium (Vosloo, 2012). Yet students also need to hone their ideas about appropriate language use: choosing an informal textspeak register in the wrong setting might suggest a shaky grasp of pragmatic competence. It all comes down to context – but, confusingly for both students and teachers, contexts and the linguistic expectations linked to them are in a state of flux.

Textspeak is slipping into ever more communication channels and spreading into advertising and the mainstream mass media. With its optional truncations and alternative spellings, it may be contributing to a wider phenomenon which Naomi Baron (2008) dubs 'linguistic whateverism', manifested in:

> a marked indifference to the need for consistency in linguistic usage. At issue is not whether to say *who* or *whom*, or whether *none* as the subject of a sentence takes a singular or plural verb, but whether it really matters which form you use. (p.169)

Possible emerging trends, says Baron, include more use of writing to record informal speech; 'an attitude toward spelling and punctuation conventions redolent of the quasi-anarchy of medieval and even Renaissance England' (ibid., p.171); and less reliance on language as a status marker. While not created by digital communication, such trends are certainly intensified by it. But even as digital writing continues to increase in speed, quantity, fragmentation and ephemerality (Baron, 2011), still broader changes in language use are becoming evident around us.

A shifting skillset

Changes to vocabulary, spelling, grammar or punctuation brought about by some combination of textspeak and linguistic whateverism are far from the end of the story. As we find ourselves reading and writing more than ever, the skills we need to process and produce written text – that is, the macroskills of reading and writing – are shifting too, both in their nature and in their relationship to each other. Though these changes are linked to digital communication in general, once again our mobile devices give them new inflections and amplify them in particular ways.

First, we *read differently*. Even e-books which simply reproduce print texts offer an extended range of functionality but, at the same time, the text can only be accessed via a reduced viewing window on a lot of mobile hardware (see Chapter 4). Both of these features make digital reading quite unique. More generally, while some reading strategies can be transferred from print contexts, others are specific to, or require more complex iterations in, online contexts (Chifari et al., 2010; Coiro, 2009, 2011; Zhang & Duke, 2008). Online reading often requires defining a purpose; searching for information; selecting search results; navigating hyperlinks; evaluating miscellaneous sources; synthesising a response; and communicating that response to others. Thus, students need guidance in developing a whole series of digital literacies like search literacy, hypertext literacy and information literacy (see Chapter 6), and in knowing when to apply them.

Second, *reading and writing are no longer separated.* Writing has become an integral part of reading. In e-books, we add annotations and share commentary and questions. In informational research, we input search terms, tag resources, and discuss emerging results in online networks (Coiro, 2009). On blogs, social networking sites or social media platforms, we intertwine passive (reading) and active (writing) skills, much as we intertwine listening and speaking in everyday conversation.

Third, *we write differently.* While print-based writing is designed to preserve text in a fixed form, digital writing is frequently a temporary artefact of quick and convenient communication in the form of an instant message, a tweet or a discussion board comment – the kinds of short texts, indeed, which are supported by the limited text entry options on mobile devices. The more synchronous the communication, the more casual the writing is likely to be, and the more it may bolster the trend towards linguistic whateverism. Digital writing is ultimately a hybrid of speech and writing with its own special twists (Baron, 2008; Baym, 2010; Crystal, 2011). There's still relatively little actual speaking and listening in digital conversational contexts; rather, our conversations take written form. But we don't really *write* – we *'talk' in 'writing'*.

Fourth, *we don't read or write alone.* Whether we're sharing highlights in e-books, collaboratively generating search terms, or chatting on social platforms, digital reading/writing is an ever more social process. Digital writing is necessarily collaborative in conversational contexts, implicitly collaborative when the end product is a hyperlinked text embedded in a web of other texts, and often explicitly collaborative when the intended outcome is a sophisticated artefact like a multimodal digital story.

Fifth, *we don't just read or write words.* Thanks to the ease of multimodal composition in the digital era, we're witnessing a shift away from communication solely through writing (Kalantzis & Cope, 2012), sometimes described as a shift away from 'telling' and towards 'showing' (Kress, 2003). It's been suggested that the design of mobile phones underlines this shift by prioritising touch navigation and visual output over written input or output (apart from the display of texts on webpages), symbolised by the hiding of the keyboard when it's not in use (Adami & Kress, 2010). While language remains essential, nowadays it's often integrated with multimedia elements, placing a premium on multimodal literacy (see Chapter 6). Discourse in the 21st century is becoming as unthinkable without multimodal elements as it would be without language.

Changes in language use must inevitably lead to changes in language teaching. Educators need to consider textspeak when teaching vocabulary (even if they attempt to head off linguistic whateverism!). They need to consider the shifting, intertwined functions of reading and writing when they teach these macroskills and, as we'll see, when they teach listening and speaking too. Moreover, we should remember that digital language is not just something teachers can teach *about;* it's something teachers can and must teach *through.* Digital settings are perfectly valid contexts for language use – and for some students they may be more important than the face-to-face contexts for which teachers used to prepare them. It's no longer simply a case of technology use supporting language learning. For many students, it's a case of language learning, especially English learning, supporting technology use (Heift & Schulze, 2007; Warschauer, 2004).

Teaching vocabulary & grammar

Without a doubt, the single most common MALL activity reported in the literature is vocabulary learning. This is the ground of classic tutorial MALL, but recent initiatives involving gaming, AR and IMALL demonstrate that the possibilities don't stop there. While textspeak isn't much of an issue with foundational content of the kind typically covered in tutorial MALL, it may become a consideration with more sophisticated pedagogies and at more advanced levels.

Email drilling or, more commonly nowadays, *SMS drilling* involves regular transmission of words or phrases, accompanied variously by translations, definitions, examples or quiz questions, depending on what can fit within the limit of 160 characters (or fewer in non-Roman languages). In some contexts, this enables language learning which would otherwise be unavailable. In other contexts, it can extend and reinforce learning, boosting communicative time in the classroom by moving basic practice into students' own time in a flipped model. Because mobile devices are typically carried everywhere, they lend themselves to SMS drilling involving *spaced repetition,* which is known to be more effective than massed repetition (Levy & Kennedy, 2005; Thornton & Houser, 2005). Texts might be pushed to learners once a day, as in the British Council/Nokia Life Learn English project in China (see Case Study 9); two to three times a day, as in an early

SMS project with learners of Italian in Australia (Kennedy & Levy, 2008; Levy & Kennedy, 2005); three times a day, as in an early mobile email project, Learning on the Move (LOTM), with learners of English in Japan (Thornton & Houser, 2005); or many times a day, as in the Pakistani Post-literacy project, whose focus went beyond vocabulary (see Case Study 3). But if, as in the Australian and Japanese studies, some learners save messages to read later when they have more time to focus on them, this may undermine the spacing effect. Ideally, learners should have to make an effort to retrieve past learning and actively produce vocabulary rather than just passively receiving content (Levy & Kennedy, 2005). Complementary quiz questions may be delivered separately in push or pull mode, with learners receiving correct responses pushed out to them at a later time as in the Chinese Learn English project (see Case Study 9) or receiving automated responses to their answers as in the British Council's Sudanese SMS project (see Case Study 4).

Building on the foundations established by earlier research, many recent studies have compared push mode SMS vocabulary learning by a test group with some other kind of vocabulary learning by a control group or groups. Significantly higher post-test vocabulary gains by the test groups are typically reported, with a current strong concentration of such research in Iran (e.g., Hayati et al., 2013; Kimyayi, 2012; Motallebzadeh & Ganjali, 2011). In one project with a more active format, high school level Iranian learners of English sent a researcher and several classmates text messages containing new words covered in class, receiving prompt teacherly feedback; again, the test group significantly outperformed the control group, who worked on paper and brought responses to class (Tabatabaei & Goojani, 2012).

Many of these principles – such as spaced repetition and the inclusion of quizzes to encourage learners to activate their knowledge – are illustrated in the Learn English project, with content provided by the British Council through the Nokia Life service (see Case Study 9 below). Notwithstanding the limitations of SMS, even richly formatted SMS as used here, such a project can bring language learning to literally millions of users who were previously left out of the digital learning loop. While the Mobiledu project (see Case Study 6) and the newer Nokia Life+ service (in the form of a web app that works through the Nokia Xpress browser) have opened up more options for those with higher end feature phones and smartphones, projects like Learn English are vital to reaching poorly served populations with limited hardware and connectivity.

Case Study 9   Spreading vocabulary learning in China (Learn English Project)

Figure 5.1   Learn English service in China. © Nokia, reproduced by permission.

Project:	Learn English from the British Council via Nokia Life.
Language:	English.
Focus:	Vocabulary.
Level:	Three levels (easy, medium & difficult) pegged to Levels A1, A2 & B1 of the Common European Framework of Reference (CEFR) for Languages.
Format:	Richly formatted messages containing a phrase of the day, followed by a quiz question & a quiz answer at the weekend, delivered through the Nokia Life platform, which uses SMS as the bearer.
Hardware:	The messages are delivered to users' own Nokia feature phones in a BYOD model.
Key partners:	British Council (content provider); Nokia (mobile manufacturer); China Mobile & China Unicom (mobile network operators).
Timeline:	2010 – ongoing.
Location:	China.
Participants:	The learners are primarily from a low income demographic in both cities & rural areas in China. To date there have been 2.5 million users of the Learn English service.
Funding model:	Users supply their own devices. Learn English is a free value-added service provided to Nokia Life subscribers for a trial period, after which they pay CNY 5 (approx. US 80¢) per month.

Case Study 9   (Continued)

In this project, which targets a lower income slice of the same market as the Mobiledu project (see Case Study 6), Nokia Life subscribers can register to receive richly formatted messages which use SMS as the bearer. The messages are designed to help subscribers learn English with the support of their native language, Chinese (Mandarin). They contain English vocabulary with a weekly theme, such as greetings. For five days each week subscribers receive a phrase of the day, consisting of English lexis and a Chinese translation, building up gradually into a mini-dialogue and/or a lexical set. This is followed by a quiz question on the sixth day, and the answer to the quiz question on the seventh day. There is no return SMS traffic involved, so there are no additional costs for the message recipients.

Key challenges have included the limitations of a 49-character message, which is designed to keep costs down and make the subscription fee widely affordable, but severely circumscribes the content that can be included, notwithstanding the advantages of character-based languages like Chinese used for the translations (since a word may be represented by a single character). The lack of accompanying multimedia content makes it difficult to contextualise the vocabulary appropriately. Anecdotally, users are sometimes unsure of the pronunciation of the words or phrases they receive, and do not have recourse to audio files to check. While those with more advanced phones might have been able to benefit from the Mobiledu project, the Learn English project is specifically designed for users with very basic technology and no internet connections, who otherwise would lack access to such learning opportunities. Indeed, perhaps the greatest success of this and similar projects has been the use of SMS to make the content accessible to local populations with low-end phones. Such content is, moreover, less costly to produce than multimedia materials and apps, making it more affordable for content providers, while a lack of interactivity keeps costs down for users, who are not required to reply, as well as for the providers of the service.

Evaluation is an issue in this type of project. While the subscriber figures point to its success in terms of the number of people reached, it has been more difficult to gain insights into the learning which has occurred, with users scattered across remote regions of China. Nevertheless, some positive indications have emerged. Eighty-nine per cent of those surveyed by Nokia have professed themselves to be engaged by the content, with qualitative feedback indicating that users not only enjoy it but find it useful.

Anecdotally, it appears that many parents subscribe on behalf of their children, and many teachers, both of English and other subjects, subscribe in order to improve their language skills.

Logistical challenges often occur in such projects, where it is necessary to collaborate with local network operators, not all of whom may see the value of English language services, and many of whom may be constrained by technological, infrastructural or legal limitations. In this case such issues have been alleviated by the global reach of Nokia. Revenue is typically not large in this type of project, meaning that a substantial subscriber base is needed, but Nokia's ability to advertise the service directly to its users and provide it free of charge for a trial period has led to a large take-up. Sustainability is an issue in most funded mobile projects, both large and small, but can be improved with the involvement of a range of partners, with the participation of large global or regional players being helpful.

In China, the Learn English project is one strand of the much larger Nokia Life project, which offers message subscriptions related to education, health, weather, market data for rural farmers, and so on. With over 100 million users to date, Nokia Life is the world's largest informal mobile learning platform, with a particular focus on developing markets. Similar English learning strands of Nokia Life are available in more than 20 languages in a variety of other countries, including India, Indonesia and Nigeria, with Kenya and Pakistan coming online in 2013. In the last two cases, the British Council is once again the content provider. The Council has also employed a similar concept in locations such as Kazakhstan and Uzbekistan. Although it is always necessary to bear in mind cultural issues when moving between countries, much of the vocabulary content, which is relatively global in applicability because of its low level, was able to be repurposed for these contexts with the addition of unique translations. However, levels may vary between locations, with the 'easy' level in countries like Kenya, where there is considerable integration of English vocabulary into everyday life, being more challenging than in countries such as China, where this is not the case.

The key interviewees about this project were Neil Ballantyne (Mobile Learning Manager, British Council), Gai Fan (British Council, Beijing) and Bhanu Potta (Global Product Leader, Learning & Knowledge Services, Nokia Life). For further information, see Ballantyne & Tyers (2012).

Multimodal approaches to vocabulary learning hold considerable promise (see Chapter 4). They may use pull mode, as in the Vidioms project in Japan, where learners used mobile phones and PDAs to access web-based animations and videos explaining English idioms (Thornton & Houser, 2005). They may use push mode, as in the MMS vocabulary messages containing images and audio sent to learners of English in a project in Turkey; in this study, mobile learners were found to both gain and retain more vocabulary than learners who used web- or paper-based materials, which can effectively only be accessed in pull mode (Saran et al., 2012). Word-of-the day apps, which are now available for many languages, represent a simple take on push mode delivery. By contrast, dictionaries and glossaries normally operate in pull mode, but certain personalised multimodal dictionaries combine some pull and push functionality. The Remword English–Chinese dictionary app, for instance, offers text, image and audio support for vocabulary learning, and allows users to build a lexicon of unfamiliar words which it can remind them to review at appropriately spaced intervals (Deng & Shao, 2011). Similarly, though they may lack a push mode, some of today's most sophisticated tutorial apps take the form of multimodal digital flashcards which, again, allow users to build personal wordlists whose contents can be recycled at suitable intervals by IMALL software that adapts to learners' changing competence. This kind of adaptive, spaced repetition approach to a personal lexicon also forms one element of the larger Nulu project (see Case Study 11).

Simple *multimodal games* for mobile devices, whose strengths are often in their game design rather than their pedagogy per se, can complement other vocabulary learning approaches by making foundational practice more entertaining. For example, in a small-scale study of the Butterfly Shooter game, adapted from Hangman, primary students in Iran showed improvement in spelling though not understanding of Farsi vocabulary (Fotouhi-Ghazvini et al., 2009). In the MILLEE games in India (see Case Study 7), a mixture of primary and secondary students showed improvement in English spelling, vocabulary knowledge, and simpler reading competencies. And in a study of the MOBO City game, based on a virtual space representing a motherboard where technical English terms were learned incidentally, university computing students in Iran showed improvement in vocabulary knowledge (Fotouhi-Ghazvini et al., 2009).

But just because there are many ways to learn vocabulary on mobile devices, it doesn't mean students always want to do so. Glenn Stockwell (2008) found that, given the choice of completing adaptive ICALL/IMALL vocabulary tasks on PCs or mobile phones, the majority of his university level Japanese learners of English preferred the former, with some citing cost as well as other limitations discussed earlier, including those related to screen size, keyboard input, and speed (see Chapter 3). This trend held in a later study, despite a general increase in mobile use (Stockwell, 2010; see also Vignette 8). In a study of the incidental English vocabulary learning of university students in Hong Kong, Song and Fox (2008) found that they preferred to dynamically integrate their use of the supplied PDAs with their use of computers, depending on convenience and suitability for their needs. Such studies highlight the value of a multiscreen ecosystem wherever it is feasible (which for now means in the developed world) so that individuals can make choices to suit their own circumstances. In another study, Fisher et al. (2012) found that high school level Japanese learners of English who used hard copy books, e-books with online dictionaries, and enhanced e-books with adaptive vocabulary learning support, showed no significant difference in their vocabulary gains between these modes, with some students preferring the hard copy books and others favouring the convenience of mobile devices. This highlights the value not just of a multiscreen ecosystem, but a learning ecosystem with both digital and analogue components (see Chapter 3).

If mobile devices are to be a major platform for vocabulary learning – or any other language areas or skills – then we need to exploit their points of difference from other technologies, whether digital or analogue. As Stockwell suggests (see Vignette 8 below), this may involve making more use of the distinctive push capabilities which, as we've seen, are employed in some of the most effective language learning initiatives, from technologically simple SMS to more complex MMS projects, and some of the most promising applications, from word-of-the-day to personal dictionary apps. Interestingly, there was a request for precisely such push notifications from some students in the SIMOLA project (see Case Study 1).

Vignette 8   Transforming the learning process with mobile technologies

Glenn Stockwell, Waseda University, Japan

Mobile learning has continued to carry the expectations of teachers and researchers since portable technologies such as PDAs, MP3 players and mobile phones found their way into the hands of

---

Vignette 8   (Continued)

students at universities and other educational institutions around the world. The hype surrounding the possibilities has yet to be realised in terms of learner usage, however, with some of my own earlier research showing at least 40% of students did not even try to use their mobile phone to complete activities when they had the option of using a desktop computer instead. Given that surveys did not indicate any particular resistance to using mobile devices for learning (despite some awareness that these devices have certain limitations) we might wonder what the causes of this apparent lack of use were.

A potential reason for this may simply be that mobile devices are being treated in the same way as textbooks or other materials, which require the learner to take the initiative to use them. This in itself is not necessarily a problem, but when we consider that our mobile devices constantly inform us of incoming messages or remind us of tasks we need to undertake, it seems that perhaps we are not capitalising on their potential as much as we might. Rather than only having learners access the device to solve a need (such as looking up an unknown word or completing certain learning activities), the device can also prompt the learner into a particular action (such as making the learner review their vocabulary for an upcoming test by automatically emailing them a list of items). The future of learning through mobile devices will depend on more than making tools available to learners, but rather using these tools to make learning fit – even if somewhat forcefully sometimes – into the busy lifestyles of our students.

▶ Further reading: Stockwell (2010, 2013a, 2013b).

If MALL distinguishes itself from CALL when push capabilities come into play, it distinguishes itself still further when the real-world environment is integrated into learning in *situated activities*, sometimes in the form of games and often with an AR element. In the Detective Alavi mobile game, designed to teach Iranian university students English computing vocabulary, learners solved puzzles with the help of QR code clues distributed around the building, while they interacted with peers, the teacher and distant experts, as well as having the option to draw on the real-world help of university staff and students as they moved about (Fotouhi-Ghazvini et al., 2011). Teachers could customise the game without technical knowledge, and students were found to improve in a number of areas, including spelling, vocabulary, reporting skills, and critical thinking. In the Tag Added learNinG Objects (TANGO) project for learners of English and Japanese, a PDA detected nearby objects using RFID tags; learners were prompted with vocabulary questions adapted to their level, to which they could respond by scanning RFID tags on the appropriate objects and, in gaming mode, they scored points by doing so (Ogata, 2011; Ogata et al., 2010). In the Personalised Context-aware Ubiquitous Learning System (PCULS) for learners of English in Taiwan, relevant vocabulary was delivered to high school students on PDAs based on their level, their location, the time, and their free time available (Chen & Li, 2010). On a vocabulary post-test, students who had used the context-aware version of the system significantly outperformed those who had used a non-context-aware version. In the prototype JApanese MImicry and Onomatopoeia Learning Assistant System (JAMIOLAS) 3.0 for learners of Japanese, users can receive quiz questions based on live weather information in their current location, regarding how best to describe it using mimicry or onomatopoeic language (Hou et al., 2012). These are all highly promising approaches to vocabulary development.

Some situated activities demand that students take on very active roles in creating and communicating language learning content. In the 'Move, Idioms!' project, primary school learners of Chinese in Singapore used smartphones to photograph real-life contexts for idioms and construct relevant sentences about them; this user-generated content was then shared and discussed on a wiki and in class, allowing misconceptions to be picked up and understanding to be refined (Wong et al., 2010, 2012). This initiative is now being followed up by the MyCLOUD project (see Chapter 4). With the Seamless Mobile-Assisted Language Learning (SMALL) support system, university learners of English in Japan used tablets to upload useful vocabulary encountered in everyday contexts, with accompanying multimedia files if desired (Uosaki et al., 2012). The system then hyperlinked the new words to instances of the same vocabulary in the textbook or uploaded by other users, allowed students to peruse classmates' vocabulary logs and relog items to their own pages, and provided quizzes based on the logged vocabulary. The Move, Idioms! and SMALL projects share common ground with the Lingobee app in the European SIMOLA project (see Case Study 1), where users can upload multimedia examples of contextualised language usage – thereby fostering the habit of noticing vocabulary in everyday linguistic input – and read, comment on or modify others' language examples. This user-generated content, derived from user-generated contexts, ranges from standard language to colourful informal expressions (with plenty of room for textspeak, should students wish to include it!). Because it preserves something of the contexts in which language is used, Lingobee often highlights its cultural and social embeddedness.

Going a step further, the Toponimo project currently being trialled in the UK combines AR gaming with active content creation and communication by students: after logging in through Facebook or a Toponimo account on a GPS-enabled device, players score points for collecting vocabulary from and adding it to real-world locations, again with the option of linking it to multimedia materials and rating others' vocabulary contributions (Sweeney et al., 2011; Tommy Sweeney, personal communication, April 2013). The resulting geosocial, collaborative dictionary may be further enhanced in time with the addition of minigames to encourage vocabulary learning. Another European project, MASELTOV (see Case Study 13), which operates within an integrated skills paradigm, throws push capabilities into the mix, with contextualised lexis sent to learners on geoaware phones and tied into an AR game that encourages them to make active use of newly learned language, which may in turn be evaluated using IMALL software. As always, the greater the exploitation of the affordances of mobile devices, the lower the overall affordability of these approaches. But it's here, at the interface between social, gaming and AR functions, combined with user-generated contexts and content, all situated within a creation and communication MALL framework, that the developed world is likely to see some of the most exciting growth over coming years – with results that will, hopefully, be more widely shared in time.

Grammar is often treated in a similar way to vocabulary in tutorial MALL exercises, and the two areas can be integrated in SMS services like the British Council's North African projects (see Case Study 4). It's interesting to note that in the study of Italian SMS messaging described above, which focused mainly on vocabulary, it was the grammar messages which were most valued by students (Levy & Kennedy, 2005). In fact, an isolated focus on grammar is relatively rare in MALL, perhaps because grammar so obviously lends itself to integration with vocabulary, as in the above examples, or with different types of skills practice. In an inventive approach taken with pre-intermediate English learners in Iran, for example, a test group used mobile phones to record themselves participating in class discussions designed to elicit particular grammatical structures, before reviewing their own and their peers' recordings to identify and correct grammar errors (Baleghizadeh & Oladrostam, 2010). This activity, with its combined focus on output and noticing, its integration of speaking and listening skills, and its emphasis on specific feedback, led to the test group achieving significantly better results than the control group, who received no extra treatment beyond regular grammar lessons, on a grammar post-test. At the cutting edge of current developments, we find vocabulary and grammar learning integrated on a context-aware platform in the above-mentioned MASELTOV project, where grammar is implicit in the tasks set for learners in the AR game, and where it may potentially be automatically evaluated along with vocabulary and other aspects of language use though IMALL software.

Teaching reading & writing

The opportunities for *extensive reading* are greatest on larger mobile devices, like e-readers or tablets, which make it convenient to consume e-book and e-magazine content and, what's more, to interact with it. But while mobile phone users mostly engage in short-form reading, this doesn't preclude reading longer texts, as seen in the Yoza and Worldreader Mobile projects (see Chapter 4). Naturally, it's also possible to use any internet-connected device to read general web content. At the same time, we should bear in mind that digital and print texts differ in many ways and typically demand quite different sets of reading strategies, and that many of today's increasingly common multimedia texts demand a high level of multimodal literacy (see Chapter 6).

Differences aside, there is considerable promise in *intensive reading* on mobile devices with the aid of scaffolding features, which often provide help with vocabulary and sometimes grammar, thus turning texts into comprehensible input. At one end of the scale, this might involve inbuilt dictionaries and translation apps, or traditional pre- and post-reading tasks. At the other end of the scale, it might involve IMALL software like the Personalized Intelligent Mobile learning System (PIMS), developed for learners of English in Taiwan and implemented on PDAs, which worked with fuzzy item response theory to estimate learners' reading levels and recommend appropriate news articles, accompanied by Chinese translations (Chen & Hsu, 2008). In addition, a personalised vocabulary recommendation agent automatically extracted new vocabulary and presented it in a vocabulary learning and checking interface. The system was found to reduce cognitive load and significantly improve students' reading comprehension.

Annotation is technically a kind of output, but nowadays it essentially serves as a complement to reading input on smart devices. It's valuable for language learners, who may wish to mark up key vocabulary, for instance, which could be compiled into a list and even shared with other learners. Dedicated annotation and sharing systems for language learners have begun to emerge. In Taiwan, a PDA-based system was developed to allow university level learners of English to decide on the most appropriate translations of words in a reading text after using an instant translation function, and to then collaboratively share their translation annotations, thus developing their vocabulary proficiency in the context of an intensive reading course (Chang & Hsu, 2011). Students generally found the system useful and convenient, with collaborative annotations leading to greater improvement in reading comprehension scores than individual annotations, though a later study found that collaboration was not always useful and its value depended on students' relative proficiency levels (Hsu, Hwang & Chang, 2013).

When it comes to writing, the most basic form of input (from a technology perspective) or output (from a language perspective) involves *tracing letters or characters* on a touchscreen, as in the tutorial apps now available for many languages. Sophisticated systems which push in an IMALL direction can automatically detect errors in the position, direction and sequence of the strokes in Chinese characters, for example, while the prototype iWrite software is designed to provide feedback on specific structures in which students of Chinese require more practice, and may be used to adaptively train those structures (Tam & Huang, 2011). More extensive *handwriting* is a possible input mechanism on some smart devices and is supported by a number of apps; so, just as students can practise their pronunciation with voice recognition software, they can practise forming letters or characters that are recognised by their devices.

The limitations of small screens for reading are echoed by the limitations of small screens for writing (where it's difficult to maintain an overview of a text) and compounded by the limitations of restrictive input systems (whenever typing on virtual keyboards is required). It's widely agreed that mobile devices are better suited to *making notes* and *composing short texts,* perhaps in multimedia formats and perhaps in situ, rather than producing extended written output in a classroom (see Chapters 3 & 4). Basic scaffolding, in the form of spelling and grammar checkers, is commonly available. Within the limitations of their devices, students can create texts or digital stories, perhaps using template-based multimodal apps for the latter (see Chapter 4), before publishing this user-generated content for teachers, peers or the wider public to review. In one interesting experiment with situated writing, primary school learners of English in Taiwan used mobile devices to write texts on chosen topics stimulated by real-world environments, with the ability to upload accompanying pictures, and with their writing scaffolded through the provision of suggested words and phrases; they could then read and comment on peers' texts (Hwang et al., 2011). The combination of a real-world setting with linguistic scaffolding was found to promote the writing of detailed descriptions, and students in the experimental group significantly outperformed peers in a post-test which involved making sentences about objects in context.

Written interaction involving negotiation of meaning can occur in interactive forums such as asynchronous discussion boards. Asynchronous conversation may approximate certain features of speech, but occurs at a much slower pace, leaving plenty of time for using scaffolding tools like glossaries to help make input comprehensible; for noticing new language; and for carefully preparing linguistic output. The dedicated language service Nulu (see Case Study 11) makes use of exactly this kind of discussion forum, allowing learners to engage in conversation at their own speed. Similar possibilities for asynchronous communication exist in channels ranging from SMS through to web 2.0 services like blogs, wikis, social networking sites and other social media platforms. For instance, students may converse with each other and potentially also with native speakers on Twitter (Lomicka & Lord, 2012) or alternative services like the Chinese *Sina Weibo* (新浪微博) and *Weixin* (微信) (known as WeChat in the international market), with the latter offering both audio and text chat (Chen, 2013). One advantage of Twitter's 140-character limit is that it allows only short turns, and may therefore be less linguistically demanding than discussion boards, while it can also be used for training elements of pragmatic or sociolinguistic competence and, especially if there is contact with native speakers, intercultural competence (Borau et al., 2009). Twitter can be used, too, for collaborative story writing (Kolb, 2008), thus simply and neatly linking creation and communication MALL.

Naturally, all these services can be, and often are, used synchronously. There are advantages to synchronous written communication where, as in synchronous oral communication, meaning must be negotiated in real time (Meskill & Anthony, 2010). Even so, while not as leisurely as asynchronous discussion, the communication still proceeds more slowly because it's taking place in writing. What's more, conversation logs can be revisited during or after the interaction by students and teachers (Blake, 2008; Meskill & Anthony, 2010) to facilitate comprehensible input and noticing of new language. Of course, the more synchronous the service, or the use made of the service, the more the language used will tend towards the conversational hybrid which is typical of digital and above all mobile interaction, but which involves quite different skills from conventional reading and writing. In fact, such text-based chat may be a better training ground for speaking than writing, as we'll see.

Teaching listening & speaking

Opportunities for *extensive listening* abound online. Students can practise with the copious content designed for native speakers to stream (like radio channels or news broadcasts) or download (like radio podcasts or talking books). As audio becomes a more common output format from our smart digital advisers, like Apple's Siri, Google Now, and many sat nav apps, learners will also have the chance to listen regularly (and sometimes intensively!) to information and instructions. All these materials, from digital shows to driving directions, will increasingly come in a range of World Englishes, thus allowing – if not obliging – learners of English to adopt a global approach to developing their listening skills. The same goes for learners of other widely spoken languages.

Graded content, available via podcasts, audiobooks or listening apps in varying quantities depending on the language, is ideal for providing comprehensible input to learners at different levels. Some content lends itself to extensive listening, other content to *intensive listening*. As with reading, scaffolding of various kinds may be available, often focused on vocabulary. In the Nulu project for learners of Spanish and English (see Case Study 11), users can slow down the speed of listening texts, follow the written texts, or access translations. Scaffolding may also take the form of pre- and post-listening tasks which integrate multiple skills. In one Korean study, students of English used mobile phones to access listening texts on a WAP site, completing vocabulary exercises and a peer discussion on a mobile discussion board in the pre-listening phase, and completing comprehension exercises to be sent to the teacher in the post-listening phase (Nah et al., 2008). Students were also able to exchange information and obtain help on the discussion board. Listening skills were thus embedded in a rich approach which combined tutorial-style tasks with real communication, integrating comprehensible input, negotiation of meaning and comprehensible output within a collaborative framework. In the Canadian Mobile-Enabled Language Learning Eco-System (MELLES) project, English for Special Purposes students at a community college used their own mobile devices to complete eight listening tasks, some designed as individual activities and some as collaborative activities, and some requiring students to jointly create multimedia artefacts or comment on and rate each other's audio recordings (Palalas, 2012). Students indicated a high level of satisfaction with this system which, as in the Korean study, was overtly focused on listening but built collaboration around the listening tasks and required considerable language output as a complement to language input.

Video can provide an extremely effective form of scaffolding for audio content. Captions or subtitles may support listening comprehension and vocabulary acquisition (see Chapter 4), while video itself supports understanding not only of vocabulary and grammar but of the functional, pragmatic, paralinguistic and sociocultural elements of language use. Given the value of exposure to such contextualised language usage, the Television And Mobile phone Assisted Language Learning Environment (TAMALLE) project in the UK aided learners in watching interactive television by providing scaffolding in the form of programme summaries, just-in-time comprehension assistance, and lists of recommended vocabulary with the option to save items to a personal list (Fallahkhair et al., 2007). While it used a combination of mobile phones with interactive TV, it would be possible nowadays to integrate these functions on a tablet or even a smartphone – and then display them, as desired, on a TV screen.

A more recent example of a multimedia language learning initiative, the British Council's Jobseekers project in India (see Case Study 10 below), develops users' knowledge of English while promoting their listening skills via graded conversations. This is achieved through animated videos illustrating relevant functional language and the all-important pragmatics of usage in job-seeking contexts. With the explosion of mobile video viewing noted earlier (see Chapter 4), we're bound to find more language learning video content becoming available, and it's encouraging to see its benefits already spreading beyond the developed world.

**Case Study 10 Enhancing employment prospects via video in India
(Jobseekers Project)**

Figure 5.2 Jobseekers video. © British Council, Chennai, reproduced by permission.

Project:	Jobseekers.
Language:	English.
Focus:	Functional language for job seekers.
Level:	Pre-intermediate (with wider applicability).
Format:	90 short, animated videos containing conversations which showcase language & skills for seeking employment. Initially, the video series was accessed in web app format via links sent to 3G-enabled phones. Later, a Windows version was released for PCs, followed by an Android app. Both the PC & Android app versions are still supported.
Hardware:	Users supply their own Android devices or PCs in a BYOD model.
Key partners:	British Council (content provider); Avon Mobility (software developer); Tata Docomo (original 3G mobile network operator).

Timeline:	2011 – ongoing.
Location:	India.
Participants:	There has been uptake by both individual English learners & higher education colleges, with the app in the top 50 in the Education category of the Indian Google Play store as of early 2013. Downloads are currently in the tens of thousands.
Funding model:	Users supply their own devices. There is a one-time user payment of INR 90 (approx. US $1.50) to download the PC or Android app version, with both available from the webpage (www.britishcouncil.in/english/learn-online/jobseekers) & the latter also available from Google Play. All licences are currently individual, though group payments are facilitated.

This project involves animated videos containing key lexical and functional content, graded for pre-intermediate learners and covering, for example, how to write CVs, apply for jobs, or respond to interviews. The videos are delivered to mobile devices or computers. The multimedia format provides far more context for language content than is available in typical SMS projects, thus supporting listening comprehension and highlighting the pragmatics of language use. Post-listening quizzes allow users to check their understanding of new language. While far more Indian users have access to mobile phones than computers, the use of the wider technology ecosystem beyond mobile devices maximises the reach of the project and the flexibility offered.

It is often observed in large-scale projects that regulatory and logistical requirements can be an obstacle. In the Jobseekers project, the range of different telecommunications operators in the different states of India made it difficult to roll out a country-wide 3G programme. This resulted in an eventual shift to a PC version, downloadable from the web. This was followed by an Android app launched in September 2012, designed to appeal to the rapidly growing market for low-cost Android tablets in India. There has been considerable interest amongst English learners in engineering colleges, who have the need to develop their language skills, and who were targeted in a mobile advertising campaign. A number of institutions have now also purchased the product. The possibility of state governments preloading the Jobseekers videos onto laptops or tablets provided to students is currently being explored.

Case Study 10 (Continued)

The success of the product is indicated by its continuing uptake both by individual learners and educational institutions. It is in fact designed not only to enhance users' confidence to use English in employability contexts, but to demonstrate best practice in m-learning for the improvement of language and employability. Teachers' feedback indicates appreciation not only of the English language content, but of the coverage of soft skills, ranging from negotiation strategies to body language. In order to build on this appeal, supporting materials are currently being designed for teachers.

The key interviewees about this project were Samyuktha Balakrishnan (Senior Project Manager, English Digital Partnerships, British Council, Chennai) and Neil Ballantyne (Mobile Learning Manager, British Council). For further information, see the British Council's *Jobseekers* webpage (www. britishcouncil.in/english/learn-online/jobseekers). See also Ballantyne & Tyers (2012).

At its simplest, spoken output involves *pronunciation*. This is an aspect of language which, like vocabulary or grammar, lends itself to tutorial MALL drills undertaken by students working independently, though feedback is more problematic than with grammar or vocabulary. Among today's proliferating and inexpensive pronunciation apps, some simply involve learners repeating sounds or words. Others involve manual self-assessment, where learners record their pronunciation before replaying it and comparing it to that of a proficient, usually native, speaker. Still others introduce an IMALL element, with rapidly improving automatic speech recognition software providing feedback on student language production on specific, limited tasks. The feedback may take the form of a visualisation, for example of a learner's pitch contours shown side-by-side with those of a native speaker. ICALL research has suggested this approach is helpful in the pronunciation of tones in languages like Chinese (Chun et al., 2013) and in improving intonation and prosody in a wide range of languages (Grantham O'Brien, 2006). Alternatively or additionally, apps may provide automated scoring of learners' pronunciation.

Meanwhile, with voice increasingly used not only as an output but also an input mechanism, learners can take up the challenge of honing their pronunciation so that it can be accurately parsed by their smart devices – bearing in mind the frustrations of still imperfect software, and the dangers of adaptive systems being inadvertently trained by a learner to recognise erroneous pronunciations (Sussex, 2012). IMALL is likely to open up far greater automated possibilities in the future as the analysis of natural speech becomes more feasible, allowing targeted feedback not only on pronunciation but on many other elements of communication in real-world contexts, as seen in the MASELTOV project (see Case Study 13). For now, many teachers provide detailed feedback manually, for instance in response to podcasts. Some studies of student-produced pronunciation podcasts with teacher or peer feedback have found general improvement (Lord, 2008); others have not (Ducate & Lomicka, 2009). In general, pronunciation training, whether with immediate but limited automated feedback, or delayed but richer human feedback, is a long-term commitment.

There are some indications that *oral reading fluency* can be improved with the help of mobile devices like iPod Touches. In a study of college level English learners in Japan, students used iPod Touches for 'shadowing' activities, which involved reading aloud the text provided by video clip prompts (Ono & Ishihara, 2012). They were able to work at their own pace through three levels where scaffolding was gradually removed: written text + audio track, fading written text + audio track, and fading written text only with no audio track. Learners showed improvement in numerous aspects of pronunciation. In a study of learners of English at Cyprus University of Technology, students used iPod Touches to record themselves reading a set text, then practised reading the text following a native speaker model on YouTube, before recording themselves reading the text again (Papadima-Sophocleous, in press). Students spent considerable time rehearsing their final recordings, and improvements were found in speed, word decoding accuracy, and all dimensions of prosody.

The options for less structured output in the form of self-grading, fluency-focused *speech production* are limited only by our imagination. Students can make audio recordings of reports, interviews or roleplays with mobile phones, tablets or digital voice recorders, and listen to, edit and revise them as often as they desire. Self-made video recordings of talks, which can be carefully prepared and rehearsed before being shared with teachers and peers, have been found to hold promise for improving student fluency and confidence (Gromik, 2012). There's even more of an emphasis on creation and communication as we head in a web 2.0 direction with, say, audio blogs serving as oral diaries on which teachers and peers can leave feedback, or as we head in an AR direction, with audio commentary created with apps like Woices being tagged to real-world locations where it can be accessed by other users (Peachey, 2012), and perhaps even incorporated into AR games.

Oral interaction involving asynchronous negotiation of meaning can be set up with well-designed activities on audio discussion boards and well-designed feedback tasks on audio blogs or in AR apps. Synchronous negotiation of meaning is possible through language partnerships on VoIP and IM services, many of which offer support in the form of a video link and text chat. Oral interaction, with or without negotiation of meaning, can of course be daunting for learners. When learners of French at the Open University in the UK were asked to use their mobile phones to undertake automated listening and speaking activities, they often felt put 'on the spot' (Demouy & Kukulska-Hulme, 2010, p.229). However, researchers suggested this could approximate real-life language learning situations, and students indicated some appreciation of the authenticity of the experience. In the Mobile-Assisted Language Learning (MALL) and *Foghlaim Ón Nuatheicneolaíocht* (FÓN, or Learning Through New Technology) projects in Ireland, learners of Irish (also known as Gaelic) used mobile phones to access a voice response system where they could record answers to questions, listen to their own responses and re-record them until they were satisfied, and save them for teacher feedback which could then be printed out or downloaded as a podcast (Keogh, 2011). In the latter project, they also engaged in live chat with other Irish learners, with conversations again being saved for teacher feedback. Students dealt well with the challenge of responding in real time but they also spent some time reworking their recordings. Overall, the project, supported by regular vocabulary and quiz SMSs, was found to improve students' listening comprehension, fluency, vocabulary and tense usage.

Synchronous text chat is much less daunting, largely because it proceeds more slowly than oral chat. What's more, there is evidence that it involves the same cognitive mechanisms as face-to-face conversation and may therefore indirectly develop second language (L2) oral proficiency (Payne & Whitney, 2002), including pragmatic competence (Sykes, 2005). It would seem to have considerable benefits for students with lower phonological working memory capacity, who might struggle in face-to-face synchronous conversation (Payne & Ross, 2005). Naturally, it has the pedagogical advantage of preserving conversation logs for later, more leisurely examination. It also has the logistical advantage of being easy to organise since, thanks to the spread of mobile devices, it can operate through a series of channels from simple SMS to slick IM apps, the limitations of mobile keypads notwithstanding, and may potentially be used in the developing as much as the developed world.

Unsurprisingly, the affordability and affordances of mobile devices remain in tension when it comes to teaching the four macroskills, as they do in all other areas of language learning, and in mobile learning in general. While, again, some of the most exciting developments in coming years will occur around high-end smart devices and intelligent software, more basic mobile devices and software have much to contribute in the developing world – whether that means SMS-based vocabulary learning on feature phones in China (see Case Study 9), video-based language and listening skills practice on low-cost tablets in India (see Case Study 10), or preparation for spoken conversation through text-based chat anywhere in the world. Meanwhile, it is to be hoped that today's cutting-edge developments will, in time, find their way into more affordable hardware and software and, from there, into the hands of more learners.

Teaching integrated skills

Recent developments are increasingly mitigating against the separation of language areas and skills. From a pedagogical point of view, behaviourist CALL/MALL often isolates and trains specific language areas – notably vocabulary, grammar and pronunciation – but this artificial separation is less common in communicative or sociocultural CALL/MALL. From a technological point of view, the ability to communicate multimodally makes it easy and natural to (re-)integrate language areas, skills and cultural elements. As Nina Garrett (2009) points out:

> We used to consider 'the four skills' as requiring four different kinds of lesson plan, but even the earliest multimedia allowed us to represent language holistically by integrating textual, aural, and visual input and by adding hitherto undreamt-of dimensions of cultural content. (p.720)

On a number of levels, *integration* is key to contemporary MALL. There's an integration of *language areas and skills:* even when a given area or skill is emphasised, it's studied alongside other aspects of language. There's an integration *language approaches:* it's not uncommon to find elements of behaviourist drilling supplementing communicative tasks which are embedded in a sociocultural framework. There's an integration of *language teaching and learning:* more and more initiatives are crowdsourcing content (as in SIMOLA; see Case Study 1) and conversation (as in the busuu service, which feeds into MASELTOV; see Case Study 13), empowering a wide range of people to act as both teachers and learners.

The Nulu Languages initiative (see Case Study 11 below) offers a good example of integration on all these levels. It's focused on receptive skills, but it also promotes productive skills in its discussion forums. Its approach is communicative, but it throws in behaviourist elements (such as vocabulary flashcards) and makes room for pragmatics and intercultural learning (if users choose to interact with native speakers). And, within the clearly defined structure of its discussion forums, learners can crowdsource some of their teaching, while becoming teachers, mentors and guides in discussion forums for learners of their own language. On current trends, we'll see a lot more of these kinds of integrated approaches in the future.

Case Study 11   Learning through the news in the USA & Mexico (Nulu Project)

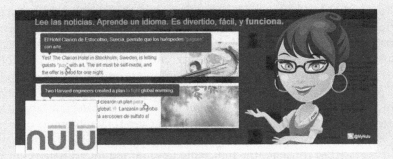

Figure 5.3 Nulu English learning mobile web app for Spanish speakers. © Nulu Languages, reproduced by permission.

Project: Nulu Languages.

Languages: Spanish & English. More will be added in 2013 & beyond.

Focus: Receptive skills (reading & listening) & vocabulary, with the option of productive skills practice (through conversation in a learning community).

Level: Two text levels (easy or hard) can be selected manually by users, but the software also adapts automatically to learners' levels.

Format:	HTML5 web app containing reading & listening texts, vocabulary flashcards & discussion forums. Native Android & iOS apps are under development.
Hardware:	Users access the mobile website on their own PCs or mobile devices, & will access the native apps on their own Android or Apple devices, in a BYOD model.
Key partners:	Development has been undertaken solely by Nulu Languages, which is in discussion with publishers & educational organisations about distribution & use of the software.
Timeline:	2012 – ongoing.
Location:	Nulu started in the USA as a Spanish learning service in January 2012 & was launched in Mexico as an English learning service in October 2012. Use of the latter service is currently expanding in Latin America.
Participants:	There are already tens of thousands of users, around half in the USA & half in Latin America, with the majority of the latter in Mexico. The greatest rate of uptake is in Latin America.
Funding model:	Users supply their own devices. The Nulu service is accessible on the website (www.nulu.com) in a freemium model (with a free basic level, but paid subscriptions for access to greater functionality).

The team behind Nulu, which stands for '*Nu* (New) *l*anguage for *u* (you)', produces texts about a variety of current news stories. Though they can be accessed on desktop or laptop devices, these succinct, chunked texts, divided up under subheadings, are designed with mobile access in mind. Users who sign up for an account to learn Spanish or English can choose to read stories on preferred topics at easy or hard levels, though the software also adapts to learners' levels. Users can listen to the stories read aloud at regular or slow speeds, and follow the written texts at the same time. When reading or listening, learners can obtain immediate translations of words or phrases in a self-scaffolding manner, select words or phrases for inclusion in a personal flashcard glossary and prioritise them as desired, and answer comprehension quiz questions. In addition to these more automated functions, which lend themselves to use on a large scale, there are options for productive language practice. Users are able to participate in discussion forums about the stories they've read, interacting not only with other

Case Study 11   (Continued)

learners but with native speakers, if they so choose. These user communities, composed entirely of voluntary participants, have proven popular. Although the forums are currently text-based, there are plans to add audio and video channels in the future.

Nulu was born out of the experiences of one of its co-founders in teaching the English language over many years in a variety of cultural and educational contexts. Firstly, it aims to capture users' interest by providing a range of fresh and varied news items, so that they can choose topics which genuinely appeal to them. Secondly, it embeds recognised best practice in language learning, such as adaptive, spaced vocabulary review of the user-generated flashcard glossary. The overall aim is to create a language learning approach which is engaging, effective and, importantly, sustainable. Given that language learning is a long-term process, sustainability is key. Because mobile devices enable bite-sized learning anywhere and anytime, they help people fit it into their busy schedules, with episodic learning adding up over time into extended learning.

The key challenge has been to deliver an intuitive, personal learning experience. To date, testing of cultural appropriateness has not revealed a need to significantly vary material between the USA and Mexico, and local US and Latin American cultural content is made available in both language versions alongside more general international content. The personalisation, both manual and automatic, which is possible within the system can help tailor it to each individual's needs and wishes. The value of the software is evidenced both by its overall number of users as well as by positive reactions from educators who have reviewed it.

The key interviewee about this project was Eitan Geft (CEO of Nulu Languages, San Diego, USA), with additional input from Kate Donahue (Account Executive, Nulu Languages). For further information, see the *Nulu Languages* website (www.nulu.com), the *Nulu* Facebook page (www.facebook.com/MyNulu), or follow @MyNulu on Twitter.

There is a growing roll call of projects which connect in-class and out-of-class language and cultural learning in an integrated skills format. In many of these, recordings of students' real-world interactions provide user-generated content which feeds into classroom teaching. In a European Social Fund project in Denmark, for instance, learners of

Danish completed pre-activities in class to prepare them to carry out set tasks in their everyday working lives, such as conducting interviews or documenting health and safety signs (Gjedde & Bo-Kristensen, 2012). These were recorded on mobile phones in text, audio, image or video formats, before being uploaded to a server to be shared with the teacher and peers as the basis for post-activity discussion and reflection.

Other projects go a step further, with the use of location-aware mobile software. In the Language-learning Outside the Classroom with Handhelds (LOCH) project in Japan, learners of Japanese carried out authentic tasks around town, which required them to interact with native speakers while the teacher tracked their locations and provided guidance and support through PDAs (Ogata, 2011; Ogata et al., 2008). Students subsequently met in class to review material they had recorded on their mobile devices, discuss difficulties encountered, and reflect on strategies to accomplish their linguistic goals. Students found the LOCH system useful for learning local language and practising class-room learning, while teachers liked the fact that students were practising Japanese in real-world settings, and reported an increase in students' confidence in speaking. Similar ideas underpin the Singaporean learning trails project (see Case Study 14).

More fully automated approaches include the proposed Context-Aware Mobile Chinese Language Learning (CAMCLL) system, which will suggest sentences to scaffold the real-world Chinese language inter-actions of learners based on location, activity, time and learner level, linked back to each student's current course of study (Al-Mekhlafi et al., 2009). An analogous approach is seen in the European MASELTOV project (see Case Study 13), whose IMALL element is likely to be used in the future to enrich many situated language learning projects. The role of teachers varies in these kinds of learner-centred, context-aware, integrated skills initiatives. In LOCH and the Singaporean Heritage Trails project, teachers are central to the support and feedback phases. But the more automated the system, the more likely it is that teachers will be central to the initial design phase rather than the support and feed-back phases. Indeed, in years to come teachers may well find themselves increasingly called upon to fuse pedagogical and technological under-standings and become designers – of digital learning tasks and activities, and potentially of digital learning software itself – in order to expand the spectrum of MALL experiences, like those covered in this chapter, which are available to their students (see Chapter 7).

It's become very evident that digital tools can play an important role in supporting the development of language. But they can also play a role in the development of literacy generally, and digital literacies specifically. Just as it's becoming more and more difficult to separate the learning of different language areas and skills on mobile devices, it's becoming next to impossible to separate the learning of old and new literacies. Nor should we try. When using digital tools, traditional literacies and digital literacies go hand in hand, as we're about to see.

6
Teaching Literacy/ies with Mobile Devices

Literacy is fundamental to educational endeavours. All around the world, governments seek to improve it and development projects seek to spread it. But literacy long ago fractured into a plural concept. Well before the digital era, we started to hear about visual literacy, media literacy and information literacy. With the advent of digital technologies, these literacies have taken on added importance and new ones have begun to emerge. But it's unsettled terrain. Both technologies and literacies are continuing to shift in mutually constitutive ways.

In this chapter we'll take a journey through some of the more salient literacies of the digital era, including multimodal literacy, code literacy, information literacy, network literacy and intercultural literacy, and we'll eventually arrive at one of today's key emerging literacies: mobile literacy. But before we begin, we need to cast an eye over more traditional approaches to literacy.

Teaching the 2 Rs

In contexts where learners are taught their own language, it's common to speak of literacy development rather than language teaching. Generally this means an emphasis on two of the so-called 3 Rs, namely *Reading* and *(w)Riting,* which are often linked to the third, *(a)Rithmetic.* In the Pakistani Post-literacy project (see Case Study 3), for instance, girls learn to read and write in Urdu, as well as learning basic maths, with the newly learned language serving as a vehicle for the dissemination of health and other information. Meanwhile, in the Australian OLPC project (see Case Study 12), XO laptops are used in remote Indigenous communities to support students' literacy development, as well as supporting maths and other areas; here, literacy means the development of both the local Aboriginal language and Standard Australian English.

Thus, in many locations the use of mobile devices is not, in the first instance, about digital literacies – that is, the skills to effectively decode and encode meaning in digital channels – or the broad set of 21st century skills to which they can open the gates (see Chapter 2). In poor countries there is an average of only one book for every 19 children; and even in a developed country like the UK, a third of children don't have a single book at home (UNESCO, 2013b). But mobile phones are increasingly widely distributed in locations with few books and, sometimes, few qualified teachers. Unsurprisingly, it was agreed at the 2013 UNESCO Mobile Learning Week Symposium that mobile phones should be enlisted in the struggle against illiteracy. As Ronda Zelezny-Green indicates (see Vignette 9 below), there is a very strong argument for using mobile phones to teach literacy in Africa and other developing regions.

Vignette 9   Building more MALLs in Africa

Ronda Zelezny-Green, GSMA, UK

I have been involved in education projects in Africa for more than six years, but I remain surprised by the inexplicable dearth of MALL initiatives on the continent. While projects like the Jokko Initiative in Senegal have provided strong evidence of the literacy and language learning gains that can be made by people who participate in programmes that use mobile devices as teaching aids, these kinds of projects are often ended or significantly scaled back after just a few years instead of being replicated.

Many people mention that a book is a more durable and affordable technology to help promote literacy and language skills acquisition. Yet, in Africa books are perhaps even rarer than mobile phones. People cannot use something that is not there to begin with. The lack of content in local languages is another perennial issue that is in part being addressed by innovative offerings like Yoza, with its mobile phone stories in local languages and English, and Worldreader Mobile, which compresses books in both local and more commonly spoken languages for reading on basic mobile devices.

Cost, as ever, remains a challenge to building more MALLs in Africa. But one could argue for the investment given that literacy rates on the continent remain far below the rest of the world, while mobile device ownership continues to skyrocket. If a tool is already in the hands of the people (with growing access, especially through shared ownership), why not help them use the tool to achieve the lives that they desire?

I believe one of the greatest missed opportunities in education in the next decade could be ignoring the potential of mobile devices to address the scarcity of literacy-building opportunities, particularly for women and girls, in developing areas of the world. With a chance to build reading, writing and mobile literacies all at once, MALL initiatives present a powerful people-centered development mechanism.

▶ Further reading: Zelezny-Green (2011, 2013b).

Yet it's not only about traditional literacy skills. As Zelezny-Green points out, it's entirely possible to teach reading and writing in tandem with mobile and other digital literacies. This can be seen in both the Pakistani and Australian projects mentioned above: some Pakistani girls were able to move on to using computers within eight months; Australian Aboriginal children have been able to integrate text and multiple media to create digital stories and e-books. In reality, once mobile devices are introduced, it may be difficult *not* to teach digital literacies alongside traditional language and literacy.

In the developed world, there is much concern over what are seen as falling literacy standards, and much attention is paid to preparing students for standardised national and international exams which emphasise traditional skills. But at the same time, many policy and curriculum documents in the developed world – not to mention similar documents and more than a few project briefs in the developing world – now refer to the need to complement traditional language and literacy learning with a focus on digital literacies, often as part of a broader 21st century skills agenda, and sometimes with an emphasis on subsets of skills like multimodal literacy (Jewitt, 2008; NCTE, 2013; Selwyn, 2011). While the educational potential which exists at the intersection of new technologies and new literacies is greater in wealthier locations, the cases outlined here show just how much can be achieved in the developing world or among underserved populations in the developed world.

Teaching digital literacies

Nowadays, effective communication includes digital (self-)expression. In the developed world, and increasingly in the developing world, digital literacies are integral to social life, employment prospects and engaged citizenship (Dudeney et al., 2013). It's therefore vital that language and literacy teaching incorporates a range of literacies which go beyond the 2 Rs. Otherwise, we'll see a new inflection of the digital divide open up between those whose active language use is restricted to face-to-face and paper-based channels, and those who use language productively in the myriad digital channels which carry so many of today's communications and open up so many of today's personal, social, educational, economic and political opportunities.

There are many digital literacies. Some, like multimodal (or multimedia), information and intercultural literacy, are old literacies which have been thrust into new prominence. Some, like network literacy, have only come to our attention as shifting technological and social patterns have lent them greater everyday relevance. Some, like code and mobile literacy, have arisen only within the digital era. These literacies may be loosely grouped into four categories (see Figure 6.1). Some are associated with the communication of meaning through language and its supplementary channels, like the texting literacy needed to communicate in textspeak, or the hypertext literacy necessary to read (and write) online. Others are associated with finding, evaluating and

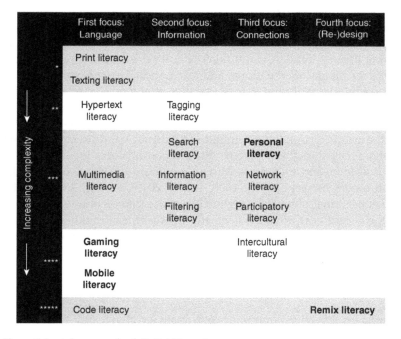

Figure 6.1   A framework of digital literacies.
Source: Dudeney et al. (2013), Table 1.1, p.6, reproduced by permission.

cataloguing information, like the search literacy needed to make effective use of search engines, or the tagging literacy necessary to build data trails. Some are associated with initiating, managing and leveraging connections, like the personal literacy needed to project an identity in digital networks, or the participatory literacy necessary to take part in collaborative digital endeavours. And finally there's remix literacy, arguably the hallmark literacy of our digital age. It is a macroliteracy which draws together multimodal and many other literacies, but it simultaneously stands apart from them as perhaps the ultimate realisation of the contemporary principle of redesign, as discussed below. Of course, there's a great deal of overlap between the four categories and between many of the literacies within them – with the latter being not so much separate skillsets as key points of emphasis in the broad landscape of digital literacies. But while they're all important in their own ways, some stand out as particularly crucial in the mobile era.

Multimodal literacy

More and more, full participation in contemporary social and working life demands multimodal literacy (Jewitt, 2008; Kalantzis & Cope, 2012; Takayoshi & Selfe, 2007). In recent years we've seen a dramatic cultural shift away from writing and towards the image, away from the book and towards the screen, and away from *telling the world* and towards *showing the world*, with a concomitant shift from a time-based logic to a space-based logic of representation (Kress, 2003). Digital technologies, which make it easy to create multimedia artefacts, have been a major catalyst for this shift (Takayoshi & Selfe, 2007). Texts, especially digital texts, no longer necessarily privilege writing. Instead, they're ever more multimodal, combining linguistic, visual, audio, gestural and spatial semiotic systems to produce meaning (Bull & Anstey, 2010). As Carey Jewitt (2005) explains:

> Screen-based texts are complex multimodal ensembles of image, sound, animated movement, and other modes of representation and communication. Writing is one mode in this ensemble and its meaning therefore needs to be understood in relation to the other modes it is nestled alongside. (p.316)

It's easy to assume that youth know how to handle multimedia texts, but the cohort of 'digital natives' is no more uniformly tech-savvy when it comes to multimodal practices than any other digital practices (see Chapter 2). Although they may have latent knowledge, most students require scaffolding and support to develop and extend their skills (Miller & McVee, 2012; Mills, 2010). Specifically, they need guidance in interpreting multimodal texts, as they develop an explicit understanding of how each mode represents meaning differently, how an overall meaning can be constructed from an ensemble of various modes, and how to interact with, respond to and ultimately critique these texts and their meanings. This is more demanding than it seems. Because multimodal texts are not linear or closed in the way of many traditional written texts, they may allow readers to find multiple entry points and follow multiple pathways, and may encourage them to adopt multiple interpretations (Jewitt, 2005, 2008). And, of course, students also need to learn how to fashion their own multimodal texts and disseminate them, whether through social media or social networking platforms, or even by building them into AR apps or mixed reality games. Literacy may be seen as a process of design, or indeed redesign, linked to agency and identity (Jewitt, 2008; Kalantzis & Cope, 2012; Kress, 2010). In a digital context one of the most obvious forms of redesign is remix, which involves taking pre-existing cultural artefacts and reworking them to create new meanings (Dudeney et al., 2013). In some ways this is the culmination of multimodal digital potential, and holds up a mirror to contemporary culture.

Among underresourced populations, affordable mobile devices are making multimedia materials much more available, whether via SD cards inserted into mobile phones connected to audio speakers or microprojectors (see Case Studies 16 & 17), or via XO laptops which encourage students not only to consume but to create multimodally (see Case Study 12). In much of the developed world, multimodal literacy was already being explored by teachers and students in the desktop era. Naturally, larger screens, physical keyboards and more powerful software have some advantages when it comes to manipulating multimedia materials. Mobile devices, on the other hand, have advantages when it comes to capturing and sharing media, while a new generation of smart devices has opened up accessible template-based multimodal creation options (see Chapter 4). As Grace Oakley points out (see Vignette 10 below), devices like iPads can play a major role in promoting multimodal literacy, with special benefits for young learners.

Vignette 10 Multimodal texts for literacy learning

Grace Oakley, The University of Western Australia

Language and literacy learning is changing every day as teachers and students find new ways of using mobile technologies, inside and outside the classroom. For quite some time now, students have had access to multimodal texts on the internet but have not had the chance to easily create them – but tablets like the iPad are changing this, even for children in their preschool years. In research I have conducted with colleagues, we have seen young children, including kindergarten children, easily creating multimodal stories using simple apps such as My Story and Play School Art Maker. Here, they can combine spoken and written text, images and animations to create multimodal stories. Text creation is the flip side of text comprehension so, although much more research is needed, any increase in children's multimodal text creation should theoretically result in improved comprehension of multimodal texts and how they work.

The creation of photomontages using apps like iMovie for iPads or Movie Studio for Android tablets is another addition to children's literacy repertoire, enabling multiple modes of knowledge representation and communication. We have seen older children build augmented reality into their multimodal storytelling through the use of apps like Aurasma. With such apps, students can create exciting animated pop-up books, adding a completely new layer of meaning to texts. There are also indications that creating multimodal texts using mobile technologies can be very engaging – we have seen this, for example, with Australian Aboriginal children in an outback school where the use of iPads transformed their engagement in writing tasks.

These current uses of mobile technology are, I suspect, the tip of the iceberg in terms of literacy transformation – the purposes of texts and thus the variety of text types will continue to change as technology opens up new possibilities.

▶ Further reading: Oakley et al. (2012); Pegrum et al. (2013).

The importance of multimodal literacy is becoming more recognised in mainstream education, especially in the developed world (Jewitt, 2008; NCTE, 2005, 2013), though there remains some tension with traditional assessments (Jewitt, 2005; Kalantzis & Cope, 2012). It's high time to foreground multimodality in L2 teaching as well, both in CALL and MALL (Gonglewski & DuBravac, 2006; Lotherington & Jenson, 2011). Students need to practise interpreting language input embedded in multimodal ensembles, from advertisements to instructions. They need to practise embedding their own language output in such ensembles, from infographics to slideshows, as they learn how to convey their meanings appropriately to their target audiences. And they need to practise negotiating meaning in multimodal interchanges, whether through social networking conversations or social media curation. Many integrated skills and, especially, geoaware mobile initiatives provide relevant kinds of multimodal practice (see Chapter 5).

Multimodal materials may be extremely important in multicultural settings, as Pamela Takayoshi and Cynthia Selfe (2007) indicate: 'In internationally networked digital environments, texts must be able to carry meaning across geo-political, linguistic, and cultural borders, and so texts must take advantage of multiple semiotic channels' (p.2). On the other hand, the meanings of images, sounds and gestures vary across social and cultural contexts. The appropriate design and redesign of multimodal materials therefore depends very much on social and cultural knowledge, making a sociocultural approach essential. Since language learners who are exploring multimodality will always face additional burdens compared to proficient target language speakers – burdens, that is, of limited linguistic competence and sociocultural understanding – they will require considerable support as teachers introduce them to multimodal L2 materials and, over time, help them to use their newly acquired language to communicate their ideas and their identities multimodally.

Code literacy

Nowadays, proficiency in human language needs to be complemented by proficiency in computer language. We don't all have to become programmers, but we all need a basic understanding of how computers and computer code work, and how they shape what we read and what we write. On the one hand, as Clay Johnson (2011) points out, the programmers at Apple, Facebook, Google and Microsoft 'build the lenses that the rest of us look through to get our information' (Kindle location 3200). On the other, they also build the channels and templates through which we are obliged to express ourselves – unless we have the ability to read and modify the code underpinning those channels and templates, or, better still, build our own websites and our own apps (Abelson, 2011; Prensky, 2012a). Without some level of code literacy, our whole literacy skillset, and the agency we can exercise through it, is potentially compromised (Dudeney et al., 2013). Arguably, the ability to build apps will become a skill of special importance in the mobile-dependent developing world.

While this area is not yet well-established, a number of language learning initiatives show that it's feasible to acquire at least some elements of code literacy and/or related skills alongside more traditional literacy skills. One example is the creation of user-generated AR trails by collaborative teacher-student teams in Singapore (see Case Study 14); a second is the achievement by students of XO-Champion and XO-Mechanic certifications in the OLPC Australia project (see Case Study 12 below). While these don't involve programming as such, they represent forays in the direction of more technological literacies. In fact, OLPC Australia provides a clear illustration of how digital education projects can integrate the old and the new to the benefit of underserved populations. This can be seen in the way it combines the teaching of standard language with new literacies, including multimodal and technological literacies, as well as numeracy and other skills.

Case Study 12   Laptops for literacy in Australia (OLPC Project)

Figure 6.2 The OLPC Australia project at a remote Indigenous school, Western Australia. © Rangan Srikhanta/OLPC Australia, reproduced by permission.

Case Study 12   (Continued)

Project: OLPC (One Laptop Per Child) Australia.
Focus: Various, notably literacy (including digital literacies) & numeracy development.
Languages: Standard Australian English & Aboriginal languages.
Level: Primary school (with students aged approx. 6–13).
Format: Various activity apps, many productive & generative in nature, running in the open source Sugar desktop environment.
Hardware: Sets of XO laptops (small, robust, low-power laptops) &, more recently, XO-duos (hybrid laptop-tablet devices) are purchased by schools for use in a 1:1 model.
Key partners: Australian Federal Government (financial supporter); Commonwealth Bank, Droga5, News Limited, Salesforce & Telstra (corporate sponsors); OLPC Australia (hardware, software & training provider).
Timeline: 2008 – ongoing.
Location: Australia.
Participants: The focus is on disadvantaged schools. By mid-2013, the programme involved 7,430 XOs in 114 schools around Australia, most rural or remote & many with a high proportion of Indigenous students. By the end of 2013, with the government-supported deployment of 50,000 additional XOs, the number of schools is set to increase to around 600, including some in metropolitan areas, with around 90% of new schools receiving XO-duos.
Funding model: The programme is now subsidised by the Australian Federal Government, with schools paying AUD $100 (approx. US $95) per XO device.

While OLPC is an international movement, there is no overarching organisation, which has allowed OLPC Australia to forge its own pathway. XO devices are available to any Australian schools classified as disadvantaged (including National Partnership schools and those with lower rankings on the Index of Community Socio-Educational Advantage, or ICSEA). They are provided on a classroom-by-classroom basis after school principals have bought into the 1:1 programme at a cost of $100 per device, and the relevant class teachers have each completed 15 hours of online training.

XOs are borderline mobile devices, lacking the greater mobility of smaller smartphones or tablets, though the newer XO-duos share some features of tablets. However, unlike smartphones or tablets, XOs have not been repurposed for education but are designed specifically for learning. Thanks to preloaded apps and peer-to-peer connections, students can work and collaborate on them even when an internet connection is unavailable or unreliable. They are also very robust, with screens that can be read in sunlight.

The pedagogical advantages are elucidated in case studies reported at *One News*, where, amongst other things, teachers describe using XOs to support students in the learning of Aboriginal languages as well as Standard Australian English, and to differentiate their teaching as they help students with a variety of disabilities and special needs. Rather than providing consumption or tutorial apps, XOs are largely equipped with productive and generic apps that allow students and teachers to collaboratively create content, with students frequently engaging in peer sharing and support. Teachers report using the devices for everything from consolidating spelling to 'tak[ing] narrative writing to another level' (Collinsville, North Queensland Case Study). There is a strong emphasis on the integration of print literacy with multimodal literacy in digital storytelling and e-book initiatives. Codeswitching between Aboriginal languages and Standard Australian English is in evidence in some of these digital tasks.

Logistical challenges have included maintenance and support of the devices in the context of the high teacher turnover in rural and remote communities. This has been rather spectacularly turned into an advantage by training a number of interested students in the requisite skills to diagnose, repair and rebuild computers, if necessary using the spare parts shipped along with the class sets. The XO-Champion and XO-Mechanic certifications recognise these students' growing hardware and software skills, along with related life skills like responsibility and customer service, and signal their readiness to support peers and indeed teachers. By mid-2013, 41 students had been certified as XO-Mechanics. An XO-Bots robotics programme being developed with Lego will allow children to acquire even more sophisticated technological literacies.

Overall, the greatest success has perhaps been in developing the capacity of both teachers and students so that they can take over the implementation of the project in their own classes and schools, with OLPC Australia in a facilitation role. It is this success that the Australian Federal Government

Information literacy

In our era, '[f]inding information rather than possessing it or knowing it becomes the defining characteristic of learning generally and of mobile learning especially' (Traxler, 2007). The problem is that digital information has few gatekeepers. Within broad social and educational limits, and subject to the affordability and affordances of their devices, anyone can say anything in any mode on any platform. The onus is on all of us to act as our own gatekeepers, critically evaluating whatever comes our way. We often imagine that young people are already information literate, but research shows that many lack the skills to conduct effective web searches (Livingstone, 2009; Weigel et al., 2009) and evaluate online content (Lumley & Mendelovits, 2012). Given the importance of effective search and evaluation, it's essential to help students develop information literacy or, as it's sometimes called, critical literacy. This is perhaps even more of an issue in developing contexts, where mobile users may be receiving digital information and communication (and, very likely, advertising) for the first time in their lives. It's certainly an issue for learners who may have a limited command of the language needed for searches, and of the linguistic skills and sociocultural understanding needed to critique search results.

Exercising information literacy involves at least four interlinked strategies: asking critical questions about each source of information or communication (who wrote this SMS or made this video, and why?); comparing each source to our existing baseline of knowledge (does it make sense in light of what I already know?); triangulating, or comparing, sources where our baseline of knowledge is inadequate (does a given source agree with other sources I can find?); and tracking the development of information over time (has it been changed or updated, by whom, and why?) (Dudeney et al., 2013). These questions are relevant to students whenever they consume, analyse or synthesise information (as in content or communication MALL), and they're relevant to their audiences whenever they produce, publish or disseminate it (as in creation or, again, communication MALL). This can be explicitly flagged up in language tasks until, in time, a critical attitude to information and communication becomes second nature to learners.

But information literacy is slippery when digital materials are constantly in flux, and the latest version of a news story or the newest iteration of an app is never more than provisional. It's made still more slippery by search engines which return ever more personalised results, and news feeds which present ever more narrowly focused selections of updates, tailored to each of us on the basis of information tracked or inferred about us (Pariser, 2011). The scale of the issue is evident if we consider that Google, which leads search engine personalisation, is used for close to 95% of mobile searches (gs.statcounter.com); and Facebook, which leads news feed personalisation, dominates mobile social networking. Not only do students need to know how to search for and critique digital content, they also need strategies for breaking out of a hyperpersonalised informational space to explore ideas and views which don't automatically surface in their search results or news feeds. Strong teacherly guidance is needed on how students can expand their range of sources and resources as they curate content within their PLEs and share it within their PLNs. Their PLNs, however, might hold part of the answer.

Network literacy

'[P]eople can be smarter because they have access to networked intelligence, whether it is technologically or socially distributed, or both', suggests Nicholas Burbules (2009, p.17). As our mobile devices increasingly augment our brains and senses, our knowledge is becoming more widely distributed, we ourselves are becoming 'the sum of our connections and relationships' (Khanna & Khanna, 2012, Kindle location 865), and network literacy is becoming indispensable (Pegrum, 2010; Rainie & Wellman, 2012; Rheingold, 2012). Network literacy involves, firstly, the ability to use trusted digital networks as informational filters to decrease the volume and increase the relevance of the material we encounter online, effectively providing a first level of curation before it even reaches us. To avoid overly narrow curation – such as that automatically performed by search engines and social networks – we need to ensure our networks, or PLNs, are both broad and diverse (Dudeney et al., 2013). Students will need guidance here; the luckiest among them will have teachers who model the value of rich, multilingual, multicultural PLNs as platforms for lifelong learning. Secondly, network literacy involves the ability to use digital networks to share and debate ideas, build collaboration and support, and even establish a reputation to promote further online engagement. Language learning initiatives which involve students communicating through digital social networks or social media platforms (typically in creation and, even more so, communication MALL) provide fertile ground for drawing students' attention to networking practices and possibilities.

Today's digital divide is, or will become, a networking divide (Pegrum, 2010; Rainie & Wellman, 2012). Digital networks are already playing an ever greater role in informal everyday learning, which can feed into formal learning through mechanisms like PLEs in some settings, but may partly or wholly substitute for formal learning in other settings (Pimmer et al., 2012). While more and more people are gaining at least some access to the global space of flows through their mobile devices, those who are unable to leverage their digital networks to learn and share – as in George Siemens' theory of connectivism – will remain peripheral to those networks and those flows (Pegrum, 2010). As Christakis and Fowler (2009) write: 'This is the real digital divide. Network inequality creates and reinforces inequality of opportunity' (p.301). But it's a divide we can start bridging by teaching digital literacies alongside language and traditional literacy skills.

From intercultural competence to intercultural literacy

Language teaching has long extended its remit beyond language and literacy to take in culture. In the communicative era, students learned about culture in addition to learning a language, with the implicit but almost unattainable goal of eventually assimilating into a target linguaculture. The shift towards a sociocultural perspective brought with it the more realisable goal of *intercultural communicative competence* (Byram, 1997). Here, the learner carves out a 'third place' (Kramsch, 1993) – or finds they have entered a 'third space' (Bhabha, 1994) – between cultures, from where they can negotiate and mediate cultural differences as they explore and develop their own identities (Pegrum, 2008). The third space is not necessarily a comfortable place to be, but it does present rich opportunities: students may learn as much about themselves and their own culture(s) as about any target culture. Of course, opportunities for third space learning occur not only in cultural encounters abroad, but in interactions with migrants and tourists within one's own culture, and in multicultural online spaces.

With growing interest in multiple literacies, and in the wake of debates around cultural literacy, the term *intercultural literacy* has also come into use. As Mark Heyward (2002) explains in a well-known early account:

> The interculturally literate person...possesses the understandings, competencies, attitudes and identities necessary for successful living and working in a cross-cultural or pluralist setting. He or she has the background required effectively to 'read' a second culture, to interpret its symbols and negotiate its meanings in a practical day-to-day context. (p.10)

In a later definition which situates intercultural literacy within a larger framework of digital literacies (see Figure 6.1), Dudeney et al. (2013) describe it as: 'the ability to interpret documents and artefacts from a range of cultural contexts, as well as to effectively communicate messages and interact constructively with interlocutors across different cultural contexts' (p.35). Clearly, the concept of intercultural literacy has much in common with intercultural competence. Linking it with digital literacies reminds us that as digital technologies bring disparate cultures into ever closer contact, learning to mediate between and among shifting cultural constellations is a skill of growing importance. It signals, moreover, that the development of intercultural literacy can be supported and furthered within digital networks.

There were and are many telecollaboration projects using desktop computers, where students from different countries engage in online interaction or co-operate on joint projects. In the process, there is the potential to develop intercultural competence/literacy. While much can be learned from these projects – including about the danger of failure if they are not carefully prepared and scaffolded (Lamy & Goodfellow, 2010; O'Dowd & Ritter, 2006) – there is a rather more elongated spectrum of possibilities with mobile devices.

Low-end mobile devices can give access to multimedia cultural resources, possibly preloaded onto SD cards, which may go beyond anything previously available to students who've never had the chance to travel outside their own cultures. If well-designed, these may seed understandings, challenge perceptions and stimulate discussions. Going a step further, most feature phones can be used to capture and share culturally revealing moments in everyday life. In one South African-US cross-cultural (though not cross-linguistic) initiative, students used mobile phones to document aspects of their daily lives, built these into multimedia vignettes, and shared and discussed them on a blogging platform (Botha et al., 2011). As they interacted around this content, they developed an understanding of each other's cultures (and subcultures) and came to see, above all, how much they had in common. In a project at Zayed University in the UAE, Emirati students used mobile phones to take photos of their everyday lives to inform and stimulate discussion with new foreign staff (Palfreyman, 2012). Students gained language practice, developed cultural and intercultural awareness as they responded to staff understandings and misunderstandings, and learned to express aspects of their identities for this audience. Staff found their preconceptions challenged, developed their own cultural and intercultural awareness, and gained a much better understanding of how to link their teaching to their students' lives.

High-end mobile devices are ideal tools for informing and supporting intercultural encounters, as well as providing a platform for recording, reflecting on and sharing those encounters. Students can learn about another culture in the context of a local space of places (say, on a visit to a foreign city or even an ethnic neighbourhood in their own city) while remaining anchored in the global space of flows where they have access to explanatory content, supportive networks and, potentially, educational prompts to foster the noticing of language and culture. Thus, mobile devices can become 'a platform for reflecting on how we inhabit and embody the languages we learn' (Ros i Solé et al., 2010, p.51), and indeed how we inhabit, and develop an identity in, a third space between linguacultures. Like telecollaboration projects, such learning experiences need careful design. They also demand from students a level of technological and social readiness which is only now becoming commonplace, as a few pioneering academics have discovered.

In a 2006 mobile blogging project at the Norwegian University of Science & Technology, Norwegian students of French who travelled to Caen, France, were provided with a platform for interacting with classmates who remained in Trondheim, Norway (Petersen et al., 2008). The travellers were to share key linguistic and cultural experiences and insights with those at home, with the latter commenting as well as updating the former on events in Norway. The level of student contributions ultimately proved disappointing, partly due to a lack of a sense of community among the students, partly due to reluctance to publish in a foreign language, and partly due to the fact that the mindset of recording and sharing everyday experiences was not yet well-established (Sobah Abbas Petersen, personal interview, March 2013). A 2007 Spanish mobile blogging project at the Open University (OU), UK, was also felt to be ahead of its time in spite of encouraging student feedback, as explained by Anna Comas-Quinn and Raquel Mardomingo (see Vignette 11 below). But both of these projects broke new ground, pointing to the promise of mobile devices for establishing user-generated learning contexts in the real world, and for sharing user-generated records and reflections as a basis for intercultural learning.

Vignette 11 Mobile intercultural blogging

Anna Comas-Quinn & Raquel Mardomingo, The Open University, UK

The OU Spanish blogging project, in which upper intermediate students of Spanish collected and reflected on their intercultural experiences on a communal blog, was first piloted during students' residential week abroad in 2007. It was later extended to encompass students' other intercultural experiences, both at home (such as their encounters with Spanish speakers, events or cultural artefacts) and abroad (such as leisure travel or living abroad). Despite positive student reactions, the project was subsequently discontinued for organisational reasons, although the concept has been adapted to other courses as diverse as linguistics, geology and a teacher training programme in Africa.

In many ways the project was ahead of its time. Both technology and habits have now moved on: on the one hand, most students now have mobile phones, and key software like Google Maps is accessible and user-friendly; on the other hand, people are now in the habit of taking photos and uploading, commenting on and sharing them on platforms like Facebook. Indeed, this kind of activity has become part of the popular imaginary.

Vignette 11   (Continued)

There is considerable scope for a crossover between mobile devices and intercultural competence. In the current context, mobile devices have great potential to capture and thus facilitate exploration of those brief moments of culture shock where your awareness is heightened and you find yourself in a state of flux about your own cultural identity. Asking students to harvest their real experiences in a mobile blogging project represents a move away from a teacher-led or materials-led process. Instead, students have the autonomy and agency to create content which can be shared with peers and teachers, and used to generate questions which can be answered collaboratively.

▶ Further reading: Comas-Quinn et al. (2009); Comas-Quinn & Mardomingo (2012).

If we jump forward a few years to the SIMOLA project (see Case Study 1), which started in 2010, it's evident that everyday experience with mobile social networking and social media has shifted students' mindsets and practices enough to make this kind of project very viable. And while SIMOLA's focus is on language, it's striking how often cultural elements are foregrounded in students' records of language-in-action in real-world contexts.

Indeed, it's difficult to separate language and culture in situated learning projects. The MASELTOV project (see Case Study 13 below) meshes together a number of elements supporting the linguistic, cultural and social integration of migrants into European countries. Context-aware AR software is designed to offer contextually appropriate linguistic content in push mode, simultaneously helping develop users' pragmatic and cultural competence. Like the earlier AMbient Intelligence as a Compelling Instructional Tool for Interlinguistic And intercultural Skills (AMICITIAS, or AMI for short) project in Europe, which also sought to develop both linguistic and intercultural competence (Robison, 2012), MASELTOV specifically aims to foster real-world interactions outside the software by setting carefully structured tasks. Learners are invited to record their interactions as they carry out suggested tasks, with the aim of having them evaluated not just linguistically but for overall effectiveness, once again potentially highlighting pragmatic and

Case Study 13   Persuasive mobile in Europe (MASELTOV Project)

Figure 6.3   Using MASELTOV in the street. © Peter Ramspacher/Joanneum Research, Graz, reproduced by permission.

Project:	MASELTOV (partial acronym for Mobile Assistance for Social Inclusion & Empowerment of Immigrants with Persuasive Learning Technologies & Social Network Services).
Languages:	English, German & Spanish. More may be added in the future.
Focus:	Language learning, cultural learning & social integration.
Level:	Beginners, with potential for progress to higher levels.
Format:	All-in-one Android app which functions as an integrated portal to a range of learning, assistance & social integration options. After testing, it will be available in Google Play, & may also be integrated into services developed by the business partners.
Hardware:	Users supply their own Android smartphones or tablets in a BYOD model.
Key partners:	European Commission (funding provider); Joanneum Research, Austria, Centre for Usability Research & Engineering, Austria, Athens Information Technology, Greece, Universitat Oberta de Catalunya, Spain,

Case Study 13 (Continued)

	The Open University, UK, Coventry University, UK, Czech Technical University, Czech Republic, & University of Applied Sciences FH Joanneum, Austria (research partners); busuu.com, UK, Fluidtime Data Service, Austria, & Telecom Italia, Italy (business partners); Fundación Desarrollo Sostenido, Spain, Migrants Resource Centre, UK, & Verein DANAIDA, Austria (NGO partners).
Timeline:	2012–2014.
Location:	The three demonstrator cities are Vienna, Madrid & London. Turin is under consideration as a fourth city.
Participants:	The current focus is on Turkish migrants learning German in Vienna; Arabic & Latin American migrants in Madrid, with the former learning Spanish & the latter learning more about the culture; as well as Arabic & Latin American migrants learning English in London. In 2012, participants contributed to the development of a user-centred design through focus groups & interviews. In 2013–2014, they will be involved in usability testing.
Funding model:	The project is funded by the European Commission through an eInclusion grant. Users supply their own devices. The app will be available from Google Play in a freemium model (with a free basic version & a paid premium version).

MASELTOV is one of three initiatives clustered under the overarching EU *Digital Games for Empowerment and Inclusion (DGEI)* project. With 85% of EU population growth now derived from migration, MASELTOV is designed to support the linguistic, cultural and social integration of immigrants. The name of the project is a partial acronym linked to the Yiddish phrase 'mazel tov', meaning 'good luck' or 'congratulations', to symbolise the bridging of cultures. Given a high level of smartphone ownership amongst migrants, MASELTOV takes the form of an app, which is currently in development and testing.

MASELTOV consists of a number of interrelated strands tied together by a *recommender system* and an *AR* (or mixed reality) *game*. Language learning is provided through lessons designed for immigrants' needs by the busuu service (www.busuu.com); these incorporate the full spectrum of learning activities from automated tutorial tasks through to live communication with native speakers. Language assistance is provided through a 'text lens' optical character recognition service, which scans text, recognises it, and provides a translation and/or makes links to relevant language being covered in lessons. Both language and cultural assistance are provided through a context-aware recommender system which offers pertinent language or information; for example, on a visit to a medical centre, a user might be presented with key expressions to use with a doctor, foregrounding not only lexis but pragmatics. Support for social integration is provided by a 'geosocial radar', which allows a user to call volunteers (identified and approved by NGOs and able to be rated by users) whose profiles indicate relevant linguistic and content expertise, and who are physically nearby. For example, a Turkish migrant who needs help with transport options in Vienna can call a Turkish-speaking volunteer with knowledge of the local underground system, thus obtaining key information while potentially also practising the target language and beginning to forge social links with local citizens.

In the AR game, a friendly avatar encourages users (and ideally persuades them, hence the project catchphrase 'persuasive assistance') to actively practise language and build familiarity with the local area and culture to acquire gaming points. Based on the user's language development, the abovementioned recommender system might suggest that they visit an office to obtain particular information; or when it detects that the user is near the railway station, it might suggest that they go there and complete a task. Conversations could be recorded and, using sophisticated IMALL software currently under development, automatically analysed to offer feedback not just on vocabulary or grammar but on the effectiveness of the interaction (including, for example, an assessment of underlying emotions, stress levels and even eye contact).

Key challenges have included ensuring migrants' input into app design, and ethical issues around privacy and surveillance of pedestrians' trajectories. Work is continuing on how to evaluate the benefits of the project. Linguistic progress indicators are still in development. More broadly, the project is studying how participants evolve over time, not just linguistically, but in terms of adjustment to the local culture and interaction with local citizens, with whom cultural exchanges should ideally be bi- or multidirectional.

MASELTOV's combination of cutting-edge technology (like AR and automated speech processing) with social networking opportunities

Case Study 13   (Continued)

(through the geosocial radar) holds considerable promise. It fuses a high level of automated personalisation (such as in the recommender system) with the option for deliberate personalisation (such as in the choice of crowdsourced native speaker chat partners or volunteer contacts) to produce an individually tailored, context-sensitive, and yet still scalable learning tool.

The key interviewee about this project was Lucas Paletta (R&D Project Manager, Joanneum Research, Graz, & Project Co-ordinator, MASELTOV). For further information, see the *MASELTOV* website (www.maseltov.eu), the *MASELTOV.EU* Facebook page (www.facebook.com/MASELTOV.EU), or follow @MASELTOV_EU on Twitter.

cultural competence. Significantly, the social contacts which MASELTOV helps users establish are predicated on the idea of two-way cultural exchanges, where both locals and immigrants learn about each other's cultures. Everyone thus becomes a teacher and a learner in the process of developing intercultural literacy.

Mobile literacy in a mixed reality

In the developed world, the desktop era is fading into the mobile era. In the developing world, an unconnected era is, similarly, morphing into a mobile era. Naturally, the affordances of the tools we have to hand impact on the sophistication of the literacies they engender and eventually require, especially as we move in an AR direction. But the effects of mobile technologies, and the need for mobile literacy, are felt everywhere.

At one end of the scale, with SMS available on even the most basic phones, texting literacy may acquire a heightened salience globally. With feature phones, there is likely to be an increased need for processing multimodal texts (supplied perhaps on SD cards in the absence of reliable networks), for evaluating information and communication (which may be pushed to users by mobile operators, advertisers and a range of content providers), and for networking to filter and share information (which can occur through SMS, email or Facebook Zero, which works on a similar principle to Wikipedia Zero, where other options aren't accessible). Mobile literacy, even at its simplest, is a macroliteracy which comprises elements of multimodal, information and network literacy. It is essential not only for learning but for everyday life in the mobile era.

At the other end of the scale, with smart devices, 3G and 4G connectivity, and web or native apps, mobile literacy takes on even greater significance as a skillset for navigating the mixed reality now emerging at the intersection of the virtual and the real. Multimodal literacy is an absolute must when the real world is tagged with text, image, audio and video annotations. Information literacy is a must when data is pushed at us, or pulled by us, through AR interfaces. Network literacy is a must when our social, educational and professional networks hover literally before our eyes, filtering and supplementing what we learn, and sharing and discussing what we do. Intercultural literacy is a must when AR apps invite us to explore multiple cultures and mediate our encounters with otherness. And code literacy is a must when we seek greater understanding of, and finer control over, the potential of AR. Mobile literacy, at its most sophisticated, is a macroliteracy fashioned from a complex constellation of digital literacies which are important for, and developed through, our use of mobile tools. As AR interfaces penetrate day-to-day reality more often for more people in more contexts, this skillset will become just as vital as basic mobile literacy both for learning and for everyday life.

No matter where we find ourselves, then, mobile literacy matters. And, with the spread of AR, it will matter more and more. It's been suggested that mobile literacy is not necessarily a naturally acquired skillset, but may require explicit development (Ng, 2011; Parry, 2011). Fortunately, like other digital literacies, it lends itself to development alongside language and more traditional literacy skills. Indeed, some of today's most exciting potential resides in teaching language in an integrated skills format through context-sensitive AR software, while simultaneously sharpening students' mobile literacy. Because it's a macroliteracy, developing mobile literacy entails developing all of the other literacies that underpin it.

The Heritage Trails project in Singapore (see Case Study 14 below) demonstrates exactly how more conventional language and literacy skills can be developed alongside 21st century skills and digital literacies, including mobile literacy and the specific literacies of which it is comprised – right down to an element of code literacy, though without a requirement for programming knowledge. Like the European

Case Study 14 Augmented reality learning trails in Singapore (Heritage Trails Project)

Figure 6.4 Mandarin version of Singapore River Heritage Trail. © LDR Pte Ltd, reproduced by permission.

Project:	Heritage Trails.
Languages:	English, Chinese (Mandarin) & Tamil.
Focus:	Inquiry-based learning integrated with language & literacy, 21st century skills & digital literacies, extensible to other areas.
Level:	All levels from primary school to junior college, with most trails available in primary & secondary school versions.
Format:	35 AR Heritage Trails, part of a larger collection of over 75 interactive mobile learning trails, which digitally enhance real-world locations with information & tasks. Trails are created with the Learning-On-The-Move (LOTM) rapid authoring tool & accessed by users in the form of native Android or iOS apps.
Hardware:	Students may be loaned Samsung Galaxy Note tablets (which run on the Android OS) preloaded with apps, or may use other Android or iOS devices which are supplied by schools or individually owned.
Key partners:	Infocomm Development Authority [IDA] of Singapore (grant provider for tool development); MOE, Singapore

	(provider of funding & Heritage Trails content, & supporter of schools deployment & teacher training); LDR (developer of LOTM tool & trails, provider of support & teacher training); Agency for Science, Technology & Research [A*STAR], Singapore (provider of additional technology).
Timeline:	2008 – ongoing.
Location:	Singapore.
Participants:	By March 2013, more than 80,000 participants had experienced an interactive mobile learning trail, with all 300,000 primary & secondary school students in Singapore expected to participate in Heritage Trails in due course.
Funding model:	The project was funded by an initial grant from IDA & a contract from the MOE. Participants may be loaned tablets or may use their schools' or their own devices. A sample app, *Battle for Singapore,* is available as a free download from iTunes.

With the aid of a grant from IDA, LDR Pte Ltd developed a rapid authoring tool, LOTM, to create AR mobile learning trails based on a combination of GPS (geofencing), Bluetooth and image recognition technology. These trails can be converted into native apps for downloading to Android or iOS devices. In collaboration with the Singaporean MOE, 35 Heritage Trails were then created to run on sets of Samsung Galaxy Note tablets, which use the Android OS.

The Heritage Trails promote inquiry-based, media-rich, collaborative, situated learning experiences in which students can find out about their environment and heritage, while practising language and literacy as well as 21st century skills and digital literacies. The trails function something like sophisticated treasure hunts, with new instructions released as students complete tasks. From a central position, teachers can track students' progress, locations, activity results and multimedia submissions, re-entering their students' learning spaces at appropriate moments to scaffold their understanding. In surveys conducted with 1170 students in January–March 2013, 75% agreed or strongly agreed that the Heritage Trails helped them understand the topics they had learned about in social studies classes; 77% stated that they could participate actively; and an overwhelming 95% preferred the AR trails to pen-and-paper trails.

Case Study 14   (Continued)

With students typically working in pairs, contextually appropriate, meaningful language use is paramount: in conversations about the tasks; in reading the texts and listening to the videos which are triggered by GPS locations and pushed to the devices; in reading neighbourhood signs or interviewing local people to acquire information; in responding to quiz questions; in creating the required multimedia artefacts, such as video re-enactments of historical events; in collecting and summarising ideas to answer open-ended questions; and in responding to peers' shared submissions. All the trails were originally in English. However, with the Singaporean government keen for the country's diverse ethnic groups to maintain their linguistic heritage, two trails, including the Singapore River Trail (see Figure 6.4), were converted into Mandarin in 2012, and the first Tamil trail was released in 2013. A bilingual English–Mandarin school trail was also launched in 2013, but in fact all of the trails may already involve multiple languages: though questions are typically posed in one language, students in ethnic neighbourhoods like Chinatown, Little India or Kampong Glam may need to shift between their main language(s) and Mandarin, Hokkien, Tamil, Punjabi, Malay or other languages required to communicate with locals. In some cases they may need to co-operate with classmates with a range of mother tongues and language competencies, thus learning through linguistic and cross-cultural collaboration.

The project has faced both technological and human challenges. In a fast-moving environment, smaller technology companies like LDR benefit enormously from being part of an ecology of institutions, whether public or private, which can help them to keep up with the latest educational and technological developments, as well as providing financial support. Infrastructure remains an issue, even in highly wired Singapore, with the 3G/4G networks in central city areas becoming congested under the data load, which is an important reason for using native apps rather than web apps requiring constant internet connectivity. Singapore has one of the highest smartphone penetration rates in the world, so users are technologically well-prepared, but project developers have noted that there is a need for a shift of mindset to allow mobile devices to be seen not just as entertainment or communication tools, but learning devices.

The LOTM tool is contributing in its own way to this shift. Teachers are being trained to create their own customised trails, with more than 125 teachers having already attended a workshop on developing mother tongue, maths, science, geography, and school orientation trails for their students. This is done by dragging/dropping and cutting/pasting within the LOTM tool, without the need for programming knowledge. The trails are then converted into native apps – often iOS apps, if they are to be accessed on school devices like iPads. Recently, collaborative teacher–student teams from different schools took part in a competition to create zoo trails. Perhaps the greatest success of the project to date is the finding that user-generated trails are not only possible, but successful, and give users a much greater sense of ownership. The LOTM tool achieved wider recognition with a Best Singapore Infocomm Technology Federation Award (Mobile App category) and a Best Asia Pacific ICT Award (E-learning category) in 2012, and there is growing corporate interest in customised learning trails. As the next stage of technological development moves the trails further in an AR direction, the appeal of user-generated trails will be an important feature on which to build.

The key interviewee about this project was Png Bee Hin (CEO of LDR, Singapore). For further information, see the *LDR* website (www.ldr.sg) and the *LDR Pte Ltd* Facebook page (www.facebook.com/LDR.pteltd), watch the *Learning-On-The-Move (LOTM) Tool by LDR Pte Ltd* YouTube video (www.youtube.com/watch?v=o6jx8P4WNuA), or download the *Battle for Singapore* app from iTunes (itunes.apple.com/app/id498223166).

MASELTOV initiative (see Case Study 13), this project, which promotes inquiry-based learning enhanced with AR overlays of information and tasks, is a sign of promising educational possibilities beginning to emerge in our ever more mixed reality.

Yet, as vital as it may be, an *instrumental mobile literacy*, which helps users employ mobile tools effectively for everyday life and learning, is not enough. It must be twinned with a *critical mobile literacy* (cf. Pachler et al., 2010) which pushes teachers, students and indeed the wider population to ask difficult questions about the impact of our mobile devices. This critical mobile literacy demands a deep familiarity with the hardware, including an understanding of its physical constraints as well as the constraints of its intertwined affordability and affordances. It demands a deep familiarity with the software that mediates many of these affordances, including an understanding of the limitations of an orientation towards appification, consumption, and template-driven self-expression. Beyond this, it demands an awareness that new technologies are situated within wider social, political and economic ecologies. In this way, we make room for the kinds of critical questions Guy Merchant (2012) suggests we should be asking:

> A critical perspective is key to interrogating the competing discourses that surround mobile technologies – the positive stories of participation and empowerment on the one hand and the more negative associations with consumerism, exploitation and bullying on the other. A citizen of the twenty-first century, it could be argued, needs to know how mobiles can be used to advantage, when they are disruptive and how they are framed by the desire-acquire-dispose discourse of consumerism, and this, I suggest, is a fitting task for public education in a digital age. (pp.779–780)

A critical perspective will inevitably encompass ethical issues around privacy and surveillance, which may well intensify with the spread of AR technologies; medical issues around physical and mental health, which may likewise intensify as we plunge into a mixed reality; and environmental issues around e-waste, which will certainly intensify unless we quell our desire to update our devices faster and faster (see Chapter 3). The last of these is an issue which feeds back into social, political and economic questions about the promotion of consumerist agendas in both the developed and developing world (see Chapter 2).

The need for critical questions is perhaps most acute when mobile technologies cross cultural boundaries, notably in connection with social justice initiatives. Successful projects, especially in the developing world, require us to step outside of powerful but sometimes simplistic global discourses about the benefits of mobile devices to ask what is needed to transform lives and learning in ways that are sensitive not only to global themes but to social and educational needs in specific local contexts. One initiative which asks the right kinds of tough questions is the Mobigam project in India (see Case Study 15 below). Having set out to improve language learning, it displays a keen awareness of its own position at the intersection of competing interests, which may affect each other in as yet unknown ways. The questions asked are a clear sign of a critically aware mobile project with the potential to join the ranks of those initiatives, some profiled in this book, which manage to achieve contextually appropriate change.

Case Study 15   Exploring mobile approaches in India (Mobigam Project)

Figure 6.5   Children with smartphone, Hansapor, Navsari, Gujarat, India. © Surendra Gohil/Mobigam, reproduced by permission.

Project:	Mobigam.
Languages:	English, Gujarati & Hindi. Codeswitching is also being researched.
Focus:	Study of the role of mobile devices in developing language & literacy, including digital literacies, & fostering social inclusion.
Level:	All levels.
Format:	Ethnographic research project.
Hardware:	The project focuses on mobile phones currently owned or used by participants.
Key partners:	The British Academy (grant provider); University of Leeds, UK, Central University, Gandhinagar, Gujarat, India, & HM Patel Institute, Vallabh Vidyanagar, Gujarat, India (research team).
Timeline:	The pilot research study is running from 2012–2013.
Location:	Gujarat, India.
Participants:	The participants will be local mobile phone users across urban, rural & Adivasi (i.e., 'tribal') areas of Gujarat, to be identified following initial survey-based research.

Case Study 15   (Continued)

Funding model: The pilot project is funded by the British Academy through a Partnership & Mobility Scheme grant.

The name Mobigam is a fusion of 'Mobi' (mobile) + 'gam' (Gujarati for 'a rural setting'). It is a pilot initiative in preparation for a bid for a large multiple-case study project examining the use of mobile technologies for language and literacy learning in Gujarat, India. In the pilot phase, Indian–UK research networks are being established, research training is being conducted in India, and research questions, methods and locations are being worked out.

Even within the pilot phase, however, the focus has begun to shift. What started as an examination of the potential of mobile technologies for language learning is evolving into a study of mobile technologies, digital literacy practices and social justice. Indeed, an important success of the project so far has been the growing realisation of the need for a deep understanding of the current context of mobile language and literacy practices in Gujarat, combined with an understanding of issues of digital inclusion and inequality and how mobile devices may or may not impact on those issues. This entails a critical perspective on how best to promote language learning and literacy development in ways appropriate for this particular context.

In terms of language itself, Mobigam started out with a focus on English language education in Gujarat, but soon broadened out to an interest in language use in general. This was prompted by a deepening understanding of the extensive multilingualism 'on the ground' – mainly involving Gujarati, Hindi and English, but with other languages and dialects mixed in, and widespread codeswitching and translanguaging practices – and the extent to which this must be incorporated in any work relating to language in India.

One challenge may be to persuade a range of local partners of the importance of adopting a more critical stance and placing less emphasis, at least initially, on the practicalities of promoting language learning. Future success will depend, from a research point of view, on developing common understandings of these issues among all research partners. Beyond this, practical challenges in the implementation of the research may well lie ahead. In the first instance, continuation of the research will depend on a successful bid for further funding.

The key interviewee about this project was James Simpson (School of Education, University of Leeds, UK). For further information, see the *Mobigam* blog (mobigam.wordpress.com), or follow @mobigam1 on Twitter.

Operating within a suitably critical and contextual framework, there are many ways to gainfully promote language and literacy, including digital literacies, through mobile devices. But, while the tools are essential, effective learning is a product more of pedagogy than technology. That means we need teachers who are well-trained in the possibilities (and the risks) of m-learning and MALL to be closely involved in the design and implementation of mobile education. Teachers in turn need the support of educational policymakers, leaders and researchers. In the final chapter, we'll look at how we can collaboratively prepare for a mobile educational future.

7
Preparing for a Mobile Educational Future

There's a pressing need for teacher training about mobile technologies. In fact, it's hard to find a point more widely made in the research literature (e.g., Pachler et al., 2010; UNESCO, 2013c; West, 2012a). In the developed world we're just starting to see a shift, with ICTs finding their way into teacher standards and national curricula (e.g., Oakley et al., 2012), and more in-service professional development (PD) courses covering ICTs; in both cases, room is increasingly made for mobile tools. In the developing world, on the other hand, it's estimated that up to half of all teachers lack adequate training (GSMA, 2010a) – that is, general training, not just ICT training. This issue is compounded by the need to recruit millions more teachers in coming years (West, 2012a). Thus, the need for teacher training about mobile tools is part of a much larger problem – where, curiously, teacher training *through* mobile tools might be part of the answer.

However, it's not just a question of *more* digital or mobile training, but *different* training. Teachers who do receive training, most of them in the developed world, often express a wish for PD which focuses less on the technology itself and more on the pedagogy of its use (Fritschi & Wolf, 2012a; Pegrum et al., 2013). As stated in the recent *UNESCO Mobile Learning Week Symposium Report*: 'Technology – and perhaps mobile learning in particular – requires re-conceptualizing the role of the teacher and models of pre- and in-service training' (UNESCO, 2013b). As we reconceptualise our training models, a pedagogical focus is crucial.

Yet it's not enough to consider how technology can enrich pedagogy. We should also ask how it can serve literacy. Across the board, there's a distinct lack of teacher training in digital literacies or, as the 2013 *Horizon Report* (Higher Education edition) calls it, 'digital media literacy':

Despite the widespread agreement on the importance of digital media literacy, training in the supporting skills and techniques is rare in teacher education and non-existent in the preparation of faculty. As lecturers and professors begin to realize that they are limiting their students by not helping them to develop and use digital media literacy skills across the curriculum, the lack of formal training is being offset through professional development or informal learning, but we are far from seeing digital media literacy as a norm.

(Johnson et al., 2013, p.9)

The time has come to promote the notion of a *digitally trained teacher* who is also a *digitally literate teacher* and indeed a *digitally networked teacher*, and who can liaise with policymakers, educational leaders and researchers to help shape our mobile learning future.

The digitally trained teacher

The most commonly used model for teacher training in new technologies is Punya Mishra and Matthew Koehler's (2006) TPACK (formerly TPCK) framework (see Figure 7.1). Here, new technologies, mobile or otherwise, aren't treated as a separate field of knowledge, but as interlinked with *content knowledge (CK)* and *pedagogical knowledge (PK)*. In other words, teachers remain content experts (who, in the case of language teachers, need a solid foundation and ideally fluency in the language they're teaching) and pedagogical experts (who need a grasp of behaviourist, communicative and sociocultural approaches to language teaching and an associated repertoire of materials and activities). *Technological knowledge (TK)* serves to enhance teachers' content and pedagogical understandings and options. Specifically, developing *technological content knowledge (TCK)* involves teachers becoming aware of how digital tools influence the content they may teach (such as textspeak, online reading and writing skills, or mobile literacy). Developing *technological pedagogical knowledge (TPK)* involves them becoming aware of how digital technologies can complement their pedagogical strategies (whether in blended or online mode).

Most teachers will begin using technology on the lower levels of Puentedura's SAMR model (see Chapter 2) before progressing to higher levels as they build their familiarity not just with the technology, but with the ways their TK intersects with their CK and especially their PK. The outer circle of the TPACK framework reminds us that teaching must be tailored to the contexts in which it occurs. But no matter

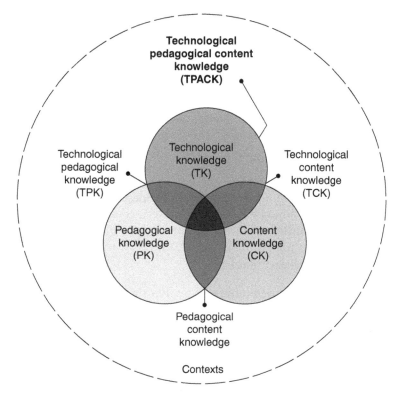

Figure 7.1 The TPACK framework.
Source: tpack.org, © 2012, reproduced by permission.

what a teacher's level of CK, PK or TK, and no matter whether they live in a developed urban centre or a developing rural village, teacher training can be built around the TPACK framework, supported by the SAMR model, as twin scaffolds for the growing integration of teachers' CK, PK and TK. It's where these overlap – represented by the centre of the TPACK framework, and correlated with teaching at the upper levels of the SAMR model – that the affordances of the technology may be best harnessed to enable a transformation of teaching and learning, one perhaps linked to 21st century skills and social justice agendas.

Indeed, digital technologies may open the gates to transformation, whether teachers are ready or not – which is why the Trojan horse (or 'Trojan mouse') metaphor has been applied to digital tools in general (Klopfer, 2008) and mobile tools in particular (see Chapter 2). Some teachers neutralise the threat of new technologies as best they can, trapping them within old pedagogical and organisational structures. But those who are open to the possibilities at the intersection of their CK, PK and TK may find their whole mindset starting to shift. As Mark Warschauer (2011) notes, 'learning to use technology well is a multi-year process, and involves not only the development of teachers' technical skill, but also an evolution of their ideas about teaching and learning' (p.107). This usually involves a shift away from transmission and behaviourist approaches towards more powerful and empowering teaching and learning, coupled with a shift away from old structures of classroom authority towards more collaborative relationships between teachers and students. Such changes are very much promoted by the affordances of mobile devices, as observed in studies from around the world (e.g., Burden et al., 2012; Cochrane, 2014; Deriquito & Domingo, 2012; Ng & Nicholas, 2013). This kind of shift was seen in the Brazilian iPads project (see Case Study 2), and we might ask ourselves whether there is a connection to the broader shift of mindset seen as necessary for teachers (as well as students and parents) to appreciate the value of mobile tools, games and activities in other projects (see Case Studies 7, 8 & 14). Notwithstanding the need to tailor teaching to the context, and to recognise the differences between using one device per class in an underresourced setting and a 1:1 model in a well-resourced setting, it may be appropriate for trainers and teachers to aim, over time, to develop greater openness to the possibilities of (more) interactive pedagogies, (more) learner-centred classrooms, and (more) transformative uses of new tools, all of which are mutually reinforcing, and whose promise is evident in projects from diverse contexts around the globe.

While numerous projects have focused on teaching students via mobile technologies, as reported in the case studies in this book, far fewer have focused on teaching teachers via the same tools (Shrestha, 2012; UNESCO, 2013c; Vosloo, 2012). Notable exceptions in the developed world include several projects funded under the UK MoLeNET programme where, for instance, trainee teachers used Skype on mobile phones to communicate with supervisors, or used video cameras to record their teaching for self-assessment (Dykes & Renfrew Knight, 2012). Notable exceptions in the developing world include a teacher training programme building on the success of the Pakistani Post-literacy project along with related projects in Mexico and Nigeria (UNESCO, n.d., c), and a teacher mentoring model under consideration in Indonesia (see Case Study 18).

In some cases, broader educational projects have a strong teacher training element. The English in Action project in Bangladesh (see Case Study 16 below) and the Great Idea project in Afghanistan (see

Case Study 16   A learning ecology in Bangladesh (EIA/Janala Project)

Figure 7.2 Primary teachers experimenting with an iPod Nano. © Prithvi Shrestha, OU, reproduced by permission.

Project:	EIA (English in Action), consisting of a *Schools Initiative* for both primary & secondary teachers & students, & a *Media & Adult Learning Initiative* commonly known as 'BBC Janala'.
Language:	English.
Focus:	Improving the English language & pedagogical skills of teachers; improving the English language skills of students & adults.
Level:	Various (including primary & secondary school teachers & students, & adult learners).
Format:	Audio, video, web, TV & print materials in a wide variety of formats (see below for examples).
Hardware:	In the Pilot phase of the *Schools Initiative*, materials were distributed to teachers via iPods & iPod Touches, accompanied by portable speakers & print materials; in the current Upscaling phase, materials are distributed via Nokia

feature phones containing SD cards, accompanied again by portable speakers & print materials; in the Institution-alisation phase, SD cards may be distributed for teachers' own devices in a BYOD model. In both phases of the *Media & Adult Learning Initiative* to date, participants' own mobile phones, computers, televisions, CD players & even newspapers have been used to access audio lessons, web lessons, TV shows & print lessons in an extended BYOD model.

Key partners: Department for International Development [DFID], UK (funding provider); BMB Mott MacDonald (project man-ager); The Open University [OU], UK (*Schools Initiative* component leader & research team); British Broadcast-ing Corporation [BBC] Media Action, UK (BBC Janala component leader & media producer); BBC Learning English (BBC Janala content designer & producer in Pilot phase); SW Multimedia, Bangladesh (animation producer); Underprivileged Children's Educational Pro-gramme [UCEP], Bangladesh, & Friends in Village Devel-opment Bangladesh [FIVDB] (NGOs involved in piloting & implementation); MOE & Ministry of Primary & Mass Edu-cation, Bangladesh (supporters of implementation); Airtel, Banglalink, Citycell, Grameenphone, Robi & Teletalk (all six local mobile network operators); Bangladesh Tele-vision (state broadcaster); *Prothom Alo* (daily Bangla newspaper).

Timeline: 2008–2017, with the following phases: 2008–2011: Pilot; 2011–2014: Upscaling; 2014–2017: Institutionalisation.

Location: Bangladesh.

Participants: The aim is to reach 25 million people by 2017, including 85,000 English teachers, ten million primary & secondary students, & many millions of adults aged approx. 15–45 years. To date, BBC Janala has reached almost 24 million learners.

Funding model: The project is being funded over nine years by DFID/UKaid, UK. In the *Schools Initiative* Pilot & Upscaling phases, both mobile devices & SD cards have been supplied free of charge, but in the Institutionalisation phase only SD

Case Study 16   (Continued)

> cards are likely to be supplied. In the *Media & Adult Learning Initiative*, participants supply their own devices. Web materials can be accessed free of charge. The two to 2.5-minute audio lessons accessed on mobile phones cost BDT 0.5 per minute (less than US 1¢) thanks to the partnership with local mobile network operators.

The EIA project was set up by DFID following an approach from the Bangladeshi government. All content has been designed specifically to suit the local social and educational context. The project as a whole relies on close co-operation with local governmental and educational bodies and is aligned with the government's *Vision 2021* and *Digital Bangladesh* initiatives.

The *Schools Initiative* made use of iPods and iPod Touches in the Pilot phase. However, due to cost, recharging problems (with the local electricity supply being unreliable) and navigational issues, these were replaced with mobile phones in the Upscaling phase. This underlines the focus of the project on educational and social goals rather than on any one particular technology (a point also evidenced in BBC Janala's multi-platform approach). In the current phase, bilingual Bangla and English PD materials, including communicative lesson guidelines, suggested activities and multimedia classroom resources linked to the national textbook, *English for Today*, are made available on SD cards on the Nokia mobile phones distributed through teacher workshops across the country. This 'trainer in the pocket' does not involve digital networking but is a self-contained set of resources accompanied by print materials. However, in addition to face-to-face peer support, there is some teacher networking via the mobile phones.

Through the mobile devices used in the *Schools Initiative*, teachers and students have access to previously unavailable language materials, particularly in the areas of speaking and listening, which have traditionally been somewhat neglected in Bangladesh. The project has helped teachers not only to improve their spoken English competence, as reflected in the Graded Examinations in Spoken English (GESE) administered by Trinity College, London, but to change their classroom practices, shifting them in a communicative direction. Teachers now use far more English in their classrooms, with a dramatic increase in the proportion of their talking time in

English observed after a year in the Pilot phase. They make their classroom activities more interactive by giving students opportunities to speak, with students' proportion of English use showing a similarly dramatic increase. GESE scores also showed an improvement in students' spoken English in the Pilot phase.

Notwithstanding the considerable successes to date, some teachers, especially more established teachers in secondary schools, have not been keen to employ new technologies or new pedagogies. This reluctance is compounded by the pressure placed on teachers by an exam-oriented education system focused on reading and writing. As in many projects, however, the greatest challenge is the sustainability of the changes achieved so far. The project still relies on outside expertise but aims to build further local training capacity and foster more local leadership. Moving to a BYOD model may well aid the technological sustainability of the project, but it is the human capacity which will matter most in the long run.

Meanwhile, in the *Media & Adult Learning Initiative*, the BBC Janala ('window' in Bangla) service provides English access through mobile phones, the web, TV, CDs, print, and English clubs. For example, audio lessons can be accessed on mobile phones; lessons and quizzes can be accessed on the web; a drama, *Bishaash*, and a game show, *Mojay Mojay Shekha*, can be viewed on TV; and learning material is printed in the daily newspaper *Prothom Alo*. While the material has a broad communicative orientation, audiolingual (behaviourist) elements and translation are used when appropriate. To date, BBC Janala materials have reached almost 24 million learners, with 6.8 million engaging regularly. Audiences are strong among women and lower socioeconomic groups, notably for TV output. It is known that learning is sometimes shared in family groups. Some 8.8 million users feel that they have learned some English, and 7.7 million say that they have used the English they have learned. Users are also more motivated to learn English, and more confident to use it in everyday life – 47% of people who are highly exposed to BBC Janala rated their motivation to learn English as higher than two years previously.

In a related but separate development, responding to a gendered divide which has been observed in the use of EIA web and mobile lessons in particular, the British Council and a local NGO, the Bangladesh Rural Advancement Committee (BRAC), have now set up community ICT clubs where girls can learn with the British Council's digital resources preloaded onto notebook

Case Study 17), which have introduced digital tools into new contexts on a class-by-class basis, both focus on teachers' CK as well as their PK, implicitly overlaid with TK development. The EIA *Schools Initiative* shows it is possible to provide teachers and students with greater access to language content while simultaneously transforming teaching practices with the help of a digital 'trainer in the pocket'. A shift towards more communicative teaching has already led to improvements in language competence for both teachers and students. EIA does not privilege a single digital tool and shows that specific technologies matter less than the chosen content and pedagogies. In particular, its *Media & Adult Learning Initiative*, also known as 'BBC Janala', demonstrates how different technologies can work together in a learning ecology.

Digitally trained leaders

Beyond teacher training, there's a need for *institutional leadership training*. It's been widely noted that effective leadership is necessary for the successful implementation of new technologies in education (Ng & Nicholas, 2013; Vosloo, 2012; Warschauer, 2011). This requires the involvement not only of teacher leaders who can enthuse and inform colleagues, but of institutional leaders, managers and administrators who are responsible for organisational vision, policies and funding. That's why the Brazilian iPads project team is educating managers to understand and support teachers' and students' use of the devices, and why the Indian MILLEE project team noted a need to educate managers about the value of ' students taking mobile phones home (see Case Studies 2 & 7). Management backing is crucial in contexts where teachers' pedagogical exploration and TPACK evolution may be hampered by restrictive IT policies. It is crucial, too, when students' rich learning outside institutional walls – whether in informal contexts or on MOOC platforms, as noted by Gary Motteram in his comments on trainee teachers (see Vignette 12 below) – goes unrecognised within their walls. By demonstrating the powerful educational affordances of new technologies, backed up by a familiarity with published research as well as, ideally, solid local research and evaluation, teachers and teacher leaders can seek to bring institutional leaders on board to help support and expand digital learning. To allow teachers to fully capitalise on new technologies and new pedagogies, and to help students move beyond what Motteram calls 'portable versions of conventional modes of study', it's imperative to have an informed institutional leadership.

Vignette 12   Mobile teacher education

Gary Motteram, The University of Manchester, UK

On our MA programmes for teachers and learning technologists at Manchester University, there is inevitably discussion about the shifting technological landscape, and mobile learning is currently part of the debate. While there is no established practice, there has been a significant growth in the number of course participants using portable devices, from wireless-enabled laptops to iPads, mobile phones, Kindles and other e-readers. For our many part-time, mostly distance learning students, a laptop can become like a portable office which is used to store reading material, take notes, write assignments and communicate. Tablet devices, mostly iPads, are also used in similar ways, but often in combination with a laptop for writing. We find that students are working in a variety of locations, from public transport to parks and even on holiday, and using iPads or Kindles to access and annotate reading material,

---

Vignette 12   (Continued)

which they might then synch to a laptop for inclusion in an assignment. There are however still a lot of copyright and access limitations with library materials, and many of our core textbooks are not yet available in e-formats.

Mobile devices are also used to listen to audio files and view videos provided by tutors; on a visit to Japan, one student showed me course videos she had downloaded onto her iPod Touch to watch on her commute to work. Communication is increasingly possible: students can use an app to access forums or blogs in our Blackboard virtual learning environment (VLE), and we now see them experimenting with joining into our synchronous tutorial and seminar sessions through mobile devices. This means they don't have to be in an office or at home to attend online sessions.

Mobile devices are certainly going to continue to have an impact in our students' personal and professional lives and will gradually have a greater impact on higher education. However, if we want students to be able to move beyond portable versions of conventional modes of study, some of the barriers that formal education erects around itself will need to be broken down. The sorts of informal learning or extra-academe learning (in the form of MOOCs, for example) that we increasingly see happening will need to be brought into our educational establishments and accredited, so that the innovative and transformative study that some of our course participants are engaging in is recognised.

In many contexts, there's also a need for *social leadership training,* as the backing of social leaders may be the key to getting new projects off the ground. In ICT4D or M4D projects in the developing world, this might involve the awareness-raising efforts of local organisations. In the Pakistani Post-literacy project, for instance, the local NGO Bunyad worked to convince community leaders of the appropriacy of providing mobile phones to adolescent girls. In the Afghan Great Idea initiative, the local NGO CHA secured the involvement of community leaders in helping to change attitudes to female education, and in allowing the project to function with community support in areas where it is unsafe for project staff to travel (see Case Studies 3 & 17). In the developed world, social leadership training might simply mean building the support of the local community for school initiatives by running parents' information sessions or setting up digital communication channels (Oakley et al., 2012), perhaps in the form of online newsletters, blogs or Twitter feeds.

Going still further, there's often a need for *political leadership training*. This may be necessary at all levels of government and policymaking, given that there are bans on the use of mobile phones in schools still in place at city level, for example in New York (Fritschi & Wolf, 2012b), and even at national level, as in France (Hylén, 2012). Some of the positive outcomes of political and policymaker support and funding at a national level can be seen in the Australian Federal Government's backing for the rollout of XOs in the OLPC project (see Case Study 12), or the Singaporean MOE's backing for the development of the AR Heritage Trails (see Case Study 14). At a global level, the support of national governments and their departments and agencies (such as the US State Department in Case Study 2 or the UK's DFID in Case Study 16), along with IGOs and NGOs (like UNESCO in Case Study 3 or the various NGOs mentioned above), as well as technology and telecommunications corporations, can make or break m-learning projects. Once again, the ability to demonstrate the value of new technologies, backed up by local and global research, is very important when teachers and teacher leaders – perhaps in tandem with institutional and even social leaders – lobby political leaders for support. The question of exactly what kind of research evidence is needed is one we'll return to at the end of the chapter.

Digitally trained students

If teachers, once trained themselves, have a role in the training of institutional leaders, social leaders, and political leaders and policy-makers, they obviously also have a role in *student training*. Teachers may well need to spend time helping to turn students from *tech-comfy* into *tech-savvy* users of mobile and other tools, as Gavin Dudeney points out in his account of the spread of everyday mobile devices in language education (see Vignette 13 below). On the one hand, students need guidance in how their devices can support not only classroom learning but informal, contextual, lifelong learning. This

---

Vignette 13   Everyday technologies

Gavin Dudeney, The Consultants-E, Spain/UK

Working with both teachers and learners in a private language school in the UK over the past 12 months I've seen exactly how tablet computers – in this case, iPads – can become embedded in daily practice. Both groups have taken to the tablets in ways I have not observed with other technologies over the past 20 years. Ease-of-use has something to do with this, as does the tactile nature of the interactions with electronic media, and the opportunity for creativity and sharing. Perhaps, most importantly, it is about the familiarity that users have with the devices, based on their daily interactions with mobile phones in their personal lives. In these classes, a global mix of English as a Second Language (ESL) learners are able to use the iPads for creative language practice, including writing digital stories, conducting audio interviews, and recording and editing videos.

Providing teachers with short bursts of 'just in time' training with the iPads, focused on practical skills, has quickly overcome any apprehension, and I've even seen a teacher opt to run a high-stakes observed class (while being assessed in a diploma course) entirely based on the iPads. This to me confirms new attitudes to these technologies. What has been particularly interesting to observe is a subtle shift as teachers working with these tools adopt more of a guiding role. Mike Sansone points to this with his distinction between 'tech-savvy' and 'tech-comfy', allowing that whilst learners are often comfortable using technologies, they are not always good at using them in the service of their learning. This may point to the new role we need to move towards as educators.

► Further reading: Dudeney et al. (2013); Hockly & Dudeney (in press); Sansone (2008).

---

involves coming to see that mobile tools are more than toys, mobile activities are more than entertainment, mobile learning is more than drills, and user-generated content is more than a lazy substitute for teacher-generated material. On the other hand, they need to develop an awareness of the risks around safety, privacy, surveillance and reputation (see Chapter 3) which often go unnoticed by tech-comfy youth. Stepping stones along this path might include acceptable use policies or, better still, responsible use policies (UNESCO, 2013c), digital safety classes for students, and seminars for parents, guardians and indeed leaders. At the same time as these structures help scaffold students' tech-savviness, they safeguard teachers and reassure institutional, social and political leadership that new technologies will not get out of control.

As teachers bring their CK and PK to bear on new technologies and vice versa, they may sometimes find themselves teaching students whose technological expertise exceeds their own, and who can therefore contribute to teachers' TK development. In fact, when the old structures of classroom authority break down, teachers and students are freed up to explore emerging tools together, effectively becoming 'technological co-learners' (Oakley et al., 2012, p.31). Teachers should be prepared to learn not only from trainers, but from and with their students, in what may become rich teaching and learning partnerships (Dudeney et al., 2013).

The digitally literate teacher

In settings where educational opportunities are limited and teacher training is inadequate, digital literacy may be a gateway to improved learning for both teachers and students. This is evident in the EIA project in Bangladesh (see Case Study 16) as well as in the Great Idea project currently running in war-ravaged Afghanistan (see Case Study 17 below). As in EIA, the upcoming second phase of the Afghan project will not rely primarily on telecommunications networks but on content distributed on SD cards for mobile phones. This will consist of video lessons which can be shown publicly in classrooms via microprojectors, or viewed privately on individual devices. The latter option will give teachers more flexibility to improve their CK (based on the curriculum content covered) and PK (based on the modelling by master trainers), as they prepare their teaching in their own private time and space. While the level of digital literacy skills required of teachers – and acquired by them in the process of learning to use these tools – may be relatively low, the effects in a drastically underserved context are potentially quite revolutionary, and even more so when students are encouraged to develop some of the same skills.

Case Study 17　Making mobile inroads in Afghanistan (Great Idea Project)

Figure 7.3　Girls using a mobile phone in a school in Jabal Saraj, Parwan Province, Afghanistan. © Merel van der Woude/Butterfly Works, reproduced by permission.

Project:	Great Idea.
Languages:	In Phase I, maths & science broadcasts were delivered in Dari. In Phase II, maths & science videos will be delivered in Dari & possibly Pashto; English will be included as a curriculum subject.
Focus:	Maths, science & English curriculum delivery to secondary school students; curriculum & pedagogical training for secondary school teachers.
Level:	Secondary school students & teachers.
Format:	Television broadcasts & live mobile phone calls in Phase I; videos & mobile phone calls in Phase II; supplementary radio broadcasts & face-to-face meetings in both Phases I & II.
Hardware:	In Phase I, satellite televisions & mobile phones were supplied to schools; in Phase II, SD cards containing video lessons will be distributed for classroom use with supplied feature phones or Android phones & microprojectors, or

for personal use on participants' own mobile phones in a BYOD model.

Key partners: Oxfam Hong Kong (funding provider for Phase I); Oxfam Novib Netherlands (overall project manager & funding provider between Phases I & II); Coordination of Humanitarian Assistance [CHA] (NGO involved in project management & implementation); Butterfly Works (creator of mobile learning concept, project & technical advisor, & organiser of co-creation workshops); SABA Media Organization [SMO] (project implementer; television, video & radio producer); Roshan (mobile phone supplier & mobile network operator); Paiwastoon (technical advisor); MOE, Afghanistan (curriculum designer).

Timeline: 2011 – ongoing, with the following phases: 2011–2012: Phase I; 2013: Between Phases (continuation & expansion of Phase I & preparation of Phase II); 2014 onwards: Phase II (Upscaling).

Location: Parwan Province, Afghanistan & potentially Balkh, Farah, Faryab, Ghor, Herat & Kabul Provinces, with the final list of locations dependent on fundraising.

Participants: The focus is on improving education for youth, especially girls, & upskilling teachers in the new Afghan MOE curriculum. Phase I targeted 21 schools in Parwan Province, involving 5,500 students & 800 teachers of grades 7–9; in the Between Phases period, grades 10–12 have been added; Phase II is intended to target 77 schools in seven provinces, involving 37,000 students & 1,222 teachers of grades 7–12, with the final numbers dependent on funding.

Funding model: Phase I was funded by Oxfam Hong Kong, with mobile phones supplied by Roshan. The Between Phases period is being funded by Oxfam Novib Netherlands. Funding options are currently being explored for Phase II. In Phase I, television sets, satellite dishes, mobile phones & roof solar panels (to provide power) were supplied to schools. In Phase II, SD cards containing video lessons, mobile phones, microprojectors & roof solar panels will be

Case Study 17   (Continued)

> supplied to schools for classroom viewing of videos, but
> teachers & students will supply their own mobile phones
> for personal viewing. Teachers, students & parents may
> be able to purchase additional SD cards containing more
> video lessons.

After three decades of war and repression, including bans on female
education and employment by the Taliban, education levels are extremely
low in Afghanistan. The adult literacy rate is estimated at 28% but only
13% for women (which is rather lower than neighbouring Pakistan; see
Case Study 3). The formal education system is in poor shape, and few
teachers have adequate knowledge of curriculum content or effective
pedagogy. As of 2008, only 44% of boys and 27% of girls in rural areas
attended schools.

In Phase I of the Great Idea project, master trainers in Kabul were filmed
giving well-designed lessons on new curriculum content in maths and science, with two to three lessons broadcast every day by satellite television to
each of the three grades 7, 8 and 9 in schools in the Parwan region. A level of
interactivity was introduced though a live mobile helpline, where teachers
and students could pose questions to the trainers after each lesson. Students' active participation was further encouraged through a competition
announced by the trainers each week in each subject area, with students
phoning the helpline and leaving their answers, and the winners being
announced in television broadcasts the following week. Radio and face-
to-face meetings were used as supplementary channels to enhance teachers' pedagogical knowledge, and in particular to promote learner-centred,
participatory approaches and offer tips on classroom management.

In order to upscale the project in Phase II, a more cost-effective and
easier to implement approach is being developed. Video lessons will be
pre-recorded, following the MOE curriculum and informed by the kinds of
questions asked by students on the live mobile helpline in Phase I. They
will be distributed on SD cards to be viewed in classrooms using phones
connected to microprojectors. Participating schools will receive a package
consisting of several SD cards containing the lessons, a feature phone or
Android phone, a microprojector, and a rooftop solar panel and batteries
(since most schools are not on the electricity grid). It is important that the
mobile phones selected can have software installed to automatically log

video use – how often and for how long they are watched – in order to assist in further materials development. This would be easier with an Android phone, but it is also possible with some feature phones, and a decision is yet to be made on which to use. In addition to being viewed in the classroom, the videos will be able to be viewed on teachers' or students' own personal phones. There will still be a helpline that teachers and students can call, though it will not be live. The weekly competitions will be retained, though the media format for distributing competition questions, providing feedback and announcing winners is yet to be determined. Radio and face-to-face meetings will again be used, this time largely to raise awareness among parents and the community of the importance of education, especially for girls.

The project has been very much shaped by a series of co-creation workshops run by Butterfly Works. Based on the idea that local communities should not be treated as passive recipients of educational development projects, but should be involved as co-creators, these workshops have drawn – and will continue to draw – a wide range of stakeholders and community members into every phase of the design cycle. This process helps ensure that projects are informed by local expertise and are contextually appropriate; that there is local ownership and engagement; and that there is local capacity- and skills-building. All of these factors support long-term sustainability.

Community involvement has in fact been crucial to the successful implementation of the project. CHA, a local NGO with a strong community presence, has been instrumental in disseminating information about the project, bringing community leaders on board, and even holding monthly meetings with community members to discuss how the project is working in schools. In this way, it is helping to raise awareness and has already begun to change attitudes towards girls' education. The involvement of local communities is all the more important in a country where it is not safe for project staff to travel to rural areas.

A number of educational successes have been achieved to date, for both students and teachers. Student dropout rates have decreased, and girls in particular are more likely to stay in school. Test results for both girls and boys have increased and are considerably higher than in schools which have not taken part in the project. Teachers have appreciated the support, as many were struggling with the new curriculum, and some have been promoted.

Case Study 17   (Continued)

Attention is currently focused on finding appropriate donors to allow upscaling in Phase II, with each school package likely to cost around US $2000. More female master trainers are being sought as role models for girls. English videos are already being recorded between phases, as English will be included as a curriculum subject in Phase II. This was a subject requested by girls, for whom English can open doors to work with NGOs and foreign companies. Girls have also requested computer lessons, though these are not being created at the moment due to a lack of computers in schools. One possibility might be to explore the teaching of digital literacy skills on mobile phones. In time it may also be possible to distribute far more lesson content on SD cards. Teachers have indicated that they would be willing to pay around AFN 150 (approx. US $2.70) for SD cards, and it is anticipated that parents who are already investing in additional university entrance exam preparation classes for their children might also purchase these cards. Families often send sons and perhaps one daughter to school, but keep other daughters at home. If families purchased SD cards, they could be shared among siblings, thus supporting the education of girls who don't have the chance to attend school.

The key interviewee about this project was Merel van der Woude (Butterfly Works, Amsterdam). For further information, see the *Great Idea* website (afghanlearning.wordpress.com), the *Butterfly Works* website (www.butterflyworks.org), or follow @butterflyworks on Twitter.

As development levels increase, so do the technological possibilities along with the associated literacy demands on teachers. With appropriate technology at their disposal, effective teachers can and should become *creators* and *curators* of learning materials for their students. This entails a broad swathe of digital literacies. As creators, teachers need experience in the productive aspects of multimodal literacy (see Chapter 6) and an awareness of the principles of multimodal instruction (see Chapter 4). As curators, teachers must add to their repertoire the information literacy skills to identify, evaluate and catalogue relevant content, complemented by the network literacy skills to leverage online connections to help discover as well as disseminate this content. Not only will this support their teaching; it will allow them to mentor their students in developing the very same digital literacies as they, too, learn to become creators and curators of digital content within a creation or communication MALL paradigm.

But to be maximally effective, teachers need to be more than designers or collectors of materials; they need to become *designers of learning experiences* for their students. The value of seeing teaching as a design science, a point which has long been made by Diana Laurillard (2012), is not restricted to the digital era, but learning design takes on an added salience when education entails effectively and efficiently integrating pedagogy and technology (along with content, of course, as in the TPACK framework). Learning design is crucial to e-learning (Churchill, 2006) and CALL (Levy & Stockwell, 2006), and to m-learning (Milrad et al., 2013), MOOCs (see Chapter 2) and MALL. As a white paper from the 2011 Sustaining Technology Enhanced Learning at a LARge scale (STELLAR) Alpine Rendez-Vous puts it:

> The challenge of education is no longer about delivery of knowledge: it is about designing environments, tools and activities for learners to construct knowledge. In order for educators to effectively orchestrate learning within this landscape they need to perceive themselves, and indeed to be perceived by society, as techno-pedagogical designers.
>
> (Mwanza-Simwami et al., 2011, p.5)

Alongside other literacies, this requires code literacy, which feeds into the TK component of teachers' TPACK. A command of creation, curation and communication demands some understanding of coding and programming; so, too, does a command of the learning design options opened up by new technologies. An ability to work at the TPK juncture at the centre of the TPACK framework will permit teachers to contribute effectively to the array of pedagogically rich CALL and MALL materials available to students (see Chapter 5).

At the same time, the spread of user-friendly software for creating learning materials has dramatically reduced entry levels. While this software is more about shaping the details than designing the overall form of learning, it greatly expands the capacity of teachers with little or no code literacy to customise materials to better suit their pedagogical purposes and their students' learning needs. Games like the Iranian Detective Alavi are designed to be modified by teachers without technical knowledge (see Chapter 5); ARIS software and LOTM software allow AR games and AR learning trails, respectively, to be built without programming skills (see Case Studies 8 & 14); and more intuitive interfaces will soon enable teachers to create their own ICALL and IMALL materials (see Chapter 4). Ideally, however, teachers should be encouraged to see such user-friendly software as the beginning, not the end, of their development of code literacy – since it is code literacy which will allow them to design not just tasks, or even websites and apps, but integrated techno-pedagogical learning experiences.

Of course, the design of digital experiences should not simply be the province of teachers; students should become 'designers of their own learning and of their personal learning environment' (Mwanza-Simwami et al., 2011, p.5). In some cases, teachers may share their code literacy skills as part of broader learner training approaches; in others, they may provide pedagogical input while developing their code literacy skills alongside their students. Once they have a base in code literacy, students can extend their technological knowhow as they gradually take control of generating their own learning contexts and content, recording the outcomes in their PLEs, and disseminating and discussing their learning in their PLNs.

With digital literacies still underrepresented in both pre-service and in-service training, few teachers are likely to feel confident of their ability to do all of the above. In an era of rapidly developing technologies and rapidly expanding possibilities, teachers need to be learners, perhaps more so than ever before. Beyond attending courses and learning with students, one of teachers' most important assets is a network of colleagues – which places a premium on their *network literacy*. This is true of teachers in both developed and developing regions, who might sometimes use different tools, but can benefit from similar kinds of network support structures.

The digitally networked teacher

PLNs are an essential counterpart to teachers' pre-service and in-service development, no matter how much training they have received, but especially if they have received little training. PLNs can help them keep abreast of new developments, exchange ideas with and receive feedback from colleagues, and indeed model lifelong learning to their students. Mobile tools give anywhere, anytime access to these networks, allowing teachers to become 'life-long and life-wide learners themselves through their personal use of mobile technologies to reflect on their teaching practices and to extend their knowledge' (Kukulska-Hulme, 2010b, p.10).

Mobile social networking provides an ideal platform for teachers' PLNs, with 'professional Facebooking' prevalent from Italy (Ranieri et al., 2012) through Nepal (Pimmer et al., 2012) to South Africa (Isaacs, 2012a). In a UNESCO (n.d., c) teacher development project for early childhood educators which began in 2012 in Pakistan, videos and resources delivered on mobile phones through the Nokia Education Delivery (NED) platform, and SMS questions delivered through the mobile operator, Mobilink, are complemented by a Facebook page set up by the UNESCO Islamabad office. Here, teachers can share resources and content, including in multimedia formats, which allows them, for example, to exchange photos of their classroom layouts (Steve Vosloo, personal interview, May 2013). In a related project for teachers of Spanish to indigenous language learners in Mexico, videos delivered through NED are complemented by a Wordpress blog, which serves as a similar forum for teachers to engage in multimedia communication and sharing (ibid.). Other services like Twitter, where teachers can follow experts and converse with colleagues, or LinkedIn, where they can join professional interest groups and message peers, can also support teacher development (Fritschi & Wolf, 2012a; West, 2012a).

Mobile phones lend themselves to more traditional forms of networking, too. In the EIA project in Bangladesh, teachers have used SMS to maintain a professional network, co-ordinate cluster meetings and send discussion questions to project staff (Shrestha, 2011). In a UNESCO (n.d., c) teacher development project for primary teachers of English in Nigeria, daily messages delivered through the Nokia Life+ platform are supplemented by calls and messages from master teachers, with teachers encouraged to network with peers via voice calls, SMS, email or social networking sites (Steve Vosloo, personal interview, May 2013). In the British Council's TALULAR project in Indonesia (see Case Study 18 below), a model is being considered in which VoIP and SMS would form the basis of a mentoring arrangement linking trainers in Jakarta with teachers in remote schools, as well as allowing teachers to network with colleagues. Such approaches are likely to play an ever larger role in teacher PD, notably in underresourced regions where such development has traditionally been lacking.

Case Study 18   SMS teacher mentoring in Indonesia (TALULAR Project)

Figure 7.4   British Council teacher training school visit. © British Council, Jakarta, reproduced by permission.

Project:	TALULAR (Teaching And Learning Using Locally Available Resources).
Language:	English.
Focus:	Mentoring for English teachers in remote areas of Indonesia.
Level:	Secondary school teachers.
Format:	Weekly mentor–mentee VoIP calls &/or SMS messages, with mentees having the option to contact other mentees as desired.
Hardware:	Teachers would supply their own mobile phones in a BYOD model.
Key partners:	British Council (training provider).
Timeline:	The model is currently under consideration.
Location:	Remote areas of Eastern Indonesia.
Participants:	It is likely that there would be around 30 initial participants, who would be English teachers at junior secondary or senior secondary schools.

Funding model: The funding model is in development. To promote sustainability, teachers would supply their own devices.

The teacher training model under consideration in this project is one of a new wave of networked teacher PD concepts. It would use mobile devices to network teacher trainers with teacher trainees, and trainees with each other. The aim is to provide ongoing support for teachers of English who have attended training with the British Council in Jakarta, or who have received training visits in their own locations. This is likely to involve weekly messages exchanged between British Council mentors and mentee teachers working in remote areas of Eastern Indonesia, notably on distant islands. Content would be related to offline weekly self-access materials, using loop input throughout to reinforce prior learning.

The programme is intended to be motivational, and to encourage participants to share best practice, observations and ideas along with any worries or concerns. Not only would this ongoing support build on the initial enthusiasm of teachers, helping them to continue putting into practice what they have learned in training sessions, but the one-to-one contact would allow the training to be customised to the conditions in which individual teachers find themselves working – which, in some cases, may include a lack of school buildings and an unreliable electricity supply.

Financial sustainability would be achieved through a BYOD model where teachers use the devices already at their disposal. Sustainability within the teaching community could be enhanced by encouraging mentees not only to interact with their mentors but to network with each other, thus building a supportive community of practitioners.

The key interviewees about this project were Danny Whitehead (Head of English Language Development, British Council, Jakarta) and Neil Ballantyne (Mobile Learning Manager, British Council), with additional input from Winda Wastu Melati (Programme Manager, British Council, Jakarta).

Researching our mobile educational future

The current proliferation of mobile educational opportunities shows no signs of letting up. It's apparent that teachers can't rely on pre-service training or in-service PD to cover everything they should know. But neither can they expect their PLNs to supply them with all of the new insights and learning they need – unless they're prepared to regularly and systematically contribute their own insights and learning to their PLNs.

Teacher research

One of the best ways for teachers to build their TK, TCK and TPK, and to enhance their TPACK, is by conducting *action research* on the effectiveness of their use of mobile technologies for teaching, and on their students' use of these technologies for learning. Although action research has a number of variations, it's always based on an action-reflection cycle, in which a teacher might follow a series of steps including some or all of the following: develop a question related to their teaching and/or their students' learning; consult relevant literature; seek ideas from online and offline sources and colleagues; develop an overview of the possibilities; develop a plan for action to improve their teaching and/or their students' learning; implement the action; collect data about the effectiveness of the action (often through observations, surveys or assessments); evaluate the data; develop a new or revised plan, which might extend, modify or replace the original plan; start a second research cycle; and disseminate the results of the first research cycle (Dudeney et al., 2013).

Action research findings can be disseminated through a variety of channels, including the many online networks that bring together CALL and MALL practitioners; m-learning conferences with CALL streams; CALL conferences with m-learning streams; and relevant journals from these fields. This is a way for a teacher to obtain feedback, contribute to the learning of others, and draw others with shared interests into an expanding PLN. Over time, such a PLN will provide an ever richer context for the exchange of ideas about teaching and learning with mobile tools. What's more, action research can help build bridges between practitioners and researchers, to the benefit of both.

It's become clear that mobile technologies are embedded in complex ecologies of use. Successful MALL projects – those that transform teaching and learning, develop 21st century skills, and bring education, often at scale, to underserved populations – must work within these ecologies by building partnerships with international, national and local organisations, institutions and companies, as well as political, social and educational leaders. Teachers' action research has much to contribute to developing appropriate pedagogical approaches and providing research-based evidence of effectiveness to educational leaders. But the ecologies are too large and complex for teachers to do all the research by themselves.

Wider research agendas

A number of state and national governments, and national and international organisations, have begun to develop educational policies to promote ICTs and support the spread of 21st century skills. Tellingly, however, mobile learning does not yet feature explicitly in many countries' educational policies (Vosloo, 2012; West, 2012b). The aim of the 2013 *UNESCO Policy Guidelines for Mobile Learning* is precisely to address this mobile policy gap (UNESCO, 2013c). While research alone won't lead to the creation of mobile learning policies, it can certainly play a role in demonstrating the value and impact of m-learning. But this means that action research on a micro-scale must be complemented by large research projects like those covered in some of the case studies in this book, in order to more clearly establish the benefits of m-learning and MALL, and to communicate those benefits to the many actors who need to work together to realise the full global potential of mobile education.

It's often commented that research on the effectiveness of m-learning and MALL has been rather limited to date. Where it has occurred, it has frequently lacked rigour (Traxler, 2007, 2013; UNESCO, 2013b) or scale and scope (Rushby, 2012; UNESCO, 2013b; Viberg & Grönlund, 2012). While the projects described in the case studies and elsewhere in this book provide a good start, there is still much to be learned, and demonstrated, and disseminated. There is a need for further funded development projects, in particular, which are: *integrated* into a network of IGOs, NGOs, government bodies, educational bodies and commercial bodies; *aligned with* and *embedded in* local cultures with the support of local leaders, and ideally *co-designed* with local actors; *piloted* before full implementation; *scalable* after the pilot phase; *sustainable* and self-supporting once initial funding dries up; *long-term* in focus; and *capacity-building,* so that in time they can be ably taken over by local populations. Despite the difficulties inherent in assessing all mobile learning (see Chapter 4), such projects and the learning they engender need to be *regularly evaluated* to identify strengths and weaknesses, preferably with input from a wide spectrum of stakeholders, and the projects need to be *iteratively modified* in light of these evaluations.

In tandem with, and building on, these evaluations, the projects need to generate research which can be leveraged to inform and persuade political, corporate, social and educational leaders of the value of mobile learning, and feed into future policy and project development. Not only is m-learning difficult to assess, as noted above, but it may be difficult even to pin down because it can flow across space and time, the real and virtual, and the formal and informal (Looi et al., 2010; Pachler, 2009; Vavoula & Sharples, 2009). However, without such research our claims for mobile learning remain anecdotal or aspirational. Challenges notwithstanding, m-learning research should ideally incorporate many of the characteristics outlined below.

Framing the research – the research should be:

- *theoretically informed* or *theoretically generative*: it should apply appropriate theoretical lenses (Looi et al., 2010), which may be philosophical, epistemological and/or pedagogical, or alternatively it should seek to generate new mobile-specific theories (Vavoula & Sharples, 2009; Viberg & Grönlund, 2012) which may be based on but differ from established educational theories, though it should not necessarily be grounded solely in Western approaches (Kukulska-Hulme, 2009; Selwyn, 2013);
- *agenda-oriented*: it should be underpinned by pedagogical, skills, social justice or other explicitly identified agendas (see Chapter 2) rather than by specific technologies, given the rapid development and obsolescence of the latter (JISC, n.d.; Looi et al., 2010);
- *cumulative*: it should acknowledge and build on past theoretical work (Viberg & Grönlund, 2012) and empirical work, rather than starting afresh theoretically or empirically.

Contextualising the research – the research should be:

- *co-designed*: it should involve learners as co-designers and co-researchers where appropriate (Kukulska-Hulme, 2009; Ros i Solé, 2009), especially given that user-generated learning contexts and content may only be identifiable with the input of the individuals who have generated them;
- *ecological*: it should include ethnographic research methods (Looi et al., 2010; Ros i Solé, 2009) which can encompass the full cultural, social, political, economic, educational and institutional contexts of mobile learning (Kam, 2013; Kukulska-Hulme, 2009; Pachler, 2009), ranging from the ecology of partners in multi-stakeholder projects (Unwin, 2009a) to the interweaving of formal with informal learning (Looi et al., 2010; Vavoula & Sharples, 2009), and thus including local, episodic and personal learning.

Collecting the data – the research should be:

- *methodologically informed*: it should apply appropriate methodological lenses (Looi et al., 2010), and perhaps multiple lenses

(Kukulska-Hulme, 2009), which will make it possible to identify and collect different kinds of data, and reveal and elucidate different aspects of those data;

- *methodologically mixed*: it should collect both qualitative (including ethnographic; see above) and quantitative data where possible (Pachler, 2009; Vavoula & Sharples, 2009);
- *extensively informed*: it should draw on multiple information sources (Kukulska-Hulme, 2009) and collect multiple data sets (Looi et al., 2010);
- *aligned with the medium*: it should exploit mobile technologies where appropriate to collect data such as user logs (Pachler, 2009) as unobtrusively as possible (Looi et al., 2010);
- *longitudinal*: it should extend from project conception to deployment over time (Diaz, 2010; Vavoula & Sharples, 2009), which may necessitate finding ways of collecting data beyond initial project funding periods;
- *ethical*: it should avoid subjecting (sometimes disadvantaged) populations to intrusive or constant surveillance (cf. Chapter 3), especially given the semi-private nature of mobile devices and the amorphous nature of mobile learning integrated into everyday life (Pachler, 2009; Vavoula & Sharples, 2009), and it should consider developing 'user-generated ethics' to supplement the ethics clearances granted by Western research bodies (Traxler, 2013b).

Analysing the data – the research should be:

- *rigorously evaluated for hard outcomes*: it should provide evidence of learning outcomes on traditional assessments, using statistics where appropriate, as well as using statistical correlations to identify broader patterns in areas like educational access, employment, and economic impact;
- *broadly evaluated for soft outcomes*: it should provide evidence of more difficult-to-measure soft outcomes (Traxler, 2013a), including learning outcomes like the acquisition of 21st century skills and digital literacies and, more broadly still, changes in teaching and learning practices (Diaz, 2010; Vavoula & Sharples, 2009), as well as personal and social impact (Ros i Solé, 2009).

Sharing the results – the research should be:

- *reported in detail*: it should fully describe the context and implementation to allow readers to assess whether an initiative is reproducible elsewhere (Matthew Kam, personal communication, July 2013), as well as explaining the research framing, data collection and data analysis to allow readers to assess whether to reuse, build on or deviate from these in their own research;

- *peer reviewed*: it should demonstrate the credibility of the data analysis and conclusions by subjecting them to peer review (UNESCO, 2013b), notwithstanding the need to make room for non-Western and/or more creative approaches which may opt to use other forums, from edited books to social media, to bypass the strictures of narrow international conference and journal reviewing procedures;

- *well-disseminated*: it should be widely communicated (GSMA, 2010a), allowing insights to be shared between projects and, moreover, generalisations to be abstracted across projects in order to give our policymakers – and ourselves – a clearer sense of the big picture (Traxler, 2013b). This in turn could promote a new cycle of cumulative, theoretically and empirically informed research (see 'Framing the research' above).

Such research will help establish the still emerging, and still undertheorised, fields of m-learning and MALL. In an era and an area which are suspicious of unifying theories (Traxler, 2007; cf. Levy & Stockwell, 2006, on CALL), it may be that we don't need one theory but a cluster of interrelated theories of mobile learning and MALL. These should shed light on different mobile learning contexts; different agendas for mobile learning; different kinds of mobile hardware, connectivity, and software; different approaches to mobile teaching and learning; and different aspects of language, literacy and culture that can be taught or learned through mobile devices. Drawing on varied experiences around the world, of the kind presented in the vignettes and case studies, these theories should be expansive rather than constrictive, providing scaffolds for enhancing learning potential in multiple ways in multiple settings. In short, they should be *theories of the possible*, with the caveat that what is 'possible' must be grounded in what has been, or can be, demonstrated empirically with real teachers and real students in real contexts.

Of course, these theories of mobile learning should also be temporary, designed to serve us during our transitional mobile stage on the way to ubiquitous technology-enhanced learning – that is, 'just learning', with no prefixes. In the meantime, the spread of mobile devices across the world is exposing our commonalities as well as our differences, and compelling us to explore what it means to learn in ways that are both locally and globally viable. If we're open to developing a broader perspective, not just on *mobile language learning,* nor even just on *mobile learning,* but on *learning* in general, we may find ourselves entering a space of educational and social possibilities that go far beyond what we've imagined so far. And so we return, finally, to the question posed at the end of the first chapter: are we ready to take this journey?

Recommended Reading

Getting up to date

Berge, Z.L. & Muilenburg, L.Y. (Eds.) (2013). *Handbook of Mobile Learning*. New York: Routledge.

Cope, B. & Kalantzis, M. (Eds.) (2009). *Ubiquitous Learning*. Urbana, IL: University of Illinois Press.

Díaz-Vera, J.E. (Ed.) (2012). *Left to My Own Devices: Learner Autonomy and Mobile-assisted Language Learning*. Bingley, West Yorkshire: Emerald Group.

Dikkers, S., Martin, J. & Coulter, B. (Eds.) (2011). *Mobile Media Learning: Amazing Uses of Mobile Devices for Learning*. Pittsburgh, PA: ETC Press.

Float Mobile Learning Primer [app]. http://floatlearning.com/apps/float-mobile-learning-primer/

Hockly, N. & Dudeney, G. (in press). *Going Mobile: Teaching with Hand-held Devices*. Surrey: Delta.

JISC. (n.d.). *Mobile Learning Infokit*. http://www.jiscinfonet.ac.uk/infokits/mobile-learning/

Pachler, N., Bachmair, B. & Cook, J. (2010). *Mobile Learning: Structures, Agency, Practices*. New York: Springer.

Parsons, D. (Ed.) (2011). *Combining E-learning and M-learning: New Applications of Blended Educational Resources*. Hershey, PA: Information Science Reference.

Parsons, D. (Ed.) (2012). *Refining Current Practices in Mobile and Blended Learning: New Applications*. Hershey, PA: Information Science Reference.

Parsons, D. (Ed.) (2013). *Innovations in Mobile Educational Technologies and Applications*. Hershey, PA: Information Science Reference.

Quinn, C. (2012). *The Mobile Academy: Learning for Higher Education*. San Francisco: Jossey-Bass.

Stodd, J. (2012). *A Mindset for Mobile Learning: A Journey through Theory and Practice*. Smashwords.

UNESCO. (2013). *UNESCO Policy Guidelines for Mobile Learning*. Paris: UNESCO. http://unesdoc.unesco.org/images/0021/002196/219641E.pdf

Vavoula, G., Pachler, N. & Kukulska-Hulme, A. (Eds.) (2009). *Researching Mobile Learning: Frameworks, Tools and Research Designs*. Oxford: Peter Lang.

Vosloo, S. (2012). *Mobile Learning and Policies: Key Issues to Consider*. Paris: UNESCO. http://unesdoc.unesco.org/images/0021/002176/217638E.pdf

West, M. (2012). *Mobile Learning for Teachers: Global Themes*. Paris: UNESCO. http://unesdoc.unesco.org/images/0021/002164/216452E.pdf

West, M. (2012). *Turning on Mobile Learning: Global Themes*. Paris: UNESCO. http://unesdoc.unesco.org/images/0021/002164/216451E.pdf

Woodill, G. (2011). *The Mobile Learning Edge: Tools and Technologies for Developing your Teams*. New York: McGraw-Hill.

Keeping up to date

Business Insider: Tech. http://www.businessinsider.com/sai
Development Gateway. http://www.developmentgateway.org/
IAmLearn. http://www.iamlearn.org/
ICT for Development Network. (CI Global). http://www.comminit.com/ict-4-development/
ICT in Education: Mobile Learning. (UNESCO). http://www.unesco.org/new/en/unesco/themes/icts/m4ed/
infoDev: Mobile. http://www.infodev.org/mobile
M-learning References. (Mark Pegrum). http://e-language.wikispaces.com/m-references
mLearnopedia. (Aggregage). http://cc.mlearnopedia.com/
Mobile for Development. (GSMA). http://www.gsma.com/mobilefordevelopment/
Mobiles for Education Alliance. http://www.meducationalliance.org/
NMC Horizon Project. http://www.nmc.org/horizon-project
Our Mobile Planet. (Google, Ipsos, MMA & IAB). http://www.thinkwithgoogle.com/mobileplanet/
Pew Internet: Mobile. http://pewinternet.org/topics/Mobile.aspx
ReadWrite: Mobile. http://readwrite.com/mobile
Ubiquitous Learning. (Mark Pegrum). http://www.scoop.it/t/ubiquitous-learning
WorkLearnMobile. (Qualcomm Learning Center). http://www.worklearnmobile.org/

References

Abdous, M., Camarena, M.M. & Facer, B.R. (2009). MALL technology: Use of academic podcasting in the foreign language classroom. *ReCALL*, 21(1), 76–95.

Abelson, H. (2011). Mobile ramblings. *EDUCAUSE Quarterly*, 34(1). http://www. educause.edu/ero/article/mobile-ramblings

Adami, E. & Kress, G. (2010). The social semiotics of convergent mobile devices: New forms of composition and the transformation of *habitus*. In G. Kress, *Multimodality: A Social Semiotic Approach to Contemporary Communication*. London: Routledge.

Aljohani, N.R. & Davis, H.C. (2012). Learning analytics in mobile and ubiquitous learning environments. In M. Specht, M. Sharples & J. Multisilta (Eds.), *mLearn 2012: Proceedings of the 11th International Conference on Mobile and Contextual Learning 2012*, Helsinki, Finland, 16–18 October (pp.70–77). http://ceur-ws.org/ Vol-955/papers/paper_70.pdf

Al-Mekhlafi, K., Hu, X. & Zheng, Z. (2009). An approach to context-aware mobile Chinese language learning for foreign students. In X. Hu, E. Scornavacca & Q. Hu (Eds.), *Proceedings: Eighth International Conference on Mobile Business (ICMB 2009)*, Dalian, China, 27–28 June (pp.340–346). Los Alamitos, CA: CPS/IEEE Computer Society.

Al-Shehri, S. (2011). Mobile social networking in language learning: A transformational tool. *International Journal of Mobile Learning and Organisation*, 5(3/4), 345–359.

Baddeley, A. (1998). *Human Memory: Theory and Practice* (revised ed.). Boston: Allyn & Bacon.

Baleghizadeh, S. & Oladrostam, E. (2010). The effect of mobile-assisted language learning (MALL) on grammatical accuracy of EFL students. *MEXTESOL Journal*, 34(2), 1–10.

Ballantyne, N. & Tyers, A. (2012). British Council's mobile learning projects in terms of international development. *mLearning Solutions for International Development: Rethinking What's Possible. Proceedings from Pre-conference Workshop*, mLearn 2012, Helsinki, Finland, 15 October. http://ceur-ws.org/Vol-955/ workshops/WS4International.pdf

Ballvé, M. (2013, 31 January). Facebook reaches mobile tipping point. *BI Intelligence*. https://intelligence.businessinsider.com/facebook-passes-mobile-tipping-point-2013-1

Barber, M., Donnelly, K. & Rizvi, S. (2012). *Oceans of Innovation: The Atlantic, the Pacific, Global Leadership and the Future of Education*. London: IPPR. http://www.ippr.org/images/media/files/publication/2012/09/oceans-of-innovation_Aug2012_9543.pdf

Baron, N.S. (2008). *Always On: Language in an Online and Mobile World*. New York: Oxford University Press.

——. (2011). Assessing the internet's impact on language. In M. Consalvo & C. Ess (Eds.), *The Handbook of Internet Studies* (pp.117–136). Malden, MA: Wiley-Blackwell.

Barton, D. & Lee, C.K.M. (2012). Redefining vernacular literacies in the age of web 2.0. *Applied Linguistics*, 33(3), 282–298.

Baym, N.K. (2010). *Personal Connections in the Digital Age*. Cambridge: Polity Press.

Belshaw, D.A.J. (2011). *What is 'Digital Literacy'? A Pragmatic Investigation*. Ed.D. thesis. http://neverendingthesis.com/doug-belshaw-edd-thesis-final.pdf

Bennett, S., Maton, K. & Kervin, L. (2008). The 'digital natives' debate: A critical review of the evidence. *British Journal of Educational Technology*, 39(5), 775–786.

Berge, Z.L. (2011). If you think socialisation in mLearning is difficult, try personalisation. *International Journal of Mobile Learning and Organisation*, 5(3/4), 231–238.

Bhabha, H.K. (1994). *The Location of Culture*. London: Routledge.

Bjerede, M. & Bondi, T. (n.d.). *Learning is Personal: Stories of Android Tablet Use in the 5th Grade*. Learninguntethered.com. http://www.learninguntethered.com/wp-content/uploads/2012/08/Learning-is-Personal.pdf

Blake, R.J. (2008). *Brave New Digital Classroom: Technology and Foreign Language Learning*. Washington, DC: Georgetown University Press.

Borau, K., Ullrich, C., Feng, J. & Shen, R. (2009). Microblogging for language learning: Using Twitter to train communicative and cultural competence. In M. Spaniol, Q. Li, R. Klamma & R.W.H. Lau (Eds.), *Advances in Web Based Learning – ICWL 2009*, 8th International Conference, Aachen, Germany, August (pp.78–87). Berlin: Springer.

Borgia, L. (2009). Enhanced vocabulary podcasts implementation in fifth grade classrooms. *Reading Improvement*, 46(4), 263–272.

Botha, A., Vosloo, S., Kuner, J. & van den Berg, M. (2011). Improving cross-cultural awareness and communication through mobile technologies. In D. Parsons (Ed.), *Combining E-learning and M-learning: New Applications of Blended Educational Resources* (pp.308–318). Hershey, PA: Information Science Reference.

boyd, d. & Crawford, K. (2012). Critical questions for big data: Provocations for a cultural, technological, and scholarly phenomenon. *Information, Communication & Society*, 15(5), 662–679.

Broadband Commission for Digital Development (n.d.). *Broadband Targets for 2015*. http://www.broadbandcommission.org/Documents/Broadband_Targets.pdf

Buchanan, R. (2011). Paradox, promise and public pedagogy: Implications of the Federal Government's Digital Education Revolution. *Australian Journal of Teacher Education*, 36(2), 67–78. http://ro.ecu.edu.au/cgi/viewcontent.cgi?article=1524&context=ajte

Bull, G. & Anstey, M. (2010). *Evolving Pedagogies: Reading and Writing in a Multimodal World*. Carlton South, VIC: Curriculum Press.

Bunyad (n.d.). *Mobile Based Post Literacy Programme: Mobile as a Tool for Illiterate Women*. http://www.bunyad.org.pk/Mobile%20Based%20Literacy.htm

Burbules, N.C. (2009). Meanings of 'ubiquitous learning'. In B. Cope & M. Kalantzis (Eds.), *Ubiquitous Learning* (pp.15–20). Urbana, IL: University of Illinois Press.

Burden, K., Hopkins, P., Male, T., Martin, S. & Trala, C. (2012). *iPad Scotland Evaluation*. Hull: University of Hull. http://www.janhylen.se/wp-content/uploads/2013/01/Skottland.pdf

Byram, M. (1997). *Teaching and Assessing Intercultural Communicative Competence.* Clevedon: Multilingual Matters.

Campigotto, R., McEwen, R. & Demmans Epp, C. (2013). Especially social: Exploring the use of an iOS application in special needs classrooms. *Computers & Education*, 60, 74–86.

Carlson, S. (2004, 17 September). With this enrollment, a toy surprise. *The Chronicle of Higher Education.* http://chronicle.com/article/With-This-Enrollment-a-Toy/12432

Carmigniani, J. & Furht, B. (2011). Augmented reality: An overview. In B. Furht (Ed.), *Handbook of Augmented Reality* (pp.3–46). New York: Springer.

Carr, N. (2008). *The Big Switch: Rewiring the World, from Edison to Google.* New York: W.W. Norton.

Castells, M. (2008). Afterword. In J.E. Katz (Ed.), *Handbook of Mobile Communication Studies* (pp.447–451). Cambridge, MA: MIT Press.

——. (2010). *The Rise of the Network Society* (2nd ed.). Chichester: Wiley-Blackwell.

——, Fernández-Ardèvol, M., Qiu, J.L. & Sey, A. (2007). *Mobile Communication and Society: A Global Perspective.* Cambridge, MA: MIT Press.

Centre for Community Child Health [Australia]. (2009). *Television and Early Childhood Development.* Policy Brief No.16. The Royal Children's Hospital Melbourne/Murdoch Children's Research Institute. http://www.rch.org.au/uploadedFiles/Main/Content/ccch/PB_16_template_final_web.pdf

Chan, T.-W., Roschelle, J., Hsi, S., Kinshuk, Sharples M., Brown, T., Patton, C., et al. (2006). One-to-one technology-enhanced learning: An opportunity for global research collaboration. *Research and Practice in Technology Enhanced Learning*, 1(1), 3–29.

Chan, W.M., Chen, I.R. & Döpel, M.G. (2011). Podcasting in foreign language learning: Insights for podcast design from a developmental research project. In M. Levy, F. Blin, C. Bradin Siskin & O. Takeuchi (Eds.), *WorldCALL: International Perspectives on Computer-Assisted Language Learning* (pp.19–37). New York: Routledge.

Chang, C.-K. & Hsu, C.-K. (2011). A mobile-assisted synchronously collaborative translation-annotation system for English as a Foreign Language (EFL) reading comprehension. *Computer-Assisted Language Learning*, 24(2), 155–180.

Chapelle, C.A. (2009). The relationship between second language acquisition theory and computer-assisted language learning. *The Modern Language Journal*, 93, 741–753.

Chen, B.X. (2011). *Always On: How the iPhone Unlocked the Anything-Anytime-Anywhere Future – and Locked Us In.* Cambridge, MA: Da Capo.

Chen, C.-M. & Hsu, S.-H. (2008). Personalized intelligent mobile learning system for supporting effective English learning. *Educational Technology & Society*, 11(3), 153–180. http://www.ifets.info/journals/11_3/12.pdf

—— & Li, Y.-L. (2010). Personalised context-aware ubiquitous learning system for supporting effective English vocabulary learning. *Interactive Learning Environments*, 18(4), 341–364.

Chen, X.-B. (2013). Tablets for informal language learning: Student usage and attitudes. *Language Learning & Technology*, 17(1), 20–36. http://llt.msu.edu/issues/february2013/chenxb.pdf

Chifari, A., Chiazzese, G., Seta, L., Merlo, G., Ottaviano, S. & Allegra, M. (2010). A reflection on some critical aspects of online reading comprehension. *Informatica*, 34, 491–495.

Chinnery, G.M. (2006). Going to the MALL: Mobile-assisted language learning. *Language Learning & Technology*, 10(1), 9–16. http://llt.msu.edu/vol10num1/pdf/emerging.pdf

Chonchaiya, W. & Pruksananonda, C. (2008). Television viewing associates with delayed language development. *Acta Pædiatrica*, 97, 977–982.

Christakis, N.A. & Fowler, J.H. (2009). *Connected: The Surprising Power of Our Social Networks and How They Shape Our Lives*. New York: Little, Brown & Co.

Chun, D.M. (2006). CALL technologies for L2 reading. In L. Ducate & N. Arnold (Eds.), *Calling on CALL: From Theory and Research to New Directions in Foreign Language Teaching* (pp.69–98). San Marcos, TX: CALICO.

——, Jiang, Y. & Ávila, N. (2013). Visualization of tone for learning Mandarin Chinese. In J. Levis & K. LeVelle (Eds.), *Proceedings of the 4th Pronunciation in Second Language Learning and Teaching Conference*, August 2012 (pp.77–89). Ames, IA: Iowa State University.

Churchill, D. (2006). Teachers' private theories and their design of technology-based learning. *British Journal of Educational Technology*, 37(4), 559–576.

Cisco. (2012). *Cisco Visual Networking Index: Global Mobile Data Traffic Forecast Update, 2011–2016*. White Paper. http://www.cisco.com/en/US/solutions/collateral/ns341/ns525/ns537/ns705/ns827/white_paper_c11-520862.pdf

——. (2013). *Cisco Visual Networking Index: Global Mobile Data Traffic Forecast Update, 2012–2017*. White Paper. http://www.cisco.com/en/US/solutions/collateral/ns341/ns525/ns537/ns705/ns827/white_paper_c11-520862.pdf

Clark, R.C. & Mayer, R.E. (2011). *E-learning and the Science of Instruction: Proven Guidelines for Consumers and Designers of Multimedia Learning* (3rd ed.). San Francisco: Pfeiffer.

——, Nguyen, F. & Sweller, J. (2006). *Efficiency in Learning: Evidence-based Guidelines to Manage Cognitive Load*. San Francisco: Pfeiffer.

Cochrane, T.D. (2014). Critical success factors for transforming pedagogy with mobile web 2.0. *British Journal of Educational Technology*, 45(1), 65–68.

Cocotas, A. (2013, 31 January). *2013 – The Year Ahead in Mobile*. Business Insider. http://au.businessinsider.com/2013--the-year-ahead-in-mobile-slide-deck-2013-12

Coiro, J. (2009, March). Rethinking online reading assessment. *Educational Leadership*, pp.59–63.

——. (2011). Predicting reading comprehension on the internet: Contributions of offline reading skills, online reading skills, and prior knowledge. *Journal of Literacy Research*, 43(4), 352–392.

Comas-Quinn, A. & Mardomingo, R. (2012). Language learning on the move: A review of mobile blogging tasks and their potential. In J.E. Díaz-Vera (Ed.), *Left to My Own Devices: Learner Autonomy and Mobile-Assisted Language Learning* (pp.47–65). Bingley, West Yorkshire: Emerald Group.

——, Mardomingo, R. & Valentine, C. (2009). Mobile blogs in language learning: Making the most of informal and situated learning opportunities. *ReCALL*, 21(1), 96–112.

Constantinides, M. (2013, 20 May). From curation to creation. *TEFL Matters*. http://marisaconstantinides.edublogs.org/2013/05/20/from-curation-to-creation/

Cook, J. (2010). Mobile learner generated contexts: Research on the internalization of the world of cultural products. In B. Bachmair (Ed.), *Medienbildung in neuen Kulturräumen: Die deutschsprachige und britische Diskussion* (pp.113–125). Wiesbaden: VS Verlag für Sozialwissenschaften.

Couros, A. (2010). Developing personal learning networks for open and social learning. In G. Veletsianos (Ed.), *Emerging Technologies in Distance Education* (pp.109–128). Edmonton, AB: Athabasca University Press. http://www.aupress. ca/books/120177/ebook/06_Veletsianos_2010-Emerging_Technologies_in_ Distance_Education.pdf

Crystal, D. (2006). *Language and the Internet* (2nd ed.). Cambridge: Cambridge University Press.

———. (2008). *Txtng: The Gr8 Db8*. Oxford: Oxford University Press.

———. (2011). *Internet Linguistics: A Student Guide*. London: Routledge.

DEECD (Department of Education and Early Childhood Development) [Victoria, Australia]. (n.d.). Evaluation. *iPads for Learning*. http://www.ipadsforeducation. vic.edu.au/ipad-student-trial/ipad-research

Deloitte/GSMA. (2012). *Sub-Saharan Africa Mobile Observatory 2012*. London: GSMA.

Demouy, V. & Kukulska-Hulme, A. (2010). On the spot: Using mobile devices for listening and speaking practice on a French language programme. *Open Learning*, 25(3), 217–232.

Deng, H. & Shao, Y. (2011). Self-directed English vocabulary learning with a mobile application in everyday context. In *10th World Conference on Mobile and Contextual Learning: mLearn 2011 Conference Proceedings*, Beijing, China, 18–21 October (pp.24–31). Beijing: Beijing Normal University. http://mlearn. bnu.edu.cn/source/Conference_Procedings.pdf

Deriquito, M. & Domingo, Z. (2012). *Mobile Learning for Teachers in Asia: Exploring the Potential of Mobile Technologies to Support Teachers and Improve Practice*. Paris: UNESCO. http://unesdoc.unesco.org/images/0021/002162/216284E.pdf

de Waard, I. (2013). mMOOC design: Ubiquitous, open learning in the cloud. In Z.L. Berge & L.Y. Muilenburg (Eds.), *Handbook of Mobile Learning* (pp.356–368). New York: Routledge.

Diaz, V. (2010). *Mobile Teaching and Learning: Engaging Students and Measuring Impact*. ECAR Symposium. http://net.educause.edu/ir/library/pdf/ ECR1005.pdf

Dikkers, S. (2011). Dewey buys a smartphone. In S. Dikkers, J. Martin & B. Coulter (Eds.), *Mobile Media Learning: Amazing Uses of Mobile Devices for Learning*. Pittsburgh, PA: ETC Press.

Dourish, P. (2004). What we talk about when we talk about context. *Personal and Ubiquitous Computing*, 8(1), 19–30.

Driver, P. (2012). Pervasive games and mobile technologies for embodied language learning. *International Journal of Computer-Assisted Language Learning and Teaching*, 2(4), 50–63.

Ducate, L. & Lomicka, L. (2009). Podcasting: An effective tool for honing language students' pronunciation? *Language Learning & Technology*, 13(3), 66–86. http://llt.msu.edu/vol13num3/ducatelomicka.pdf

Dudeney, G., Hockly, N. & Pegrum, M. (2013). *Digital Literacies*. Harlow, Essex: Pearson.

Dykes, G. & Renfrew Knight, H. (2012). *Mobile Learning for Teachers in Europe: Exploring the Potential of Mobile Technologies to Support Teachers and Improve Practice*. Paris: UNESCO. http://unesdoc.unesco.org/images/0021/002161/216167E.pdf

The Economist. (2012, 21 November). Live and unplugged. http://www.economist.com/news/21566417-2013-internet-will-become-mostly-mobile-medium-who-will-be-winners-and-losers-live-and

——. (2013, 5 January). Conquering Babel. http://www.economist.com/news/science-and-technology/21569014-simultaneous-translation-computer-getting-closer-conquering-babel

EIA (English in Action). (2013). About EIA. *English in Action*. http://www.eiabd.com/eia/index.php/abouts/about-eia

Engeström, Y., Miettinen R. & Punamäki, R.-L. (Eds.). (1999). *Perspectives on Activity Theory*. Cambridge: Cambridge University Press.

Facebook. (2013, 30 January). *Facebook Reports Fourth Quarter and Full Year 2012 Results*. http://goo.gl/6TlQA

Fallahkhair, S., Pemberton, L. & Griffiths, R. (2007). Development of a cross-platform ubiquitous language learning service via mobile phone and interactive television. *Journal of Computer-Assisted Learning*, 23, 312–325.

Farago, P. (2013, 18 February). China knocks off U.S. to become world's top smart device market. *Flurry Blog*. http://blog.flurry.com/bid/94352/China-Knocks-Off-U-S-to-Become-Top-Smartphone-Tablet-Market

Fisher, T., Sharples, M., Pemberton, R., Ogata, H., Uosaki, N., Edmonds, P., Hull, A., et al. (2012). Incidental second language vocabulary learning from reading novels: A comparison of three mobile modes. *International Journal of Mobile and Blended Learning*, 4(4), 47–61.

FitzGerald, E., Adams, A., Ferguson, R., Gaved, M., Mor, Y. & Thomas, R. (2012). Augmented reality and mobile learning: The state of the art. In M. Specht, M. Sharples & J. Multisilta (Eds.), *mLearn 2012: Proceedings of the 11th International Conference on Mobile and Contextual Learning 2012*, Helsinki, Finland, 16–18 October (pp.62–69). http://ceur-ws.org/Vol-955/papers/paper_49.pdf

Fotouhi-Ghazvini, F., Earnshaw, R.A. & Haji-Esmaeili, L. (2009). Mobile-assisted language learning in a developing country context. In H. Ugail, R.S.R. Qahwaji, R.A. Earnshaw & P.J. Willis (Eds.), *Proceedings: 2009 International Conference on Cyberworlds*, Bradford, UK, 7–11 September (pp.391–397). Los Alamitos, CA: CPS/IEEE Computer Society.

——, Earnshaw, R., Robison, D., Moeini, A. & Excell, P. (2011). Using a conversational framework in mobile game based learning – Assessment and evaluation. In R. Kwan, C. McNaught, P. Tsang, F.L. Wang & K.C. Li (Eds.), *Enhancing Learning through Technology. Education Unplugged: Mobile Technologies and Web 2.0*, International Conference, ICT 2011, Hong Kong, China, 11–13 July (pp.201–213). Berlin: Springer. http://scim.brad.ac.uk/staff/pdf/drobison/Springer-HK-FF.pdf

Fritschi, J. & Wolf, M.A. (2012a). *Mobile Learning for Teachers in North America: Exploring the Potential of Mobile Technologies to Support Teachers and Improve Practice*. Paris: UNESCO. http://unesdoc.unesco.org/images/0021/002160/216084E.pdf

—— & Wolf, M.A. (2012b). *Turning on Mobile Learning in North America: Illustrative Initiatives and Policy Implications*. Paris: UNESCO. http://unesdoc.unesco.org/images/0021/002160/216083E.pdf

Gallen, C. (2012, 28 November). Cellular penetration in Africa expected to surpass 80% in 1Q-2013, says ABI research. *Business Wire*. http://www.businesswire.com/news/home/20121128005874/en/Cellular-Penetration-Africa-Expected-Surpass-80-1Q-2013

Garrett, N. (2009). Computer-assisted language learning trends and issues revisited: Integrating innovation. *The Modern Language Journal*, 93, 719–740.

Gee, J.P. (2003). *What Video Games Have to Teach Us about Learning and Literacy*. New York: Palgrave Macmillan.

Gjedde, L. & Bo-Kristensen, M. (2012). Workplace mobile-assisted second language learning: Designing for learner generated authenticity. In J.E. Díaz-Vera (Ed.), *Left to My Own Devices: Learner Autonomy and Mobile-Assisted Language Learning* (pp.183–195). Bingley, West Yorkshire: Emerald Group.

Global Partnership for Education. (n.d.). *Towards Reading for All: Early Grade Reading Assistance in Cambodia*. http://www.globalpartnership.org/media/docs/our_work/ACR_Asia_Workshop/presentations/day1/1210_Towards_Reading_for_All.pdf

Gonglewski, M. & DuBravac, S. (2006). Multiliteracy: Second language literacy in the multimedia environment. In L. Ducate & N. Arnold (Eds.), *Calling on CALL: From Theory and Research to New Directions in Foreign Language Teaching* (pp.43–68). San Marcos, TX: CALICO.

Grantham O'Brien, M. (2006). Teaching pronunciation and intonation with computer technology. In L. Ducate & N. Arnold (Eds.), *Calling on CALL: From Theory and Research to New Directions in Foreign Language Teaching* (pp.127–148). San Marcos, TX: CALICO.

Gray, J.H., Bulat, J., Jaynes, C. & Cunningham, A. (2009). LeapFrog learning design: Playful approaches to literacy, from LeapPad to the tag reading system. In A. Druin (Ed.), *Mobile Technology for Children: Designing for Interaction and Learning* (pp.171–194). Burlington, MA: Morgan Kaufmann.

Greenfield, S. (2008). *ID: The Quest for Identity in the 21st Century*. London: Sceptre.

Gromik, N.A. (2012). Cell phone video recording feature as a language learning tool: A case study. *Computers & Education*, 58, 223–230.

GSMA (Global System for Mobile Communications Association). (2010a). *mLearning: A Platform for Educational Opportunities at the Base of the Pyramid*. London: GSMA. http://www.gsma.com/mobilefordevelopment/wp-content/uploads/2012/04/mlearningaplatformforeducationalopportunitiesatthebaseofthepyramid.pdf

——. (2010b). *Women and Mobile: A Global Opportunity*. London: GSMA. http://www.gsma.com/mobilefordevelopment/wp-content/uploads/2013/01/GSMA_Women_and_Mobile-A_Global_Opportunity.pdf

Gulati, S. (2008). Technology-enhanced learning in developing nations: A review. *International Review of Research in Open and Distance Learning*, 9(1), 1–16.

Hague, C. & Williamson, B. (2009). *Digital Participation, Digital Literacy, and School Subjects: A Review of the Policies, Literature and Evidence*. Bristol: Futurelab. http://archive.futurelab.org.uk/resources/documents/lit_reviews/DigitalParticipation.pdf

Hall, J. (2012, 26 December). MP3 players are dead. *Business Insider.* http://www.businessinsider.com/mp3-players-are-dead-2012-12

Han, J. (2012). Robot assisted language learning. *Language Learning & Technology,* 16(3), 1–9. http://llt.msu.edu/issues/october2012/emerging.pdf

Harel, I. & Papert, S. (Eds.). (1991). *Constructionism: Research Reports and Essays, 1985–1990.* Norwood, NJ: Ablex.

Hargittai, E. (2010). Digital na(t)ives? Variation in internet skills and uses among members of the 'net generation'. *Sociological Inquiry,* 80(1), 92–113.

HARP (Handheld Augmented Reality Project). (n.d.). *Handheld Augmented Reality Project (HARP) & Alien Contact! Unit Overview.* http://isites.harvard.edu/fs/docs/icb.topic135310.files/AlienContactOverview012907.pdf

Hayati, A., Jalilifar, A. & Mashhadi, A. (2013). Using short message service (SMS) to teach English idioms to EFL students. *British Journal of Educational Technology,* 44(1), 66–81.

Heift, T. & Chapelle, C.A. (2012). Language learning through technology. In S.M. Gass & A. Mackey (Eds.), *The Routledge Handbook of Second Language Acquisition* (pp.555–569). London: Routledge.

—— & Schulze, M. (2007). *Errors and Intelligence in Computer-Assisted Language Learning: Parsers and Pedagogues.* New York: Routledge.

Heyward, M. (2002). From international to intercultural: Redefining the international school for a globalized world. *Journal of Research in International Education,* 1(1), 9–32.

Ho, J. & Thukral, H. (2009). *Tuned In to Student Success: Assessing the Impact of Interactive Radio Instruction for the Hardest-to-Reach.* Washington, DC: EDC. http://idd.edc.org/sites/idd.edc.org/files/EDC%20Tuned%20in%20to%20Student%20Success%20Report.pdf

Hockly, N. & Dudeney, G. (in press). *Going Mobile: Teaching with Hand-held Devices.* Surrey: Delta.

Holden, C. & Sykes, J. (2011). Mentira: Prototyping language-based locative gameplay. In S. Dikkers, J. Martin & B. Coulter (Eds.), *Mobile Media Learning: Amazing Uses of Mobile Devices for Learning.* Pittsburgh, PA: ETC Press.

Hou, B., Ogata, H., Miyata, M., Li, M., Liu, Y. & Yano, Y. (2012). JAMIOLAS 3.0: Supporting Japanese mimicry and onomatopoeia learning using sensor data. In D. Parsons (Ed.), *Refining Current Practices in Mobile and Blended Learning: New Applications* (pp.98–112). Hershey, PA: Information Science Reference.

Hourcade, J.P., Beitler, D., Cormenzana, F. & Flores, P. (2009). Early OLPC experiences in a rural Uruguayan school. In A. Druin (Ed.), *Mobile Technology for Children: Designing for Interaction and Learning* (pp.227–243). Burlington, MA: Morgan Kaufmann.

Hsu, C.-K., Hwang, G.-J. & Chang, C.-K. (2013). A personalized recommendation-based mobile learning approach to improving the reading performance of EFL students. *Computers & Education,* 63, 327–336.

——, Hwang, G.-J., Chang, Y.-T. & Chang, C.-K. (2013). Effects of video caption modes on English listening comprehension and vocabulary acquisition using handheld devices. *Educational Technology & Society,* 16(1), 403–414. http://www.ifets.info/journals/16_1/35.pdf

Hwang, W.-Y., Chen, C.-Y. & Chen, H.S.L. (2011). Facilitating EFL writing of elementary school students in familiar situated contexts with mobile devices. In *10th World Conference on Mobile and Contextual Learning: mLearn 2011*

Conference Proceedings, Beijing, China, 18–21 October (pp.15–23). Beijing: Beijing Normal University. http://mlearn.bnu.edu.cn/source/Conference_Proceedings.pdf

Hylén, J. (2012). *Turning on Mobile Learning in Europe: Illustrative Initiatives and Policy Implications*. Paris: UNESCO. http://unesdoc.unesco.org/images/0021/002161/216165E.pdf

IDC (International Data Corporation). (2013, 25 April). More smartphones were shipped in Q1 2013 than feature phones, an industry first according to IDC. *IDC*. http://www.idc.com/getdoc.jsp?containerId=prUS24085413

Isaacs, S. (2012a). *Mobile Learning for Teachers in Africa and the Middle East: Exploring the Potential of Mobile Technologies to Support Teachers and Improve Practice*. Paris: UNESCO. http://unesdoc.unesco.org/images/0021/002163/216358E.pdf

——. (2012b). *Turning on Mobile Learning in Africa and the Middle East: Illustrative Initiatives and Policy Implications*. Paris: UNESCO. http://unesdoc.unesco.org/images/0021/002163/216359E.pdf

ISTE (International Society for Technology in Education). (2012). *NETS*. http://www.iste.org/standards

ITU (International Telecommunication Union). (2012). *Measuring the Information Society: 2012*. Geneva: ITU. http://www.itu.int/en/ITU-D/Statistics/Documents/publications/mis2012/MIS2012_without_Annex_4.pdf

——. (2013). *The World in 2013: ICT Facts and Figures*. Geneva: ITU. http://www.itu.int/en/ITU-D/Statistics/Documents/facts/ICTFactsFigures2013.pdf

Jabr, F. (2013, 11 April). The reading brain in the digital age: The science of paper versus screens. *Scientific American*. http://www.scientificamerican.com/article.cfm?id=reading-paper-screens

James, K.H. & Engelhardt, L. (2012). The effects of handwriting experience on functional brain development in pre-literate children. *Trends in Neuroscience and Education*, 1, 32–42.

Jewitt, C. (2005). Multimodality, 'reading', and 'writing' for the 21st century. *Discourse: Studies in the Cultural Politics of Education*, 26(3), 315–331.

——. (2008). Multimodality and literacy in school classrooms. *Review of Research in Education*, 32, 241–267.

JISC. (Joint Information Systems Committee) [UK]. (2012, 13 December). Using interactive posters with learners. *JISC Regional Support Centre East Midlands*. http://www.jiscrsc.ac.uk/eastmidlands/news/2012/december/using-interactive-posters-with-learners.aspx

——. (n.d.). *Mobile Learning Infokit*. http://www.jiscinfonet.ac.uk/infokits/mobile-learning/

Johnson, C.A. (2011). *The Information Diet: A Case for Conscious Consumption*. Sebastopol, CA: O'Reilly Media.

Johnson, L., Adams, S. & Cummins, M. (2012). *NMC Horizon Report: 2012 K–12 Edition*. Austin, TX: New Media Consortium. http://www.nmc.org/pdf/2012-horizon-report-K12.pdf

——, Adams Becker, S., Cummins, M., Estrada, V., Freeman, A. & Ludgate, H. (2013). *NMC Horizon Report: 2013 Higher Education Edition*. Austin, TX: New Media Consortium. http://www.nmc.org/pdf/2013-horizon-report-HE.pdf

Joseph, S.R.H. & Uther, M. (2009). Mobile devices for language learning: Multimedia approaches. *Research and Practice in Technology Enhanced Learning*, 4(1), 7–32.

Kagohara, D.M., van der Meer, L., Ramdoss, S., O'Reilly, M.F., Lancioni, G.E., Davis, T.N., Rispoli, M., et al. (2013). Using iPods and iPads in teaching programs for individuals with developmental disabilities: A systematic review. *Research in Developmental Disabilities*, 34, 147–156.

Kaku, M. (2011). *Physics of the Future: How Science Will Shape Human Destiny and Our Daily Lives by the Year 2100*. London: Allen Lane.

Kalantzis, M. & Cope, B. (2012). *Literacies*. Port Melbourne, VIC: Cambridge University Press.

Kam, M. (2013). Mobile learning games for low-income children in India: Lessons from 2004–2009. In Z.L. Berge & L.Y. Muilenburg (Eds.), *Handbook of Mobile Learning* (pp.617–627). New York: Routledge.

Kemp, N. (2011). Mobile technology and literacy: Effects across cultures, abilities and the lifespan. *Journal of Computer-Assisted Learning*, 27(1), 1–3.

Kennedy, C. & Levy, M. (2008). L'italiano al telefonino: Using SMS to support beginners' language learning. *ReCALL*, 20(3), 315–330.

Kenning, M.-M. (2007). *ICT and Language Learning: From Print to the Mobile Phone*. Basingstoke, Hampshire: Palgrave Macmillan.

Keogh, K.A. (2011). Using mobile phones for teaching, learning and assessing Irish in Ireland: Processes, benefits and challenges. In W. Ng (Ed.), *Mobile Technologies and Handheld Devices for Ubiquitous Learning: Research and Pedagogy* (pp.237–258). Hershey, PA: Information Science Reference.

Khanna, A. & Khanna, P. (2012). *Hybrid Reality: Thriving in the Emerging Human-Technology Civilization*. New York: TED Conferences.

Kimyayi, K. (2012). *Effective Mobile-Assisted Language Learning: A New Way to Educational Success*. Saarbrücken: Lambert Academic Publishing.

Klopfer, E. (2008). *Augmented Learning: Research and Design of Mobile Educational Games*. Cambridge, MA: MIT Press.

——. (2011). New section. In S. Dikkers, J. Martin & B. Coulter (Eds.), *Mobile Media Learning: Amazing Uses of Mobile Devices for Learning*. Pittsburgh, PA: ETC Press.

Kolb, L. (2008). *Toys to Tools: Connecting Student Cell Phones to Education*. Eugene, OR: ISTE.

Kramsch, C. (1993). *Context and Culture in Language Teaching*. Oxford: Oxford University Press.

Krashen, S. (1985). *The Input Hypothesis: Issues and Implications*. London: Longman.

Kress, G. (2003). *Literacy in the New Media Age*. London: Routledge.

——. (2010). *Multimodality: A Social Semiotic Approach to Contemporary Communication*. London: Routledge.

Kukulska-Hulme, A. (2009). Conclusions: Future directions in researching mobile learning. In G. Vavoula, N. Pachler & A. Kukulska-Hulme (Eds.), *Researching Mobile Learning: Frameworks, Tools and Research Designs* (pp.351–363). Oxford: Peter Lang.

——. (2010a). Mobile learning as a catalyst for change. *Open Learning*, 25(3), 181–185. http://oro.open.ac.uk/23773/2/Open_Learning_editorial__Accepted_Manuscript_.pdf

——. (2010b). *Mobile Learning for Quality Education and Social Inclusion*. Policy Brief. Moscow: UNESCO Institute for Information Technologies in Education. http://iite.unesco.org/pics/publications/en/files/3214679.pdf

——. (2011). Learning a language from your mobile phone – A good idea? In E. Jackson Stuart (Ed.), *Upgrading Development: Can Technology Alleviate Poverty?* (p.28). Cambridge: The Humanitarian Centre. http://www.humanitarian centre.org/wp-content/uploads/2010/09/2011-International-Development-Report.pdf

——. (2012). Prospects for inclusive mobile learning. In M. Allegra, M. Arrigo, V. Dal Grande, P. Denaro, D. La Guardia, S. Ottaviano & G. Todaro (Eds.), *Mobile Learning for Visually Impaired People* (pp.13–25). Palermo: Consiglio Nazionale delle Ricerche, Istituto per le Tecnologie Didattiche. http://oro.open.ac.uk/34206/1/Agnes1.pdf

——. (2013a). *Aligning Migration with Mobility: Female Immigrants Using Smart Technologies for Informal Learning Show the Way.* Presented at UNESCO Mobile Learning Week Symposium, Paris, France, 18–19 February. http://www.unesco.org/new/en/unesco/themes/icts/m4ed/unesco-mobile-learning-week/keynote-speakers/agnes-kukulska-hulme/

——. (2013b). Limelight on mobile learning: Integrating education and innovation. *Harvard International Review,* Spring, 12–16.

—— & Bull, S. (2009). Theory-based support for mobile language learning: Noticing and recording. *International Journal of Interactive Mobile Technologies,* 3(2), 12–18. http://online-journals.org/i-jim/article/view/740/873

—— & Shield, L. (2008). An overview of mobile-assisted language learning: From content delivery to supported collaboration and interaction. *ReCALL,* 20(3), 271–289.

Kumaravadivelu, B. (2006). *Understanding Language Teaching: From Method to Postmethod.* Mahwah, NJ: Lawrence Erlbaum.

Lam, W.S.E. & Kramsch, C. (2003). The ecology of an SLA community in a computer-mediated environment. In J. Leather & J. van Dam (Eds.), *Ecology of Language Acquisition* (pp.141–158). Dordrecht: Kluwer Academic.

Lamy, M.-N. & Goodfellow, R. (2010). Telecollaboration and learning 2.0. In S. Guth & F. Helm (Eds.), *Telecollaboration 2.0: Language, Literacies and Intercultural Learning in the 21st Century* (pp.107–138). Bern: Peter Lang.

Larsen-Freeman, D. & Cameron, L. (2008). *Complex Systems and Applied Linguistics.* Oxford: Oxford University Press.

Laurillard, D. (2012). *Teaching as a Design Science: Building Pedagogical Patterns for Learning and Technology.* New York: Routledge.

Lave, J. & Wenger, E. (1991). *Situated Learning: Legitimate Peripheral Participation.* Cambridge: Cambridge University Press.

Leadbeater, C. (and 257 other people). (2008). *We-think.* London: Profile Books.

Leier, V. (2012). Facebook used in a German film project. *The EUROCALL Review,* 20(1), 95–99. http://www.eurocall-languages.org/review/20/papers_20/22_leier.pdf

Leigh Bassendowski, S. & Petrucka, P. (2013). Are 20th-century methods of teaching applicable in the 21st century? *British Journal of Educational Technology,* 44(4), 665–667.

Lenhart, A., Arafeh, S., Smith, A. & Rankin Macgill, A. (2008). *Writing, Technology and Teens.* Washington, DC: Pew Internet. http://www.pewinternet.org/~/media//Files/Reports/2008/PIP_Writing_Report_FINAL3.pdf.pdf

Leone, S. & Leo, T. (2011). The synergy of paper-based and digital material for ubiquitous foreign language learners. *Knowledge Management &*

E-learning, (3)3, 319–341. http://www.kmel-journal.org/ojs/index.php/online-publication/article/viewFile/123/101

Levy, M. (2009). Technologies in use for second language learning. *The Modern Language Journal*, 93, 769–782.

—— & Kennedy, C. (2005). Learning Italian via mobile SMS. In A. Kukulska-Hulme & J. Traxler (Eds.), *Mobile Learning: A Handbook for Educators and Trainers* (pp.76–83). London: Routledge.

—— & Stockwell, G. (2006). *CALL Dimensions: Options and Issues in Computer-Assisted Language Learning*. New York: Lawrence Erlbaum.

Livingstone, S. (2009). *Children and the Internet: Great Expectations, Challenging Realities*. Cambridge: Polity Press.

——. (2012). Critical reflections on the benefits of ICT in education. *Oxford Review of Education*, 38(1), 9–24.

Lomicka, L. & Lord, G. (2012). A tale of tweets: Analyzing microblogging among language learners. *System*, 40, 48–63.

Long, M.H. (1996). The role of the linguistic environment in second language acquisition. In W.C. Ritchie & T.K. Bhatia (Eds.), *Handbook of Language Acquisition. Vol. 2: Second Language Acquisition* (pp.413–468). New York: Academic Press.

Looi, C.-K., Seow, P., Zhang, B., So, H.-J., Chen, W. & Wong, L.-H. (2010). Leveraging mobile technology for sustainable seamless learning: A research agenda. *British Journal of Educational Technology*, 41(2), 154–169.

Lord, G. (2008). Podcasting communities and second language pronunciation. *Foreign Language Annals*, 41(2), 364–379.

Lotherington, H. & Jenson, J. (2011). Teaching multimodal and digital literacy in L2 settings: New literacies, new basics, new pedagogies. *Annual Review of Applied Linguistics*, 31, 226–246.

Luckin, R. (2010). *Learning, Context and the Role of Technology*. Hoboken, NJ: Taylor & Francis.

Lugo, M.T. & Schurmann, S. (2012). *Turning on Mobile Learning in Latin America: Illustrative Initiatives and Policy Implications*. Paris: UNESCO. http://unesdoc.unesco.org/images/0021/002160/216080E.pdf

Lumley, T. & Mendelovits, J. (2012). How well do young people deal with contradictory and unreliable information on line? What the PISA digital reading assessment tells us. *ACEReSearch*. http://research.acer.edu.au/pisa/3

MacKinnon, R. (2012). *Consent of the Networked: The Worldwide Struggle for Internet Freedom*. New York: Basic Books.

Mangen, A. & Velay, J.-L. (2010). Digitizing literacy: Reflections on the haptics of writing. In M.H. Zadeh (Ed.), *Advances in Haptics* (pp.385–401). Vukovar, Croatia: In-Tech.

Mayer, R.E. (2009). *Multimedia Learning* (2nd ed.). New York: Cambridge University Press.

Meeker, M. (2012). *Internet Trends @ Stanford – Bases*, 3 December. KPCB. http://www.kpcb.com/insights/2012-internet-trends-update

—— & Wu, L. (2013). *Internet Trends: D11 Conference*, 29 May. KPCB. http://www.kpcb.com/insights/2013-internet-trends

Melhuish, K. & Falloon, G. (2010). Looking to the future: M-learning with the iPad. *Computers in New Zealand Schools*, 22(3). http://education2x.otago.ac.nz/cinzs/mod/resource/view.php?id=114

Merchant, G. (2012). Mobile practices in everyday life: Popular digital technologies and schooling revisited. *British Journal of Educational Technology*, 43(5), 770–782.

Meskill, C. & Anthony, N. (2010). *Teaching Languages Online*. Bristol: Multilingual Matters.

Milgram, P. & Kishino, F. (1994). A taxonomy of mixed reality visual displays. *IEICE Transactions on Information Systems, E77-D*(12). http://etclab.mie.utoronto.ca/people/paul_dir/IEICE94/ieice.html

Miller, S.M. & McVee, M.B. (2012). Changing the game: Teaching for embodied learning through multimodal composing. In S.M. Miller & M.B. McVee (Eds.), *Multimodal Composing in Classrooms: Learning and Teaching for the Digital World* (pp.130–152). New York: Routledge.

Mills, K.A. (2010). Shrek meets Vygotsky: Rethinking adolescents' multimodal literacy practices in schools. *Journal of Adolescent & Adult Literacy*, 54(1), 35–45.

Milrad, M., Wong, L.-H., Sharples, M., Hwang, G.-J., Looi, C.-K. & Ogata, H. (2013). Seamless learning: An international perspective on next-generation technology-enhanced learning. In Z.L. Berge & L.Y. Muilenburg (Eds.), *Handbook of Mobile Learning* (pp.95–108). New York: Routledge.

Mishra, P. & Kereluik, K. (2011). *What is 21st Century Learning? A Review and Synthesis*. Presented at SITE 2011, Nashville, USA, 7–11 March. http://punya.educ.msu.edu/presentations/site2011/SITE_2011_21st_Century.pdf

—— & Koehler, M.J. (2006). Technological pedagogical content knowledge: A framework for teacher knowledge. *Teachers College Record*, 108(6), 1017–1054.

Miyazawa, I. (2009). *Literacy Promotion through Mobile Phones*. Project brief paper. Presented at the 13th UNESCO-APEID International Conference and World Bank-KERIS High Level Seminar on ICT in Education, Hangzhou, China, 15–17 November. http://unesco.org.pk/education/documents/Project%20Brief%20Paper_ICT.pdf

MoLeNET. (2010). Welcome to the Mobile Learning Network (MoLeNET). *MoLeNET*. http://web.archive.org/web/20100830073550/http://www.molenet.org.uk/

Monahan, T. (2002). Flexible space and built pedagogy: Emerging IT embodiments. *Inventio*, 4(1), 1–19. http://www.torinmonahan.com/papers/Inventio.html

Morozov, E. (2011). *The Net Delusion: The Dark Side of Internet Freedom*. New York: Public Affairs.

Motallebzadeh, K. & Ganjali, R. (2011). SMS: Tool for L2 vocabulary retention and reading comprehension ability. *Journal of Language Teaching and Research*, 2(5), 1111–1115. http://ojs.academypublisher.com/index.php/jltr/article/view/020511111115/3616

Moyle, K. (2010). *Building Innovation: Learning with Technologies*. Camberwell, VIC: ACER Press. http://research.acer.edu.au/cgi/viewcontent.cgi?article=1009&context=aer

Murray, O.T. & Olcese, N.R. (2011, November/December). Teaching and learning with iPads, ready or not? *TechTrends*, 55(6), 42–48.

Mwanza-Simwami, D., Kukulska-Hulme, A., Clough, G., Whitelock, D., Ferguson, R. & Sharples, M. (2011). *Methods and Models of Next Generation Technology Enhanced Learning*. White Paper. Alpine Rendezvous, 28–29 March,

La Clusaz, France. http://oro.open.ac.uk/29056/1/Methods_and_models_ of_next_generation_TEL.pdf

Nah, K.C., White, P. & Sussex, R. (2008). The potential of using a mobile phone to access the internet for learning EFL listening skills within a Korean context. *ReCALL*, 20(3), 331–347.

Naismith, L., Lonsdale, P., Vavoula, G. & Sharples, M. (2006). *Report 11: Literature Review in Mobile Technologies and Learning*. Bristol: Futurelab. http://www2. futurelab.org.uk/resources/documents/lit_reviews/Mobile_Review.pdf

National Cancer Institute [USA]. (2012). *Cell Phones and Cancer Risk*. National Cancer Institute Fact Sheet. http://www.cancer.gov/cancertopics/factsheet/ Risk/cellphones

NCTE (National Council of Teachers of English) [USA]. (2005). *Position Statement on Multimodal Literacies*. [Approved November 2005.] http://www.ncte. org/positions/statements/multimodalliteracies

———. (2013). *The NCTE Definition of 21st Century Literacies*. Position Statement. [Adopted 15 February 2008; updated February 2013.] http://www.ncte.org/ positions/statements/21stcentdefinition

Ng, W. (2011). mLearning literacy. In *10th World Conference on Mobile and Contextual Learning: mLearn 2011 Conference Proceedings*, Beijing, China, 18–21 October (pp.163–172). Beijing: Beijing Normal University. http://mlearn.bnu. edu.cn/source/Conference_Procedings.pdf

—— & Nicholas, H. (2013). A framework for sustainable mobile learning in schools. *British Journal of Educational Technology*, 44(5), 695–715.

Nielsen, J. (2011, 28 February). Mobile content is twice as difficult. *NN/g*. http:// www.nngroup.com/articles/mobile-content-is-twice-as-difficult/

Norton, B. (2000). *Identity and Language Learning: Gender, Ethnicity, and Educational Change*. Harlow, Essex: Longman.

Oakley, G., Howitt, C., Garwood, R. & Durack, A.-R. (2013). Becoming multimodal authors: Pre-service teachers' interventions to support young children with autism. *The Australian Journal of Early Childhood*, 38(3), online.

———, Pegrum, M., Faulkner, R. & Striepe, M. (2012). *Exploring the Pedagogical Applications of Mobile Technologies for Teaching Literacy*. Report for the Association of Independent Schools of Western Australia. http://www.education.uwa.edu. au/research/?a=2195652

O'Dowd, R. & Ritter, M. (2006). Understanding and working with 'failed communication' in telecollaborative exchanges. *CALICO Journal*, 23(3), 623–642. https://calico.org/html/article_112.pdf

Ogata, H. (2011). Supporting awareness in ubiquitous learning. In D. Parsons (Ed.), *Combining E-learning and M-learning: New Applications of Blended Educational Resources* (pp.108–116). Hershey, PA: Information Science Reference.

———, Hui, G.L., Yin, C., Ueda, T., Oishi, Y. & Yano, Y. (2008). LOCH: Supporting mobile language learning outside classrooms. *International Journal of Mobile Learning and Organisation*, 2(3), 271–282.

———, Yin, C., El-Bishouty, M.M. & Yano, Y. (2010). Computer supported ubiquitous learning environment for vocabulary learning. *International Journal of Learning Technology*, 5(1), 5–24.

O'Malley, C., Vavoula, G., Glew, J.P., Taylor, J., Sharples, M., Lefrere, P., Lonsdale, P., et al. (2005). *Guidelines for Learning/Teaching/Tutoring in a Mobile Environment*. MOBIlearn. http://www.mobilearn.org/download/results/public_deliverables/ MOBIlearn_D4.1_Final.pdf

234 *References*

Ono, Y. & Ishihara, M. (2012). Integrating mobile-based individual activities into the Japanese EFL classroom. *International Journal of Mobile Learning and Organisation*, 6(2), 116–137.

O'Reilly, T. & Battelle, J. (2009). *Web Squared: Web 2.0 Five Years On.* Sebastopol, CA: O'Reilly Media. http://assets.en.oreilly.com/1/event/28/web2009_websquared-whitepaper.pdf

P21 (Partnership for 21st Century Skills) [USA]. (n.d.). *Framework for 21st Century Learning.* http://www.p21.org/overview/skills-framework

Pachler, N. (2009). Research methods in mobile and informal learning: Some issues. In G. Vavoula, N. Pachler & A. Kukulska-Hulme (Eds.), *Researching Mobile Learning: Frameworks, Tools and Research Designs* (pp.1–15). Oxford: Peter Lang.

——, Bachmair, B. & Cook, J. (2010). *Mobile Learning: Structures, Agency, Practices.* New York: Springer.

Paivio, A. (2007). *Mind and Its Evolution: A Dual Coding Theoretical Approach.* Mahwah, NJ: Lawrence Erlbaum.

Palalas, A. (2012). Mobile-enabled language learning eco-system. In M. Specht, M. Sharples & J. Multisilta (Eds.), *mLearn 2012: Proceedings of the 11th International Conference on Mobile and Contextual Learning 2012*, Helsinki, Finland, 16–18 October (pp.1–8). http://ceur-ws.org/Vol-955/papers/paper_35.pdf

Palfreyman, D.M. (2012). Bringing the world into the institution: Mobile intercultural learning for staff and students. In J.E. Díaz-Vera (Ed.), *Left to My Own Devices: Learner Autonomy and Mobile-Assisted Language Learning* (pp.163–181). Bingley, West Yorkshire: Emerald Group.

Papadima-Sophocleous, S. (in press). Integrating computer assisted language learning into out-of-class extended learning: The impact of iPod Touch-supported repeated reading on the oral reading fluency of English for specific academic purposes students.

Pariser, E. (2011). *The Filter Bubble: What the Internet is Hiding from You.* London: Viking.

Parry, D. (2011). Mobile perspectives on teaching: Mobile literacy. *EDUCAUSE Review*, 46(2). http://www.educause.edu/ero/article/mobile-perspectives-teaching-mobile-literacy

Payne, J.S. & Ross, B.M. (2005). Synchronous CMC, working memory, and L2 oral proficiency development. *Language Learning & Technology*, 9(3), 35–54. http://llt.msu.edu/vol9num3/pdf/payne.pdf

—— & Whitney, P.J. (2002). Developing L2 oral proficiency through synchronous CMC: Output, working memory, and interlanguage development. *CALICO Journal*, 20(1), 7–32. https://calico.org/html/article_327.pdf

Peachey, N. (2011, 30 April). Augmented reality and web 3.0. *Delta Publishing.* http://www.deltapublishing.co.uk/uncategorized/augmented-reality-and-web-3-0

——. (2012, 6 April). Getting learning out of the classroom with augmented reality. *Nik's Learning Technology Blog.* http://nikpeachey.blogspot.co.uk/2012/04/getting-learning-out-of-classroom-with.html

Pegrum, M. (2008). Film, culture and identity: Critical intercultural literacies for the language classroom. *Language and Intercultural Communication*, 8(2), 136–154.

——. (2009). *From Blogs to Bombs: The Future of Digital Technologies in Education.* Crawley, WA: UWA Publishing.

——. (2010). 'I link, therefore I am': Network literacy as a core digital literacy. *E-learning and Digital Media*, 7(4), 346–354.

——, Oakley, G. & Faulkner, R. (2013). Schools going mobile: A study of the adoption of mobile handheld technologies in Western Australian independent schools. *Australasian Journal of Educational Technology*, 29(1), 66–81. http://www.ascilite.org.au/ajet/submission/index.php/AJET/article/view/64/25

Petersen, S.A., Divitini, M. & Chabert, G. (2008). Identity, sense of community and connectedness in a community of mobile language learners. *ReCALL*, 20(3), 361–379.

——, Markiewicz, J.-K. & Bjørnebekk, S.S. (2009). Personalized and contextualized language learning: Choose when, where and what. *Research and Practice in Technology Enhanced Learning*, 4(1), 33–60.

Pettit, J. & Kukulska-Hulme, A. (2011). Mobile 2.0: Crossing the border into formal learning? In M.J.W. Lee & C. McLoughlin (Eds.), *Web 2.0-based E-learning: Applying Social Informatics for Tertiary Teaching* (pp.192–208). Hershey, PA: Information Science Reference. http://oro.open.ac.uk/22867/1/pettit_chap_lee_book.pdf

Pimmer, C., Linxen, S. & Gröhbiel, U. (2012). Facebook as a learning tool? A case study on the appropriation of social network sites from mobile phones in developing countries. *British Journal of Educational Technology*, 43(5), 726–738.

Plester, B., Wood, C. & Bowyer, S. (2009). Children's text messaging and traditional literacy. In L. Tan Wee Hin & R. Subramaniam (Eds.), *Handbook of Research on New Media Literacy at the K–12 Level: Issues and Challenges* (pp.492–504). Hershey, PA: Information Science Reference.

Potter, G. (2011). Augmented reality and mobile technologies. In A. Kitchenham (Ed.), *Models for Interdisciplinary Mobile Learning: Delivering Information to Students* (pp.212–230). Hershey, PA: Information Science Reference.

Prensky, M. (2012a, January–February). Eliminating the 'app gap'. *Educational Technology*. http://marcprensky.com/writing/Prensky-EDTECH-EliminatingtheAppGap-Jan-Feb-2012.pdf

——. (2012b). *From Digital Natives to Digital Wisdom: Hopeful Essays for 21st Century Learning*. Thousand Oaks, CA: Corwin.

Puentedura, R.R. (2011). A brief introduction to TPCK and SAMR. Freeport workshop slides, 8 December. *Ruben R. Puentedura's Weblog*. http://www.hippasus.com/rrpweblog/archives/2011/12/08/BriefIntroTPCKSAMR.pdf

——. (2012). *Building upon SAMR*. Presented at Presbyterian Ladies' College, Perth, Australia, 14 September.

Quinn, C.N. (2000). mLearning: Mobile, wireless, in-your-pocket learning. *LiNE Zine*, Fall. http://www.linezine.com/2.1/features/cqmmwiyp.htm

——. (2012). *The Mobile Academy: mLearning for Higher Education*. San Francisco: Jossey-Bass.

——. (2013). A future for m-learning. In Z.L. Berge & L.Y. Muilenburg (Eds.), *Handbook of Mobile Learning* (pp.82–94). New York: Routledge.

Quitney Anderson, J. & Rainie, L. (2012). *The Web is Dead?* . . . Washington, DC: Pew Internet. http://pewinternet.org/~/media//Files/Reports/2012/PIP_Future_of_Apps_and_Web.pdf

Rainger, P. (2005). Accessibility and mobile learning. In A. Kukulska-Hulme & J. Traxler (Eds.), *Mobile Learning: A Handbook for Educators and Trainers* (pp.57–69). London: Routledge.

Rainie, L. (2012). *Networked Learners*. Presented at The Free Learning 2.0 Conference, 22 August. http://www.pewinternet.org/~/media//Files/Presentations/2012/August/82212_NetworkedLearners_Learning20_PDF.pdf

—— & Duggan, M. (2012, 27 December). *E-book Reading Jumps; Print Book Reading Declines*. Washington, DC: Pew Internet. http://libraries.pewinternet.org/files/legacy-pdf/PIP_Reading%20and%20ebooks_12.27.pdf

—— & Wellman, B. (2012). *Networked: The New Social Operating System*. Cambridge, MA: MIT Press.

Ranieri, M., Manca, S. & Fini, A. (2012). Why (and how) do teachers engage in social networks? An exploratory study of professional use of Facebook and its implications for lifelong learning. *British Journal of Educational Technology*, 43(5), 754–769.

Reinders, H. & Wattana, S. (2012). Talk to me! Games and students' willingness to communicate. In H. Reinders (Ed.), *Digital Games in Language Learning and Teaching* (pp.156–188). Basingstoke, Hampshire: Palgrave Macmillan.

Rheingold, H. (2012). *Net Smart: How to Thrive Online*. Cambridge, MA: MIT Press.

Richardson, W. & Mancabelli, R. (2011). *Personal Learning Networks: Using the Power of Connections to Transform Education*. Bloomington, IN: Solution Tree Press.

Ring, C. & LaMarche, M. (2012). *Mobile Technology and Communication*. ABA Literature Summary E-newsletter, 10. Special Learning.

Rivers, D.J. (2009). Utilizing the quick response (QR) code within a Japanese EFL environment. *The JALT CALL Journal*, 5(2), 15–28. http://journal.jaltcall.org/articles/5_2_Rivers.pdf

Roberts, J.B. (2013). Accessibility in m-learning: Ensuring equal access. In Z.L. Berge & L.Y. Muilenburg (Eds.), *Handbook of Mobile Learning* (pp.427–435). New York: Routledge.

Robison, D. (2012). Learning on location with AMI: The potentials and dangers of mobile gaming for language learning. In J.E. Díaz-Vera (Ed.), *Left to My Own Devices: Learner Autonomy and Mobile-Assisted Language Learning* (pp.67–88). Bingley, West Yorkshire: Emerald Group.

Rosell-Aguilar, F. (2007). Top of the pods – In search of a podcasting 'podagogy' for language learning. *Computer-Assisted Language Learning*, 20(5), 471–492.

——. (2009). Podcasting for language learning: Re-examining the potential. In L. Lomicka & G. Lord (Eds.), *The Next Generation: Social Networking and Online Collaboration in Foreign Language Learning* (pp.13–34). San Marcos, TX: CALICO.

Ros i Solé, C. (2009). The fleeting, the situated and the mundane: Ethnographic approaches to mobile language learning (MALL). In G. Vavoula, N. Pachler & A. Kukulska-Hulme (Eds.), *Researching Mobile Learning: Frameworks, Tools and Research Designs* (pp.137–150). Oxford: Peter Lang.

——, Calic, J. & Neijmann, D. (2010). A social and self-reflective approach to MALL. *ReCALL*, 22(1), 39–52.

Rushby, N. (2012). Editorial: An agenda for mobile learning. *British Journal of Educational Technology*, 43(3), 355–356.

Russell, T.L. (2010). *No Significant Difference*. WCET. http://www.nosignificantdifference.org/

Sándor, S. (2012). *Introduction to Augmented Reality*. Budapest: Karmamedia.

Sansone, M. (2008, 2 October). Hey teachers! Your 'digital natives' still need you. *ConverStations*. http://www.converstations.com/2008/10/hey-teachers-yo.html

Saran, M., Seferoğlu, G. & Çağıltay, K.(2012). Mobile language learning: Contribution of multimedia messages via mobile phones in consolidating vocabulary. *The Asia-Pacific Education Researcher*, 21(1), 181–190.

Schmidt, R.W. (1990). The role of consciousness in second language learning. *Applied Linguistics*, 11(2), 129–158.

Selwyn, N. (2011). *Education and Technology: Key Issues and Debates*. London: Continuum.

———. (2013). *Education in a Digital World: Global Perspectives on Technology and Education*. New York: Routledge.

Servaes, J. (2011). The role of information communication technologies within the field of communication for social change. In A.G. Abdel-Wahab & A.A.A. El-Masry (Eds.), *Mobile Information Communication Technologies Adoption in Developing Countries: Effects and Implications* (pp.218–236). Hershey, PA: Information Science Reference.

Shaheen, R. & Lace, R. (2013). *English in Action: Innovation Using Mobile for Classroom and Adult Learning in Bangladesh*. Presented at UNESCO Mobile Learning Week Symposium, Paris, France, 18–19 February. http://www.unesco.org/new/en/unesco/themes/icts/m4ed/unesco-mobile-learning-week/speakers/richard-lace-and-robina-shaheen/

Sharples, M., Taylor, J. & Vavoula, G. (2007). A theory of learning for the mobile age. In R. Andrews & C. Haythornthwaite (Eds.), *The Sage Handbook of E-learning Research* (pp.221–247). London: Sage.

———, Taylor, J. & Vavoula, G. (2010). A theory of learning for the mobile age: Learning through conversation and exploration across contexts. In B. Bachmair (Ed.), *Medienbildung in neuen Kulturräumen: Die deutschsprachige und britische Diskussion* (pp.87–99). Wiesbaden: VS Verlag für Sozialwissenschaften.

Shrestha, P. (2011). The potential of mobile technologies for (English) language learning in Nepal. *Journal of NELTA*, 16(1–2), 107–113.

———. (2012). Teacher professional development using mobile technologies in a large-scale project: Lessons learned from Bangladesh. *International Journal of Computer-Assisted Language Learning and Teaching*, 2(4), 34–49.

Siemens, G. & Tittenberger, P. (2009). *Handbook of Emerging Technologies for Learning*. http://elearnspace.org/Articles/HETL.pdf

Simon Fraser University. (n.d.). *Learn Greek Mobile App: Odysseas Greek Language Tutor*. http://www.greeklanguagetutor.com/iphone/

Small, G. & Vorgan, G. (2008). *iBrain: Surviving the Technological Alteration of the Modern Mind*. New York: Collins.

Smith, M. & Kukulska-Hulme, A. (2012). Building mobile learning capacity in higher education: E-books and iPads. In M. Specht, M. Sharples & J. Multisilta (Eds.), *mLearn 2012: Proceedings of the 11th International Conference on Mobile and Contextual Learning 2012*, Helsinki, Finland, 16–18 October (pp.298–301). http://ceur-ws.org/Vol-955/papers/paper_31.pdf

So, H.-J. (2012). *Turning on Mobile Learning in Asia: Illustrative Initiatives and Policy Implications*. Paris: UNESCO. http://unesdoc.unesco.org/images/0021/002162/216283E.pdf

Song, Y. & Fox, R. (2008). Using PDA for undergraduate student incidental vocabulary testing. *ReCALL*, 20(3), 290–314.

Squire, K. (2009). Mobile media learning: Multiplicities of place. *On the Horizon*, 17(1), 70–80.

Sreekumar, T.T. & Rivera-Sánchez, M. (2008). ICTs and development: Revisiting the Asian experience. *Science, Technology & Society*, 13(2), 159–174.

Stead, G. (2013). *Mobilizing Teachers: Bridging the Gap between Theory, and Practice*. Presented at UNESCO Mobile Learning Week Symposium, Paris, France, 18–19 February. http://www.unesco.org/new/en/unesco/themes/icts/m4ed/unesco-mobile-learning-week/speakers/geoff-stead/

Steel, C.H. & Levy, M. (2013). Language students and their technologies: Charting the evolution 2006–2011. *ReCALL*, 25(3), 306–320.

Steinkuehler, C. (2007). Massively multiplayer online gaming as a constellation of literacy practices. In B.E. Shelton & D. Wiley (Eds.), *The Design and Use of Simulation Computer Games in Education* (pp.187–212). Rotterdam: Sense Publishers.

Stockwell, G. (2008). Investigating learner preparedness for and usage patterns of mobile learning. *ReCALL*, 20(3), 253–270.

——. (2010). Using mobile phones for vocabulary activities: Examining the effect of the platform. *Language Learning & Technology*, 14(2), 95–110. http://llt.msu.edu/vol14num2/stockwell.pdf

——. (2013a). Mobile-assisted language learning. In M. Thomas, H. Reinders & M. Warschauer (Eds.), *Contemporary Computer-Assisted Language Learning* (pp.201–216). London: Bloomsbury.

——. (2013b). Tracking learner usage of mobile phones for language learning outside of the classroom. In P. Hubbard, M. Schulze & B. Smith (Eds.), *Learner-Computer Interaction in Language Education: A Festschrift in Honor of Robert Fischer* (pp.118–136). San Marcos, TX: CALICO.

Stodd, J. (2012). *A Mindset for Mobile Learning: A Journey through Theory and Practice*. Smashwords.

Sussex, R. (2012). Text input and editing as a bottleneck in mobile devices for language learning. In F. Zhang (Ed.), *Computer-Enhanced and Mobile-Assisted Language Learning: Emerging Issues and Trends* (pp.220–234). Hershey, PA: Information Science Reference.

Swain, M. (1985). Communicative competence: Some roles of comprehensible input and comprehensible output in its development. In S. Gass & C. Madden (Eds.), *Input in Second Language Acquisition* (pp.235–253). Rowley, MA: Newbury House.

Sweeney, T., Sharples, M. & Pemberton, R. (2011). Toponimo: A geosocial pervasive game for English second language learning. In *10th World Conference on Mobile and Contextual Learning: mLearn 2011 Conference Proceedings*, Beijing, China, 18–21 October (pp.417–420). Beijing: Beijing Normal University. http://mlearn.bnu.edu.cn/source/Conference_Procedings.pdf

Sydorenko, T. (2010). Modality of input and vocabulary acquisition. *Language Learning & Technology*, 14(2), 50–73. http://llt.msu.edu/vol14num2/sydorenko.pdf

Sykes, J.M. (2005). Synchronous CMC and pragmatic development: Effects of oral and written chat. *CALICO Journal*, 22(3), 399–431. https://calico.org/html/article_142.pdf

Tabatabaei, O. & Goojani, A.H. (2012). The impact of text-messaging on vocabulary learning of Iranian EFL learners. *Cross-Cultural Communication*, 8(2), 47–55.

Tacchi, J., Kitner, K.R. & Crawford, K. (2012). Meaningful mobility: Gender, development and mobile phones. *Feminist Media Studies*, 12(4), 528–537.

Takayoshi, P. & Selfe, C.L. (2007). Thinking about multimodality. In C.L. Selfe (Ed.), *Multimodal Composition: Resources for Teachers* (pp.1–12). Cresskill, NJ: Hampton Press.

Tam, V. & Huang, C. (2011). An innovative application for learning to write Chinese characters on smartphones. In R. Kwan, C. McNaught, P. Tsang, F.L. Wang & K.C. Li (Eds.), *Enhancing Learning through Technology. Education Unplugged: Mobile Technologies and Web 2.0,* International Conference, ICT 2011, Hong Kong, China, 11–13 July (pp.85–95). Berlin: Springer.

Tanaza. (2012, 11 July). A brief history of wi-fi. *Tanaza's Cloud-based Wi-fi Vendor-Agnostic Blog.* http://blog.tanaza.com/blog/bid/183121/A-Brief-History-of-Wi-Fi

Tapscott, D. (2009). *Grown Up Digital: How the Net Generation is Changing Your World.* New York: McGraw-Hill.

Taylor, J. (2006). Evaluating mobile learning: What are appropriate methods for evaluating learning in mobile environments? In M. Sharples (Ed.), *Big Issues in Mobile Learning: Report of a Workshop by the Kaleidoscope Network of Excellence Mobile Learning Initiative* (pp.25–27). Nottingham: University of Nottingham.

Thornton, P. & Houser, C. (2005). Using mobile phones in English education in Japan. *Journal of Computer-Assisted Learning*, 21, 217–228.

Tian, F., Lv, F., Wang, J., Wang, H., Luo, W., Kam, M., Setlur, V., et al. (2010). Let's play Chinese characters – Mobile learning approaches via culturally inspired group games. In *Proceedings of ACM Conference on Human Factors in Computing Systems (CHI 2010)*, Atlanta, USA, 10–15 April. http://www.cs.cmu.edu/~mattkam/lab/publications/CHI2010b.pdf

Traxler, J. (2007). Defining, discussing and evaluating mobile learning: The moving finger writes and having writ... *The International Review of Research in Open and Distance Learning*, 8(2). http://www.irrodl.org/index.php/irrodl/article/view/346/875

——. (2010). Will student devices deliver innovation, inclusion, and transformation? *Journal of the Research Center for Educational Technology*, 6(1), 3–15.

——. (2012). Sustaining mobile learning and its institutions. In D. Parsons (Ed.), *Refining Current Practices in Mobile and Blended Learning: New Applications* (pp.1–9). Hershey, PA: Information Science Reference.

——. (2013a). Mobile learning: Starting in the right place, going in the right direction? In D. Parsons (Ed.), *Innovations in Mobile Educational Technologies and Applications* (pp.1–13). Hershey, PA: Information Science Reference.

——. (2013b). Mobiles for learning in Africa: The elephants in the room. In W. Kinuthia & S. Marshall (Eds.), *On the Move: Mobile Learning for Development* (pp.161–177). Charlotte, NC: Information Age Publishing.

Trivedi, K.R. (2013). *Brainphone for M-learning – Brainwave Enabled Multifunctional, Communication, Controlling and Speech Signal Generating Device.* Presented at UNESCO Mobile Learning Week Symposium, Paris, France, 18–19 February. http://www.unesco.org/new/en/unesco/themes/icts/m4ed/unesco-mobile-learning-week/speakers/kiran-trivedi/

Tyers, A. (2012). A gender digital divide? Women learning English through ICTs in Bangladesh. In M. Specht, M. Sharples & J. Multisilta (Eds.), *mLearn*

2012: Proceedings of the 11th International Conference on Mobile and Contextual Learning 2012, Helsinki, Finland, 16–18 October (pp.94–100). http://ceur-ws. org/Vol-955/papers/paper_16.pdf

Udell, C. (2012). *Learning Everywhere: How Mobile Content Strategies are Transforming Training.* Nashville, TN: Rockbench Publishing.

UN (United Nations). (n.d.). *We Can End Poverty 2015: Millennium Development Goals.* http://www.un.org/millenniumgoals/

UNESCO (United Nations Educational, Scientific and Cultural Organization). (2012). *Youth and Skills: Putting Education to Work.* Paris: UNESCO. http:// unesdoc.unesco.org/images/0021/002180/218003e.pdf

———. (2013a, 16 January). Mobile learning projects to empower rural women in Pakistan. *UNESCO Bangkok: ICT in Education.* http://www.unescobk. org/education/ict/online-resources/databases/ict-in-education-database/item/ article/mobile-learning-projects-to-empower-rural-women-in-pakistan/

———. (2013b). *UNESCO Mobile Learning Week Symposium Report.* http://www. unesco.org/new/fileadmin/MULTIMEDIA/HQ/ED/ICT/pdf/MLW_Report.pdf

———. (2013c). *UNESCO Policy Guidelines for Mobile Learning.* Paris: UNESCO. http://unesdoc.unesco.org/images/0021/002196/219641E.pdf

———. (n.d., a). Education for all movement. *UNESCO: Education.* http://www. unesco.org/new/en/education/themes/leading-the-international-agenda/ education-for-all/

———. (n.d., b). Mobile phone literacy – Empowering women and girls. *UNESCO: ICT in Education.* http://www.unesco.org/new/en/unesco/themes/icts/m4ed/ policy-research-and-advocacy/mobile-phone-literacy-project/

———. (n.d., c). Teacher support and development. *UNESCO: ICT in Education.* http://www.unesco.org/new/en/unesco/themes/icts/m4ed/teacher-support-and-development/

Unwin, T. (2009a). Conclusions. In T. Unwin (Ed.), *ICT4D: Information and Communication Technology for Development* (pp.360–375). Cambridge: Cambridge University Press.

———. (2009b). Development agendas and the place of ICTs. In T. Unwin (Ed.), *ICT4D: Information and Communication Technology for Development* (pp.7–38). Cambridge: Cambridge University Press.

Uosaki, N., Ogata, H., Sugimoto, T., Li, M. & Hou, B. (2012). Towards seamless vocabulary learning: How we can entwine in-class and outside-of-class learning. *International Journal of Mobile Learning and Organisation*, 6(2), 138–155.

US Dept of Education. (2010). *Evaluation of Evidence-based Practices in Online Learning: A Meta-analysis and Review of Online Learning Studies* (revised ed.). Washington, DC: US Dept of Education. http://gsehd.gwu.edu/ documents/gsehd/resources/gwuohs-onlineresources/reports/doe_evaluation onlinelearning-092010.pdf

van Lier, L. (2004). *The Ecology and Semiotics of Language Learning: A Sociocultural Perspective.* Boston: Kluwer Academic Publishers.

Vavoula, G. & Sharples, M. (2009). Meeting the challenges in evaluating mobile learning: A 3-level evaluation framework. *International Journal of Mobile and Blended Learning*, 1(2), 54–75.

Viberg, O. & Grönlund, Å. (2012). Mobile-assisted language learning: A literature review. In M. Specht, M. Sharples & J. Multisilta (Eds.), *mLearn 2012:*

Proceedings of the 11th International Conference on Mobile and Contextual Learning 2012, Helsinki, Finland, 16–18 October (pp.9–16). http://ceur-ws.org/Vol-955/papers/paper_8.pdf

Vosloo, S. (2012). *Mobile Learning and Policies: Key Issues to Consider.* Paris: UNESCO. http://unesdoc.unesco.org/images/0021/002176/217638E.pdf

——. (2013). *Yoza: m-Novels for Africa.* Presented at NetExplo, Paris, France, 15 February. http://www.slideshare.net/stevevosloo/yoza-cellphone-stories?ref=http://yozaproject.com/

Vygotsky, L.S. (1978). *Mind in Society: The Development of Higher Psychological Processes.* Cambridge, MA: Harvard University Press.

Wallace, R. (2013). Empowered learner identity through m-learning: Representations of disenfranchised students' perspectives. In D. Parsons (Ed.), *Innovations in Mobile Educational Technologies and Applications* (pp.272–283). Hershey, PA: Information Science Reference.

Walsh, C.S., Shaheen, R., Power, T., Hedges, C., Kahtoon, M. & Sikander Mondol, M. (2012). Low cost mobile phones for large scale teacher professional development in Bangladesh. In M. Specht, M. Sharples & J. Multisilta (Eds.), *mLearn 2012: Proceedings of the 11th International Conference on Mobile and Contextual Learning 2012*, Helsinki, Finland, 16–18 October (pp.101–108). http://ceur-ws.org/Vol-955/papers/paper_53.pdf

Wang, M., Shen, R., Novak, D. & Pan, X. (2009). The impact of mobile learning on students' learning behaviours and performance: Report from a large blended classroom. *British Journal of Educational Technology*, 40(4), 673–695.

Ware, P. (2008). Language learners and multimedia literacy in and after school. *Pedagogies*, 3, 37–51.

Warschauer, M. (2004). Technological change and the future of CALL. In S. Fotos & C. Browne (Eds.), *New Perspectives on CALL for Second Language Classrooms* (pp.15–25). Mahwah, NJ: Lawrence Erlbaum.

——. (2011). *Learning in the Cloud: How (and Why) to Transform Schools with Digital Media.* New York: Teachers College Press.

—— & Liaw, M.-L. (2013). *Emerging Technologies in Adult Literacy and Language Education.* National Institute for Literacy.

Weigel, M., James, C. & Gardner, H. (2009). Learning: Peering backward and looking forward in the digital era. *International Journal of Learning and Media*, 1(1). http://www.mitpressjournals.org/doi/pdf/10.1162/ijlm.2009.0005

West, M. (2012a). *Mobile Learning for Teachers: Global Themes.* Paris: UNESCO. http://unesdoc.unesco.org/images/0021/002164/216452E.pdf

——. (2012b). *Turning on Mobile Learning: Global Themes.* Paris: UNESCO. http://unesdoc.unesco.org/images/0021/002164/216451E.pdf

WHO (World Health Organization). (2011). *Electromagnetic Fields and Public Health: Mobile Phones.* Fact Sheet No.193. http://www.who.int/mediacentre/factsheets/fs193/en/index.html

Williams, R. & Edge, D. (1996). The social shaping of technology. *Research Policy*, 25, 865–899.

Wong, L.-H. (2013). Analysis of students' after-school mobile-assisted artifact creation processes in a seamless language learning environment. *Educational Technology & Society*, 16(2), 198–211. http://www.ifets.info/journals/16_2/17.pdf

——, Chai, C.-S., Chin, C.-K., Hsieh, Y.-F. & Liu, M. (2012). Towards a seamless language learning framework mediated by the ubiquitous technology. *International Journal of Mobile Learning and Organisation*, 6(2), 156–171.

——, Chin, C.-K., Tan, C.-L. & Liu, M. (2010). Students' personal and social meaning making in a Chinese idiom mobile learning environment. *Educational Technology & Society*, 13(4), 15–26. http://www.ifets.info/journals/13_4/3.pdf

Woodill, G. (2011). *The Mobile Learning Edge: Tools and Technologies for Developing Your Teams*. New York: McGraw-Hill.

World Bank. (2012). *Information and Communications for Development 2012: Maximizing Mobile*. Washington, DC: World Bank. DOI: 10.1596/978-0-8213-8991-1; http://www.worldbank.org/ict/IC4D2012

Worldreader. (2012). *Worldreader Mobile*. http://www.worldreader.org/what-we-do/worldreader-mobile/

WSIS (World Summit on the Information Society). (2013). *World Summit on the Information Society: Geneva 2003 – Tunis 2005*. http://www.itu.int/wsis/

Wu, H.-K., Lee, S.W.-Y., Chang, H.-Y. & Liang, J.-C. (2013). Current status, opportunities and challenges of augmented reality in education. *Computers & Education*, 62, 41–49.

Yacoobi, S. (2013). *Using Mobile Phones to Accelerate Literacy Education and Empower Afghan Women*. Presented at UNESCO Mobile Learning Week Symposium, Paris, France, 18–19 February. http://www.unesco.org/new/en/unesco/themes/icts/m4ed/unesco-mobile-learning-week/speakers/sakena-yacoobi/

Yarow, J. (2012, 14 December). Chart of the day: The death of the e-book reader. *Business Insider*. http://www.businessinsider.com/chart-of-the-day-e-book-readers-2012-12

Zelezny-Green, R. (2011). The potential impact of mobile-assisted language learning on women and girls in Africa: A literature review. *Ubiquitous Learning*, 3(2), 69–82.

——. (2013a). Inter-generational indigenous knowledge exchange and mobile phones: The possibilities and the potential. In W. Kinuthia & S. Marshall (Eds.), *On the Move: Mobile Learning for Development* (pp.209–226). Charlotte, NC: Information Age Publishing.

——. (2013b, 4 March). MDGs: How mobile phones can help achieve gender equality in education. *The Guardian*. http://www.guardian.co.uk/global-development-professionals-network/2013/mar/04/mobile-education-international-development

Zhang, S. & Duke, N.K. (2008). Strategies for internet reading with different reading purposes: A descriptive study of twelve good internet readers. *Journal of Literacy Research*, 40(1), 128–162.

Zickuhr, K. (2012). *Mobile is the Needle; Social is the Thread*. Presented at Comm Week 2012, Elliott School of Communications, Wichita State University, 18 October. http://pewinternet.org/Presentations/2012/Oct/WSU.aspx

Zittrain, J. (2008). *The Future of the Internet – And How to Stop it*. London: Allen Lane.

Index

Printed and bound in Great Britain by
CPI Group (UK) Ltd, Croydon, CR0 4YY